CW00554548

# CARLO

## with John Kelly

**HERO**BOOKS

**HERO**BOOKS

PUBLISHED BY HERO BOOKS
1 WOODVILLE GREEN
LUCAN
CO. DUBLIN
IRELAND

Hero Books is an imprint of Umbrella Publishing
First Published 2022
Copyright © John Kelly 2022
All rights reserved

Without limiting the rights under copyright reserved above, no part of this publication may be reproduced, stored in or introduced into a retrieval system, or transmitted in any form or by any means (electronic, mechanical, photocopying, recording or otherwise) without the prior written permission of the publisher of this book.

A CIP record for this book is available from the British Library

ISBN 9781910827536

Cover design and formatting: jessica@viitaladesign.com

Photographs: Sportsfile

# ★ DEDICATION ★

To my boys, Rian, Oran and Aodhán

And to all true Carlow supporters everywhere

# ★ CONTENTS ★

# ★ ACKNOWLEDGEMENTS ★

TO SAY IT was a dream to write this book would be an understatement. Since I was a young fella growing up in Tinryland, I have been the biggest Carlow GAA supporter. It didn't matter if it was football or hurling, league or championship, home or away, senior, minor or under-21, I was there. I have travelled the length and breadth of the country going to support Carlow across both codes and I absolutely loved it. It doesn't matter if there have been more bad days than good, if it's your county, and your team, then you just keep going back for more punishment week after week, year after year. Many years ago, I was afforded the opportunity to start doing some writing for *The Nationalist*, mainly reporting on local GAA games and I really enjoyed it. Ever since then I have had the writing bug and when the opportunity came up to write about Carlow GAA, then I wasn't going to look a gift horse in the mouth!

When I was younger, I used to be in awe if I saw a county player on the street. These fellas were my heroes and I would stare at them as they passed. It was the GAA nerd in me, I suppose. To be able to interview some of those same heroes that I was once in awe of years before was a massive highlight for me. The majority of these interviews were conducted over zoom calls which was very handy at the time. A couple took place over the phone, while a number were also done in person and I would like to thank every single player who took part and gave up their time and shared some of their memories and stories with me. Doing the interviews was the easy part, listening back then and putting it down in words was a little harder, but it was worth it when people got back to you and told you it was good or that they enjoyed reading their own story. It made me confident that I was doing these stories some justice.

I would also like to mention that this book is in no way a list of the 30 'greatest' players or anything like that. It is just 30 players who have worn the jersey at some stage and I tried to spread it across both codes – and from the 1960's right up to the modern day. I could have written another couple of books on more Carlow legends and there would still be somebody you'd be leaving out, so this book is about covering all eras. Carlow might be a small county but I think there are stories in this county as good as anywhere else and these stories deserve to be told.

I would like to say a big thank you to my wife Marie for her help whilst writing this book. To our three boys Rian, Oran and Aodhán, for just being themselves, thank you and I love you. Trying to cater for their needs while writing this every night was not easy but I wouldn't change it for the world. The word legend is easily bandied about these days but in Carlow GAA circles, there is no bigger legend than Tommy Murphy. Tommy helped me out with a number of photos for this book and was a massive guiding presence. When Tommy rings you, you better be sitting down as you know you're in for a good long chat and some great stories. There is a great book in that man if he only had the time to write it!

The biggest thank you, however, must go to Liam Hayes. He was the man who gave me the opportunity to do this and he put massive trust in me, so I felt compelled to do as good a job as possible to repay that faith and I hope it turned out that way. Liam, of course, has a big Carlow link through his father Jim, while he also managed the Carlow footballers himself for two years. With those ties to the county, it is no surprise that Liam, and indeed Jim, came in for numerous mentions while doing this book.

There are many funny stories told by players here, while also some sad ones as there are mentions of some of those who are no longer with us. I hope all Carlow gaels will get as much enjoyment out of reading this book as I had putting it together.

Carlow is as much a GAA county as any other and it is only right that these stories should be told.

Carlow Abú.

**John Kelly**
June 2022

# ★ FOREWORD ★

MEMORIES LAST FOREVER.

As a small county we have not tasted much success on the inter-county stage and so we are even more indebted to the players of past generations, who proudly represented Carlow in hurling and football, despite little chance of silverware.

They have given me and all Carlovians many great memories of their time in the red, green and yellow.

We are prisoners of geography and structures that militate against the smaller county winning silverware, but that has never quelled our spirit or prevented us producing top class competitors in our national games.

Any of us who follow the games recognise real talent, no matter the colour of the jersey, and the players who have contributed to this book would hold their own in any county.

Because victories have been few and far between, they have meant even more to us and no one can take away our memories of great performances and great wins, nor can they prevent us dreaming of great occasions in the future.

Each and every player here has left the jersey in a better place by shedding their blood, sweat and tears along the way; by spending countless hours in the practice field honing their skills and improving their fitness.

I think all of them would agree that there is no finer feeling than competing at your very best, when your body and mind are in peak physical condition, and performing comes so easily. Those days are rare for most sports people but we can all recall days when these footballers and hurlers brought fleeting joy to their families, communities and generations of Carlow supporters.

We forget the draw of home for our emigrants and the importance of news from native shores. It means so much to Carlovians in the UK, America, Australia, in every corner of the world, to pick up a newspaper and read about a great Carlow performance, in victory or defeat.

I was born into the GAA; football and hurling were the topic of conversation at the breakfast table, and at the dinner table, and so much of my youth was spent travelling with my father to games all over the country. Some of my earliest memories are travelling with the Carlow hurlers to NHL games in places like Ballycran in County Down at the height of the Troubles. These players were idols to me. As a youngster I would attend county training sessions with my father when he was county secretary and I loved to kick and puck the balls back into play for these county stars. It made my night and I couldn't wait to get to the field.

Later on, I had the privilege of playing with many of the players who have contributed to this book and indeed, in latter years, I had the great honour to be involved in managing some of these exceptionally talented county footballers.

Every one of them brought their talent and their character to the teams they played on; they moulded others around them and, to a man, they lived and died for each other in the jersey.

When I look at the list of players featured here, my chest puffs out to know that this county has produced players as talented as in the land. We have endured more sad days than happy days but nothing can take away the memories of great days out and of great performances delivered by the contributors to this book and hundreds of others not featured.

A great American Football coach is often misquoted but he once said, 'Winning isn't everything but the will to win is'. That's why I admire Carlow footballers and hurlers more than winning All-Ireland teams – it's easy to go to the field when you have a chance of outright victory, but it is much harder to do so as the underdog.

Great credit and thanks is due to John Kelly for his determination and foresight to ensure that, finally, we have the first-hand accounts of so many of our players preserved in a wonderful publication that celebrates Carlow GAA.

**Turlough O'Brien**
**June 2022**

# MOLING MORRISSEY

**CARLOW 3-9 ★ GALWAY 2-5**
**All-Ireland IHC 'Home' Final**
**St Brendan's Park, Birr**
**AUGUST 26, 1962**

*Legends together, Moling Morrissey with Paddy Quirke.*

★ **CARLOW:** J O'Connell; P Brophy, M Hogan, T Fortune; W 'Town' Walsh, P Somers, T Nolan; P McGovern, M O'Brien; W Hogan (0-1), P O'Connell (0-2), N O'Gorman; W 'Black' Walsh (2-0), **M Morrissey (1-3)**, L Walsh (0-3).

★ **GALWAY:** M Howley; W Fogarty, T Dolly, J Lyons; P Shaughnessy, M Connaughton, A Furey; S Gleeson, K Shaughnessy (0-1); P Egan (0-1), S Devlin, C Stanley; J Donoghue; P Fahy, M Curtin (2-3). Subs: L Marmion for Fahy.

## THE ACTION

BEFORE 2,500 ENTHUSIASTIC supporters, Carlow hurlers, the All-Ireland Junior 'Home' champions of 1960, added the intermediate equivalent when in driving rain and a near gale force wind, they defeated the Munster intermediate champions Galway.

At one stage it looked like Galway might haul back their two goal deficit but with the Carlow defence working like Trojans, the Galway men never got close enough. In the 12th minute of the second-half when Moling Morrissey whipped a low ball to the net the game was up for Galway. Apart from this score, Morrissey had an inspiring game all through at full-forward, and later for a spell at midfield. Carlow showed great determination all the way, especially in the second-half when Galway eventually did have a short spell where they played well. Jack O'Connell in the Carlow goal came to his sides rescue with a couple of great saves to keep his sides lead intact.

The game was only six minutes old when Carlow scored their first goal of the day when McGovern released corner-forward 'Black' Willie Walsh, who aiming a low vicious shot, found the Galway net from a difficult angle. Liamy Walsh quickly followed this up with a free for Carlow. Almost immediately, Noel O' Gorman pulled on a running ball and found Morrissey, who despite being fouled, and suffering the loss of his hurley, still managed to palm the ball over the bar. Carlow had a second goal when once again, 'Black' Willie Walsh was on the end of a loose ball.

Carlow retired at the short whistle with a 10-point lead. The second-half was almost 10 minutes old before the first score arrived as Liamy Walsh struck over a point. Mick Curtin scored Galway's second goal shortly after but any notions of a Galway comeback were quickly dashed when Morrissey, Carlow's best player on the day, burst through and whipped on a ground shot for his side's third goal.

★★★★★

**❝**

BEATING GALWAY IN the All-Ireland Intermediate hurling final was most definitely the game of my life. It was the only game I kept the newspaper report from. It is well faded at this stage, but I still have it at home. That Galway win was the 'Home' final, so after we beat them we still had to play London in the final proper but, for me, and probably a lot of lads, the Galway game was the real final. The journey to that point for that team probably started two years previous in 1960. Carlow won the Junior All-Ireland 'Home' final that year. We defeated Cork in the final which was played in Kilkenny. Christy Ring was involved with the Cork management that day, which I didn't actually realise until many years later. So you could say that junior victory sowed the seeds for the intermediate win two years later

I actually started hurling senior for Carlow during the 1958/1959 season. I was only under-16 at the time, which was crazy in itself. I was actually three months short of my 16th birthday. We ended up winning the league that season. We beat Laois in the final – that was my first game for Carlow and I have to admit I cried throughout the game as the fella marking me absolutely dogged me for the whole game. In 1960 it was basically the same team from then and we beat Cork in that junior final before London beat us in the final proper after a replay… and they were tough games to play in.

The first day we played them in London and it was a horrible day. The middle of the field was just covered in water, but the game was always going to go ahead as we had flown over and God knows when we would have made it over again, so it was going ahead regardless. In the last few minutes of the game, I was taken out of it and had to come off. Carlow never brought on a substitute and my man ended up scoring a goal right at the death and so it ended level.

The replay in Croke Park was much the same and I remember Liamy Walsh, or 'Red' Willie Walsh as he was also known, was knocked out early in the game which was a big blow to us, but anyway, they beat us fair and square, although we would get revenge a couple of years later! Even though we had lost, we had still won the 'Home' final, and beating Cork in that gave us great belief going forward. Those London games were hard games to play in. They mightn't have been the best hurlers in the world but they were all tough men and they made it really hard for us.

Going in to that 1962 intermediate final against Galway, it was their second team but they were still very strong and a lot of Galway people were very disappointed afterwards that they didn't win; they thought they would have it easy against us. Galway had won the Munster Intermediate Championship so they were no bad team. They were playing the second teams from the strong Munster counties so I think that gave our victory a little more relevance too as they had come through a tough provincial campaign.

We were told that only the previous week the Galway intermediates had beaten their senior counterparts in a challenge game, so there was a lot expected of them. We were in total control throughout. I can remember it was a wet day but that didn't deter us. Someone told me years ago that I played all my best hurling in the rain, but I disagree with that! By half-time, we had built up a 2-7 to 1-0 lead with two goals from Billy Walsh, or 'Black' Willie. We didn't let up in the second-half and carried on from where we had left off in the first period. I scored our third goal of the game, and by the time the final whistle went the scoreboard read 3-9 to 2-5 in our favour. Galway did play a bit better in the second-half but we were still the better team throughout. Mick Curtin was Galway's main man and he scored 2-3 of their total. I actually met Mick Curtin years later out in New York playing golf and we chatted about the game. Mick was a very good hurler.

Galway were shocked afterwards. They were expected to beat Carlow easy enough but we knew we'd be more than a match for them and it showed on the day with our performance where every man played well and we were convincing winners. Years later I remember reading an interview with Joe McDonagh where he said he cried after the game. Joe was only very young at the time but that stuck with me ever since.

It's funny looking back, but I can't remember too many celebrations after it. I don't even think we got a meal. Times were different back then. For the most part you just played the game and went home afterwards. A few weeks later we played London again, this time in the All-Ireland proper final in Croke Park and we hammered them on a score line of 6-15 to 3-3. It was great to be All-Ireland champions but in a way that game was a little bit of an anti-climax as, like I said, for a lot of lads the Galway game was the real final. In fairness though, no matter what lads were thinking we still had a job to do and we did what was needed, and it was nice to win it in Croke Park too.

Back then the league started before Christmas, around October time and about six weeks after we beat London we played Cork in a National League game in Dr Cullen Park. We ended up beating them in what was one of Carlow hurling's greatest ever results. That was a very good Carlow team we had and at the time I didn't think it was anything major beating Cork. It's a bigger deal now for me when I look back on it, but at the time I didn't think of it like that. I don't mean to be flippant about it but we deserved to be up in Division One and beating Cork was just proof of that.

I remember arriving home to the house that evening about 6pm. How I remember the time was because Seán Óg Ó Ceallachain was just coming on the radio with the GAA results. Only one of my brothers had gone to the match so he knew the result but I had a couple of brothers at home who hadn't gone in to it, so they still wouldn't have heard the result until it came on the radio. I came in to the house, threw the boots under the stairs and went into the kitchen. One of my brothers asked me how we got on? I knew what he was getting at and I didn't say much, but when the results came on the radio the headline was… 'Shock of the century'. I got a bigger kick out of seeing the brothers' faces than I did from actually beating Cork!

About a week later one of my friends showed me a copy of *The Nationalist* and there was a small piece with Christy Ring after the game where he apparently said about me after the game that 'I'd stay up all night just to watch him hurl'. Whatever way he said it or whoever he said it too, I got great mileage out of it. I picked the Galway game as the 'Game of my life' but it was that Cork win that really made me well known because of what Christy said. On that note, just before lockdown due to Covid-19, I gave an interview for *The Examiner* ahead of the Carlow and Laois NHL game where I mentioned the above statement.

A few weeks later I received a lovely letter from Tim Horgan. Tim had written a book on Christy a few years previously and wanted to clear something up. After we beat Cork, it was written in the paper that Christy had said that quote about Denis Murphy, the Cork hurler. Many years later, when writing his book, Tim Horgan had that quote in it about Denis. It wasn't until Denis Murphy confirmed to Tim himself that it wasn't him Christy had paid the compliment to, rather a Carlow hurler. It was only when seeing my interview then did Tim Horgan realise that I was the Carlow hurler. Only for that mix up in *The Examiner* all those years ago, I might have been in Christy's book!

I actually ran into Christy again a few years after that game, albeit in unexpected circumstances. I was part of a Laois team playing a golf tournament in Thurles. All the teams were made up of hurlers for the tournament. I was having a mineral before we went out to play and one of the lads remarked that they had spotted Christy Ring over by the scoreboard. I don't think Christy played golf, but he was there as a guest.

Despite playing against Christy, and the nice compliment he paid me after we beat them, I had never actually spoken to the man and I was going to go over and introduce myself to him but I was a little shy about doing so because I didn't even think he'd remember who I was. This was around 1978, so it was 16 years after we beat them in that league game and actually only a year before his untimely death. Anyway Christy was walking past us and I put my hand out and put it on his shoulder and I said to him, 'Christy, it's a good few years since I met you'. He turned around to me, and it was probably one of the greatest moments of my life as he stuck his finger in my stomach and he said, 'I know you boy, you hurled for Carlow'. That's something I will never forget. I got such a shock as I didn't think he'd recognise me but when he did, I'd say I probably blushed. Most of the lads I was with wouldn't have known I'd have hurled against Christy either so they got a great kick out of it too, but that was definitely a stand out moment for me and one I'm still very proud of.

Playing in Division One for those couple of years was great for Carlow and we more than held our own. I remember we played Tipperary… I think it was 1961. The Tipperary full-back line at the time, Kieran Carey, Michael Maher and John Doyle were affectionately known as 'Hell's Kitchen'. I remember getting the ball and soloing through towards their last line of defence. Someone remarked to me after, 'Jesus you're some eejit to be soloing in there' but when you're playing you don't think about those things, you just get on with it and play the match as normal. Certainly they were heady times for Carlow.

My first All-Ireland hurling final I was ever at was in 1955 when Wexford beat Galway. In 1956 I was there again for the clash of Wexford and Cork. That day Christy Ring was going for his ninth All-Ireland senior medal. Wexford won the game but afterwards Wexford's Nick O'Donnell, Bobby Rackard and Art Foley carried Christy shoulder high from the field. To be able to do that despite just being crowned All-Ireland champions took something special but I'd know a lot of those Wexford lads and they were great men.

My brother Mick was playing for Wexford at the time. Mick had a very successful career with his adopted county and won three All-Irelands with Wexford in 1955, '56 and '60. I often thought back to that 1956 final and said to myself that… *Here I was in Croke Park, my brother is playing corner back for Wexford, Christy Ring is playing corner forward for Cork.* It was surreal. Little did I know, that being a young 12-year-old boy from Carlow, that one day I'd get to be on the same pitch as Christy Ring.

After I left Carlow and St Mullins, I ended up hurling with Clonaslee in Laois. Tom Neville was training us and we had a final coming up. The last night at training before the final, Tom was giving us a little pep talk. He was talking to our goalie John Joe Carroll and he said, 'John Joe, if I see you taking a short puck out, I'm taking you straight off'. So that just shows the difference between both eras and how much things have changed as regards tactics; puck outs are such an integral part of the game whereas back then, it was just hit it as hard and as far as you could.

The reason I was playing in Laois in the first place was in part due to a dispute. St Mullins had qualified for the Carlow SHC final in 1970 where we were due to play Erin's Own (Bagenalstown). After the semi-final, three of our players had headed straight to the airport on holidays. They had originally put their holiday back by a week so they could play the semi-final. Inside in the dressing-room after, we were told that the final was on the following week, but we told the county board that we wouldn't be able to field.

You might think that how could we fail to field by only missing three players but at the time we had a very small pick. Some games we'd barely have 15. I can remember my brother Luke playing in goal for the senior side when he was only 14, so that just shows that numbers were very tight and three players missing definitely made a difference between us fielding and not fielding. The county board anyway gave Erin's Own the game, just like that and we were given no opportunity to play the game on an alternative date. I said then that I wouldn't play in Carlow again. By that stage, I had actually started a business in Laois and while there, Clonaslee got on to me so I decided to throw in my lot with them from there on in.

I never hurled in Carlow again after that, although I did carry on with Carlow for one more year and played for them in 1971. As luck would have it, my first match hurling in Laois for Clonaslee was also the same day I was supposed to play for Carlow against Wicklow. I played the club game in Laois and had the lads on the line told that if we were winning well to take me off. With about 10 minutes remaining, we had a good lead so I came off and headed for the car, still togged out. I drove straight to Gorey for the Carlow game, but I might as well have stayed at home. I was frozen by the time I got to the second game and I should have put on a tracksuit or jumper or something but it was a lesson that it wasn't good to be jumping from one place to the other in such a rush.

When I arrived to Clonaslee, they hadn't won the senior championship since 1910, but in '75 I was part of the team that brought the cup back to Clonaslee after 65 years, so no one can accuse me of going there medal hunting with a famine like that! The people in Clonaslee were very good to me and I enjoyed that victory. As much as it meant to me though, it didn't compare to winning a championship with your own club. I've won things with Carlow and St Mullins but above anything else, to win a county championship with your own is something special. The people you grew up with, your friends, all of you coming from the same place. That feeling can't be beaten. Coming from St Mullins means a lot to me. I have lived away from there for a long time now but home will always be home for me. Everything I have achieved in life, on and off the field, I owe to St Mullins. Even to this day, every time I go home, the feeling never gets old. Going through Borris and then knowing that I'm almost there.

I still get a lump in my throat. *I'm home.*

# TOMMY CORCORAN

### ÉIRE ÓG 4-7 ★ PALATINE 1-5
### Carlow SFC Semi-Final
### Dr Cullen Park, Carlow
### SEPTEMBER 30, 1962

*Tommy Corcoran (far right), who served club and county for two decades as a player, started his journey as a teenager in the county championship in 1962.*

★ **ÉIRE ÓG:** M Brophy (2-0) P Nolan (1-1), J Byrne (1-1), V Harvey (0-3), G Kelly (0-1), PJ Hogan (0-1).

★ **PALATINE:** J Byrne (1-0), S Woods (0-4), P Daly(0-1).

*\* Full teams not available*

## THE ACTION

AS A RESULT of this easy victory over Palatine, Éire Óg have qualified for a second successive 'all town' county final against O'Hanrahan's in a bid to be crowned Carlow's finest. Éire Óg were never in any danger here. The only redeeming features of the game were touches of wizardry from Genie Kelly and the great defending of Ed Hogan.

Starting on a slow note, five minutes had not gone until the game was already shaping up as a flop. Palatine's determination could not withstand the lightning Éire Óg forward thrusts. The Éire Óg forwards had a plentiful supply of ball, this was in part to their dominance at midfield where they were never beaten. At the other end, Palatine attacks on the Éire Óg goal were few and far between. Occasionally they tried the short passing game but were met with frustration each time.

From Frank Power in goal to Pat Nolan at corner-forward, the winners were on top in every department. Power, whenever he was called upon, was capable but truth be told he had little to do as Cran Hogan was on top at full-back. Hogan gave a brilliant display of fielding and clearing. Lar D'Arcy and Tom Murphy were also outstanding at the back. Genie Kelly and Denny Hyland were never troubled at midfield. All six forwards won their battles and were well on top all day, particularly Martin Brophy, Pat Nolan and Vinny Harvey.

Éire Óg led 2-3 to no score at the break and the game was already well over. Palatine, did however try to change it around for the second-half, most notably the switch of Jim Hayes to the forwards, but in reality it made little impact. Seamie Woods scored 0-4 of Palatine's total between frees and open play, while Joe Byrne got the goal.
Éire Óg didn't let up in the second-half and scored a further 2-4 to complete a comfortable 11 point victory.

★★★★★

66

THE FIRST CHAMPIONSHIP game I ever played with Éire Óg was the semi-final of the county championship. I was still a minor that year and so I wasn't involved with the seniors at all up to that point. Any preparation I had in the lead up to that game was zero, AND it was a total surprise to me to be called up. It was only two years previously, in 1960 that the club had won its first senior championship, so to be called up to play with that team was a big thing. My memories of the game itself are hazy but funny enough, it's the details before the game and how I ended up being involved that are more vivid.

There was an organisation in Carlow town at the time called the Irish National Foresters. They had a premises down in College Street. My father would have been treasurer with the INF while also being caretaker of the building they had. They used to let out the rooms some nights for meetings. This one Saturday night anyway, Éire Óg were having a meeting there. I'm not sure if it was a club meeting or just the selectors picking the team. I'd have often helped out my father down there and on this night I was there waiting to lock up.

When the meeting was finished up and everyone was leaving I was handed a card with all the details of the game on it. Obviously there were no mobile phones in those days so that was how players would find out about games. I was handed a card with all the details of the game, venue, opposition, time etc. Sometimes if it was an away game, it would have the time you were to meet up and where, because at that time not everybody would have had a car.

The game I was handed a card for was no ordinary game, but the semi-final of the senior county championship. I went home that night and showed my parents the card. I think my mother was a little bit concerned at the fact that I hadn't been involved with an adult team before and was still only playing minor. I kind of made nothing of it at the time, thinking that they just wanted me to be there to tog out and nothing else.

I went to Dr Cullen Park on the Sunday. I had my gear with me and I went in to the senior dressing-room for the very first time. I was togging out and getting ready and still not expecting to see any action at that stage. Frank Power, who was our goalkeeper and captain, was handing out the jerseys and he handed me one. I looked at it and it was the No 2. I was a little bit reluctant at the time to put it on as it was my first involvement with them. I was thinking to myself, *Has he given me the wrong jersey here? Is someone going to come along in a minute and take this back off me?* Anyway I decided to put the jersey on and it was okay. It wasn't a mistake. I had actually been picked at corner-back. I might have been that bit unsure at the start but once I knew that I was actually playing, of course I was delighted that they had shown faith in me and that day was the start of a long career playing senior for Éire Óg and indeed Carlow.

I thought I had done enough that day and was happy that we had qualified for the county final. The funny thing was, after been parachuted into the team out of nowhere for the semi-final to start the game, I didn't see any action in the final then at all as we beat O'Hanrahans the following week. I've often thought back to that game and maybe the selectors didn't think they were taking that much of a risk by starting me, as they possibly thought that we wouldn't lose to Palatine.

I might not have seen any action in the final but deep down I wasn't overly disappointed. Of course I would have loved to play but before the semi-final I had never played a senior game and now a few weeks later, I had a senior championship medal so I was delighted to have played my first game and to have gotten my foot in the door with the team.

When I think back to Shane O'Donnell's heroics for Clare in the All-Ireland hurling final where he wasn't named to start, and wasn't told he was starting until shortly before throw-in, it kind of reminded me of that day being handed the No 2 jersey right before throw-in. The previous year, 1961 had been the first 'all town' final where O'Hanrahans beat Éire Óg. After we beat Palatine then, that meant it was all set to be another town affair only this time the tables were turned and it was Éire Óg who claimed the title. Those games claimed major national attention at the time as there were opposing brothers playing against each other in those county finals.

I was still playing senior football for Éire Óg into the early 80s. In 1980, we reached the club's first Leinster senior club final where we were beaten by Walterstown of Meath by a point. That game was played in early 1981. In 1982 I won my last senior championship. I didn't play at all that year but was still on the panel. That was the only year in my career where I didn't play any championship football. Some of the earlier championships I might not have made the starting 15 in every game but I still saw action in most games. In 1982, I kind of knew that it was coming to an end.

That Palatine game might have been the start of a long career in the Éire Óg senior shirt but it was also a stepping stone to getting picked for Carlow. I was delighted to play in Croke Park three times with Carlow. We played Wicklow, Dublin and Kildare. Against Kildare, I ended up marking former great Tommy Carew. We beat Wicklow and that is still the last time a Carlow senior team won a game in Croke Park.

The GAA has played a massive part in my life, both on and off the field. I had a long playing career but some people might think that most of my success came off the field after I was finished playing.

I was involved with the Carlow senior hurlers as a selector in 1992 when they won the All-Ireland B championship. Martin Fitzpatrick was the Carlow manager for that success. I was also involved in the backroom team with the first ever Carlow hurling team to reach a Leinster minor final in 2006, where we played Kilkenny in Croke Park. Tommy Buggy from Castlecomer was in charge of that team.

Playing was great but I still loved being involved in the management side of things just as much, both at club and county level. I still would have been involved with Setanta hurling club before Covid arrived. I played a lot of hurling as well during my career with Carlow Town and would have won a number of championships there too. During my playing career I had a lot more involvement with football but since I got into the coaching I have been more involved with the hurling and I managed teams over the years, while I also had a spell as chairman of Carlow Town. I was actually over the last Carlow Town team to win the senior championship in 1988. They won the senior and junior double that year, so that was great. I also coached football teams in Éire Óg and had a spell as club secretary there as well.

I was proud to represent Carlow and I've often said that Carlow players were as good as anywhere else. I did my teacher training in St Pat's Drumcondra. It was only a two-year course back then. I'd be meeting fellas from all other counties and playing football with and against them all. A lot of these players would have been on successful minor teams around the country and had gone on to play senior, while others had been successful footballers on the college circuit. In my time at St Pat's, I was on both football and hurling college teams and was playing in the Dublin Senior Championship in both codes. Even at that time, I was playing with lads from successful counties and here I was making both teams.

I could never see why Carlow footballers couldn't be competing with these stronger teams. I felt that having made the team, that I was good enough to be there and I felt I was as good as a lot of the lads who were already there before me. At the same time, there were plenty of lads around Carlow who were as good, and better than me, and I could just never figure out how we weren't doing better than we were as a county. Maybe it was an attitude, I'm not sure, but definitely Carlow should have been doing better.

When we were playing with Éire Óg we always believed we could win, no matter who we were playing. There is just a belief there in the club. I suppose that comes with all the success that the club has had. I remember having that conversation with John O'Hara many years ago. John played senior hurling for Carlow for years and we were both selectors in 1992 for that successful B campaign for the senior hurlers. John played for Naomh Eoin and at the time they were the kingpins of hurling in Carlow and he said that it was the exact same attitude in Myshall. Because they had been so successful, they just had that belief built in to them as well and, like Éire Óg, they just believed they'd win when they'd take to the field, no matter who they were playing against, either inside or outside the county.

Back when I was playing, there were probably more opportunities for clubs to test themselves outside the county in proper meaningful games. Inter-county was straight knockout at the time. A lot of the club championships would have been knockout at the time also, so this then gave clubs an opportunity to run their own tournaments. The current provincial club championships didn't come in until 1970. Those club tournaments were really big back in those days and clubs would go all out to win them as sometimes the prizes for winning them were very good. This, and the fact that you'd be playing against teams that you wouldn't normally get to play against meant they were always fiercely competitive games. We would often play in the Shillelagh tournament down in Wicklow. We also had trips to Dublin to play against a host team or maybe a Meath team sometimes, so these were all regular occurrences. You'd be playing against lads who you'd normally only be reading about. You'd be testing yourselves against the best and that always stood to you going forward. We were as good as any teams we came up against in those games and the same as my time playing for St Pat's, you'd know that other lads in Carlow were as good as those you were playing against.

When I think back to that Palatine game and getting to make my senior championship debut, I could never have foreseen the path it would lead me down. Getting to represent my club and then my county at the top level for so long was great, and to still be involved in the GAA all these years later. For that I am grateful.

# CYRIL HUGHES

**ST PATRICK'S, MAYNOOTH 2-17 ★ UCC 1-4**
**Sigerson Cup Semi-Final**
**Mardyke, Cork**
**MARCH 3, 1973**

*Playing against the best young footballers in the country forged the Sigerson Cup games that Cyril Hughes (above, managing Carlow) has never forgotten.*

★ **MAYNOOTH:** K McGovern; B Casey, D O'Mahony, J O'Mahony; P Henry, T O'Keeffe, L Walsh; **C Hughes (0-3)**, S McCarthy (1-0); F Murray (0-1), P Burke (0-9), J Kennelly; S McKeon, M Flanagan (0-2), F McCann (1-2).

★ **UCC:** N Murphy; S Looney, M Scannell, S Kavanagh; F Looney, P O'Shea, J McMahon; N O'Sullivan, P Lynch (0-1); V Hanley (0-1), D Kavanagh, D Murray; D O' Hare (1-0), M O'Callaghan, N Brosnan. Subs: F Groarke for O'Hare, B Lynch (0-2) for Murray.

## THE ACTION

MAYNOOTH'S VICTORY OVER UCC was one of the biggest upsets in the history of the Sigerson competition. It must also have been one of the largest margins of victory in a competition noted for its close games. UCC had won five of the last seven Sigerson championships and they were hotly fancied to overcome newcomers Maynooth. This was, in fact, only Maynooth's second year to play in the university championship.

The basis for their win was laid by their vastly superior fitness which completely dispirited a poor home fifteen. Even though UCC were handicapped by the absence of rugby inter-pro Moss Keane, and only introduced their star Kerry forward Brendan Lynch in the third quarter, they were as comprehensively beaten as the score suggests. And while they had a disallowed goal near the end, the huge scoreline might have been even more damning were it not for the brilliance of their goalkeeper Noel Murphy.

Maynooth set up their success with a scoring spree while playing with the wind in the first-half. Ironically, it was Cork-born corner-forward Frank McCann who hit the goal which helped Maynooth to a 10-point lead at the break, 1-11 to 1-1.

UCC, who only had one score from play in the first-half – a goal in the 22nd minute from Derry O'Hare – never looked like getting back afterwards. Fact was, there was no combating the brilliance of Maynooth midfielder Cyril Hughes, and the impeccable score-taking of Peter Burke, who finished with nine points. Hughes was ably assisted in midfield by Sean McCarthy, himself a Cork man.

Maynooth played beautifully controlled football throughout the game. They were always much more determined, used the ball cleverly and made the host team appear like novices.

★★★★★

66

I PLAYED MY first game of senior football for Carlow in 1970, when I was just 17. I came on as a substitute in an O'Byrne cup game against Wexford. I had played an Under-21 game prior to the senior game that day. Wexford beat us after, but I went on to play in the senior championship later that year against Meath a week after I finished my Leaving cert. That was the start of my football career in a way I suppose, and it really kicked on from there.

After the Leaving Cert, I ended up going to Maynooth to do teaching, and Maynooth at that stage was not really known as a football college. Up to the end of the 1960s, Maynooth would have had mostly clerical students in the college.

In 1973, UCC were once again hot favourites to not only overcome us in the semi-final, but to win the competition outright. Our team was still full of inter-county players though and obviously being Sigerson, every other college was the same. That's one of the reasons that game stands out for me and why I enjoyed my time in Maynooth so much, because you were playing with and against great players every week. A couple of our county players might not have been from the top ranked counties, but they were still *county* players and beating UCC and making the Sigerson final showed we had very good players and we showed that day what we could do.

That UCC team was full of big names. For example, Paudie Lynch was playing midfield for them and I was never one for blowing my own trumpet but I was only a young lad and I feel that I played him off the pitch that day, so that was special for me, considering where he was in his career.

Brendan Lynch didn't actually start the game for them; he came on as a substitute, but I had actually played on Brendan before as we met them in a league match earlier in the year. Moss Keane was full-back for UCC that day.

We played that league game in Dublin. It was a home game for Maynooth but we didn't play them in Maynooth; it was in a club pitch in Dublin which I can't remember now. Brendan Lynch was starting for UCC, and he had scored 2-4 in a match against Maynooth the previous year but I held him to three kicks of the ball, and he scored 0-1. Lynch had a couple of All-Ireland medals at that stage so I was very pleased about that at the time. So, the fact we had beaten UCC in the league gave us big belief going in to play them in the Sigerson semi-final a few months later.

UCC had three Kerry footballers in their half-back line, two Kerry midfielders and two Kerry half-forwards, so they had plenty of All-Ireland winners. The basis of their team was mostly Kerry and Cork lads, with maybe one from Limerick and Clare. We were no mugs either. Mayo's John O'Mahony was corner-back. John had won an All-Ireland minor medal the year before he went to Maynooth. John's brother Dan was full-back and Dan went on to be a priest after.

Paddy Henry of Sligo, he won a Connacht championship with them in 1975. Tony O'Keeffe from Kerry was our centre-back. Tony went on to be Kerry GAA secretary. Peter Burke from Longford was our main scoring threat up front. He was a silky forward and had a great kick off the ground. Mel Flanagan from Roscommon was another good fella. Mel actually went on to be a golf course designer, but Mel would have played senior for Roscommon.

There were no two ways about it; we were massive underdogs going in to that UCC game. While they had been winning Sigerson cups regularly, Maynooth probably had about 1,500 students, and that included the Theology students so it was kind of like a big secondary school. We were very small compared to our opponents.

In the final we played UCD and in midfield they had Dave McCarthy of Cork and Kerry's John O'Keeffe. I was midfield for Maynooth, along with Sean McCarthy from Cork, so you could see the type of players we were coming up against on a regular basis playing in these competitions. We only lost the final by four points, but I believe that we would have won had we had Derry's Colum Mullan playing with us.

A few weeks previous, Colum and a few lads had gone to the wake of Tyrone footballer Brendan Dolan. Brendan had been killed in a road accident. Unfortunately, on the way back from the wake they were involved in an accident themselves. Colum had been driving and ended up breaking his neck and spending the rest of his life paralysed. Colum had been our captain up to that point. After the accident, I took up the captaincy. Colum was a big guy, he was well over six foot and he made our forward line tick. He was a massive loss for us going in to that Sigerson campaign.

Of course, what happened to Colum was massively traumatic for him and his family. We went to see him before the Sigerson started; I think he was in a hospital in Belfast. It was traumatic for the players too but, unfortunately, Colum would spend the rest of his life a paraplegic before he passed away in 2004. That was a massive blow what happened to Colum. He was a big loss on the football field, but off the field it was a massive shock for everyone and a very upsetting time.

Despite being without Colum, we still managed that shock win over UCC and of course we faced another star-studded team in the final, with that UCD team. The day of the final was an awful day. It was played in the Mardyke and I remember Cork played Limerick in a hurling match before our game, so the pitch was really cut up by the time the football came around. We had a lighter team than UCD but it was still a tight game throughout. I was playing midfield and I got the first couple of points. It was pretty much even for a lot of the game. Peter Burke got a goal in the second-half to put us ahead. We kind of held on to that lead until about 10 minutes from the end, when they got a sloppy enough goal to put them ahead then. I remember the ball barely trickling over the line and it barely made it over with all the mud but it did, just about. That put UCD ahead then and they held on to that until the end.

It was disappointing to lose of course but we had beaten UCC well in the semi-final and put it up to UCD in the final, so it showed what the smaller colleges could do once they got a good group of players. Up to that point, the Sigerson cup was only really played between the big universities and it was only really after that, that the Technological and Regional colleges started to appear in it.

One of the reasons I choose that UCC game was because what it led to for me. At that time, there were five teams in the Railway Cup – the four provinces as normal and then a combined universities team made up of the best players from the colleges. I was picked on the Combined Universities and we shocked Ulster and Leinster to make the final against Connacht. I was picked to start the first day and we ended up drawing. The Combined Universities ended up winning the replay, up in Athlone to win the Railway Cup and it's a nice thing to look back on and to say that you have a Railway Cup medal.

For the three years I was in Maynooth, I was on the Combined Universities panel. I was in and out of the team itself because the lads who were there were so strong. It was a funny set up in a way. We had no selector at any stage for that team. Queens had a selector and probably a third of the team was made up of Queens' lads. That selector was the manager too for Queens, Paddy O'Hara, so that definitely helped them lads in getting on the team.

I normally played half-back or midfield and I played most of my career in or around that area. The last time I had played as a forward was probably around under-14 but I was picked there for the Combined Universities at one stage and it didn't suit me at all. Joining me for company in the half-forward line was Kerry's Brendan Lynch and Kevin Kilmurray of Offaly so I was in good company. The full-forward line was Paddy Moriarty of Armagh, Dan Kavanagh of Kerry and Derry's Anthony McGurk. That's just a flavour of who the combined side had, but there were top players all over the field.

Irrespective of all that, it was a massive honour to be picked on that team and to be playing with such top-quality players. It was a great honour to play with the Combined Universities and to play with and against such great players, as my club career at the time was a bit all over the place. I had played some of my earlier football with Ballymurphy and I won an intermediate title with them in 1969. At some stage then, Ballymurphy then kind of decided that if you weren't from the area that you weren't going to play, so I was at a loose end on where to go. Around the same time, Ballinkillen had formed a football team, so I threw in my lot with them.

I remember being at a wedding in Galway one night and driving back to Ballinkillen for a league match on the Sunday morning, because we were playing championship the following week, but they ended up giving a walkover so that was a waste of a journey. I don't think they were overly pushed about the football as much as the hurling. At that stage, I was playing senior football for Carlow so I thought to myself that I can't have this kind of carry on; so it was then I decided to join Bagenalstown the following year. They were playing intermediate at that stage and it was definitely taken more seriously, which was what I was looking for.

At that time, you had Fenagh, Ballinkillen, Bagenalstown and Nurney all in the one parish, so that was a lot of teams for just the one parish, but football in Bagenalstown was competitive and that was good for me. Around the same time, I actually trained Kilbride to win a county intermediate title, beating Nurney in the final and, looking back now, it's a wonder how I had the time to train a team and to play both codes, but I suppose that's just the love I had for the game and still do to this day.

# PADDY QUIRKE

### NAOMH EOIN 1-8 ★ ST MULLINS 1-6
### Carlow SHC Final, Third Replay
### Dr Cullen Park
### NOVEMBER 19, 1978

*Victory for Naomh Eoin in the amazing four-game Carlow hurling final in 1978 could never quite be surpassed by other acknowledgements on the national stage.*

★ **NAOMH EOIN:** K Minchin; Peter Nolan, S Quirke, S Keogh: N Kavanagh, J O'Hara (0-1) M. Nolan; J Doyle, **P Quirke (0-1)**; Pat Nolan (0-1), E Quirke (0-3), D Murphy (0-1); A Ryan (1-1), W Eustace, S Murphy. Subs: T Foley for S Murphy, N Minchin for P Nolan.

★ **ST MULLINS:** M Kehoe; P Connors, J Kielty, M Murphy; J Treacy, P Murphy, R Ryan; S Ralph, P Kehoe (0-1); F McDonald, J Kavanagh, M Moriarty; B Walsh (0-3), L Walsh (1-2), S Purcell. Subs: O Dwyer for Purcell, S O'Hanlon for Kielty.

## THE ACTION

LEADING FROM START to finish, Naomh Eoin finally broke the deadlock in this marathon Carlow SHC final at the fourth attempt. Naomh Eoin made light work of having full-back Sean Quirke sent off five minutes before half-time. In fact, with Quirke's brother Paddy outstanding at midfield the winners seemed to gain inspiration when faced with adversity.

Naomh Eoin led by 1-5 to 0-3 at half-time and were coasting to a 1-8 to 0-6 victory minutes from the end, when St Mullins veteran corner-forward Liamy Walsh cracked in a goal. However, they couldn't cut the deficit any further and the title went to Myshall.

After almost four and a half hours of hurling, and two months since the first game was played, Carlow had a county hurling champion. This was also the fourth title in five years for the Myshall men. Naomh Eoin were the dominant team in this game but yet were still hanging on at the end. Many people in attendance thought that St Mullins had snatched it right at the death, as Liamy Walsh scored another late goal. However, the referee had blown for a free beforehand.

There were many heroes throughout this epic but none stood taller than Paddy Quirke. The dual county star was just a class above the rest in everything he did. Where the last three games had been high scoring, this game was the opposite with scores relatively hard to come by. Close marking by both sets of defences, who were reluctant to give up anything after so much effort, was the main reason for this, although playing hurling in the middle of November probably didn't help either.

★★★★★

66

LOOKING BACK THROUGH my career, there were many great days, but I find it hard to look past the county hurling final saga of 1978. I picked the fourth and final game as it was the one where we finally got over the line after a long, drawn-out saga. There was about two months or so between the first and the last game; The reason being was back then the National Hurling League started before Christmas and between each of the hurling finals Carlow played league games. We were playing against the St Mullins guys one Sunday and the following Sunday we'd be playing with them for Carlow.

By 1978 we were starting to put our mark on the senior hurling championship in Carlow. Ballinkillen beat us in the final of 1973 before we beat them in the '74 decider. We beat St Fintan's in 1975, and Ballinkillen again in '76. We didn't reach the final in 1977, but in '78 we were very determined to win it back. We had a few young players coming through.

Our goalkeeper Kevin Minchin was only 17 at the time. Kevin had just come in that year and had replaced the long-serving James Eustace. Ned Kavanagh was also 17 and a regular on the team. Noel Minchin, who was in and out of the team in the forwards, was 18. We had youth but there were plenty of us in our prime as well who had all tasted championship success in the previous years. Thirty-five players contributed to our senior hurling team that year so that kept our selectors Mick Tobin, Pat Mooney and Peter Kavanagh very busy.

There was a great build up to all the games, especially the fourth final. I was in Dublin at the time doing my teacher training course in Bolton Street and I would drive down to Myshall one night a week to train. Training that time in Myshall was in 'The Ranch'. There were no dressing-rooms and there were no floodlights. There was a laneway down the side of the field and that's where we togged out… and then straight out onto the field. We'd train under the lights of cars most nights.

Pat Nolan had an old pumphouse in the corner and there was a socket in it. He used to plug in a string of light bulbs down along the side of the field. It was all very primitive but that's just the way it was at the time.

My brother Eamon was training us then, as well as playing. He was also a dual county player. He was our most dangerous forward scoring 0-9 the first day and

0–13 the second day. We were probably favourites going in to that first game. St Mullins hadn't won the championship since 1968 but they were desperate to get their hands on that trophy again.

Ballymurphy were another good team in Carlow at the time. It might have taken four games to decide the 1978 champions, but when we played Ballymurphy in the semi-final that year the game also ended in a draw so we played six games between the semi-final and final. There was a lot of hurling going on that year!

With it taking so long to find a winner for the championship, Carlow Town hurling club were chosen to represent Carlow in the Leinster Club Championship and were beaten by Carnew Emmets in the first round. It would have been nice to go forward of course but deep down I don't think any of us minded too much at that stage, as we were all so consumed in the saga that was developing.

A big part of the county final day was marching behind the Kilkenny Majorettes accordion band in front of 4,000 or 5,000 supporters. The first three finals we played were all very high scoring, all days for the forwards. Just take a look at the scores.

Naomh Eoin 0-16, St Mullins 2-10
Naomh Eoin 1-16, St Mullins 3-10
Naomh Eoin 0-21, St Mullins 4-9 (AET)
Naomh Eoin 1-8, St Mullins 1-6.

With so much going on between all the games, little things stand out for me. The first replay was a fantastic game of hurling. The second day out was another draw and the big heading on *The Nationalist* read, *A hurling super show as Naomh Eoin force second replay*. The second replay then saw St Mullins go 10 points up at one stage, before we pulled it back and managed to get a draw. That day it went to extra-time. Once St Mullins went 10 points up it probably looked like curtains for us but, in fairness to the lads, they dug deep and pulled out all the stops. I was playing midfield with 'Black' Jimmy Doyle (RIP) and he scored 0-6 from play that day which was a massive total for a midfielder.

Right near the end of the third day, we were winning by three points when a long ball came down towards our side of the field. Peter Nolan was playing corner-back for us; he went for this ball but he ended up going down with cramp.

Pat Kehoe, unmarked, gained possession and stuck it in the back of the net for St Mullins to make it another draw.

The last day then, the day we finally won it, I can remember there was a strong wind but there was no rain. St Mullins won the toss and decided to play against the wind in the first-half. We got off to a great start with a goal after five minutes. Andy Ryan using his handball brain sent Mattie Kehoe the wrong way and rattled the net with a good ground shot. That early goal proved to be vital. Eamon was still our main man up front, but they were marking him very tightly and he wasn't scoring as freely as previous days. We went in at half-time with a five-point lead, 1-5 to 0-3, but we were dealt a blow when my other brother Sean was sent off just before the break. St Mullins used their extra man, Jim Tracey who was playing half-back, in front of our full-forward line and that kind of curtailed our scoring ability. Our half-back line was probably our strongest line with John O'Hara our regular No 6; his long striking was a feature of his game.

St Mullins had us under fierce pressure coming towards the end. With seconds remaining a bizarre thing happened and we thought we had lost it. We were two points up when Liamy Walsh scored a goal for St Mullins. The players were going wild celebrating and their supporters were doing much the same thing. However, the referee Gus Hennessy had blown for a free before the ball was hit in, but this was obviously missed by the players and they played on. Once things had calmed down, everyone quickly realised that the goal was disallowed and the ball was to be called back for a free. Almost straightaway the final whistle went and we had scraped through by two points. The cup was finally presented to our captain Michael Nolan, with our large following of supporters in full voice. Michael really played the captain's part as he was a fantastic motivator… one of Mick's great skills was his solo runs. He was a great choice for captain that year.

There was great celebrating after each game especially the last game seeing as we had won it. A lot of the St Mullins players joined us each time demonstrating the sporting nature of all four games. The real celebration was probably the following February when we had our dinner dance in The Seven Oaks Hotel, where about 300 people celebrated. Our chairman Tommy Murphy was a very proud man that night.

There were crowds of up to 5,000 at those senior games to witness surely a record length for a county final. A very unique photograph was taken of the two teams together before the last game; the teams lining up for the one photo emphasised the sporting nature of those games.

That was a golden time for Naomh Eoin in both football and hurling. In the 1980s alone we were in eight football finals, including three replays, winning one. In hurling we contested seven finals and won five. We won the senior football and hurling double in 1986 and we made several attempts to do it again, but were beaten in a few football finals. One of the football finals we lost to Éire Óg will be remembered for a very bizarre reason. We were flying it on that day and had a great run on Éire Óg. Sean Kelly from Rathvilly was refereeing the game. Next thing a woman broke in through the wire around the pitch and she planted Sean with her umbrella.

I was only a couple of yards away from Sean at the time. I'd say he was down for about five minutes. When things got going again and order was restored, he definitely played seven or eight minutes of added time. We were a point ahead with time almost up, when a long ball came in to our square. I thought I had it, only for Anthony 'Muckle' Keating to come in on my blind side at the last minute and punch the ball over the bar. The game was a draw and we lost the replay.

You can imagine my delight when I was chosen as a dual replacement All-Star in 1980. We travelled to New York, Los Angeles and San Francisco. I was very excited about making the trip. Kerry won the All-Ireland football that year and Galway the hurling. Mick Morrissey, a Carlow man living in New York, and a three-time All-Ireland winner with Wexford, presented me with a trophy to mark the occasion.

At that stage I had played on Leinster Railway Cup teams, so I knew a good few of the players but it was nice to be able to play alongside the best players and just to be part of such a trip. In later years I was selected on the Carlow GAA team of the Millennium in both football and hurling. There were many great players who were selected and, of course, many great players who weren't, but I was delighted to be chosen for them.

# TOMMY DWYER

**MEATH 1-15** ★ **CARLOW 1-12**
**Leinster SFC Quarter-Final**
**Dr Cullen Park, Carlow**
**JUNE 15, 1986**

*Tommy Dwyer (centre, back row) played for Leinster and Ireland, but almost conquering Meath in the Leinster Championship in Dr Cullen Park in 1986 was a game he can look back on with joy and regret.*

★ **MEATH:** M McQuillan; B O'Malley, M Lyons, P Lyons; C Coyle, L Harnan, T Ferguson; J Cassells (0-1), L Hayes (0-2); M O'Connell, B Stafford (0-2), D Beggy (1-2); F Murtagh (0-5), C O'Rourke (0-2), B Flynn (0-1). Sub: L Smyth for O'Connell.

★ **CARLOW:** M Hayden; J Wynne, T Cullen, L Kelly; N Molloy, J Walshe, A Curry; **T Dwyer**, L Kearns (0-1); P Kenny (0-5), P Quirke (0-1), L Molloy (0-1); J Hayden (0-1), L O'Brien, W Doyle (0-2). Subs: T O'Brien for J Hayden, D Wynne for J Wynne, P Browne (1-1) for L O'Brien.

## THE ACTION

MEATH WERE MIGHTILY relieved to escape from Dr Cullen Park with their championship hopes still alive after this scare from the home side. The Royals led 0-12 to 0-5 at the interval, and by 1-15 to 1-7 with 18 minutes left, but from there on they would not score again as Carlow came storming back into the game. At one stage it looked like Carlow would record their first ever championship victory over Meath, but they just ran out of steam right at the death.

Meath started like they meant business and Liam Hayes was having a blinder at midfield. Liam's father Jim was a former Carlow player so this was a homecoming of sorts for Hayes junior. Liam started off very well but faded towards the end when Carlow came back into the game. Instead it was the turn of Carlow's giant midfielder Tommy Dwyer to have total control of the midfield battle as he caught a plentiful supply of ball during Carlow's spell on top.

Carlow kicked the last five scores of the game. Up front, Paddy Quirke and Pat Kenny were making use of whatever meagre possession they were getting. Special mention must go to Carlow goalkeeper Martin Hayden, however, as on five occasions Meath looked like scoring certain goals only for Hayden to foil them each time. Meath converted only one of their six clear goal chances, while Carlow converted the one clear opportunity they had.

That Carlow goal came 13 minutes into the second-half when a Pat Kenny free came back off the post and Paddy Browne was quickest to react to finish to the back of the net. It didn't take Meath long to respond after this as David Beggy, the championship debutant, netted with the calmness of a man who had been there for years. Incredibly that was to be Meath's last score of the game, while it seemed to kickstart Carlow. They had Meath on the rack and looked on course to carry out one of the biggest shocks in championship football but self-doubt started to creep in once they got close. They kicked four wides in succession and with each wide you could sense the relief from the Meath faithful. For Carlow, unfortunately it was another moral victory.

★★★★★

66

ONE OF THE highlights of my time playing with Carlow was when we won promotion in the National League in 1984/85. As a result of this, it meant we qualified for the league quarter-final where we played Armagh in Croke Park. I put out my shoulder that day after I ended up getting caught between Joe Kernan and Fran McMahon. I knew Joe, and I had played football with Fran in America; it was just one of those unfortunate incidents. A week later, Carlow played Kerry in Dr Cullen Park. It was the GAA open draw competition, which was a follow on from the Centenary Cup the previous year. Kerry only beat us by two points that day and because of that injury against Armagh I missed that Kerry game which was tough to take at the time.

Carlow footballers had a very good team around that time. We had achieved promotion out of Division Four and everything was looking rosy. Unfortunately, the GAA shifted the goalposts and restructured the leagues over the winter by putting Division Three and Four together and calling it Division Three South and North, so we were still playing some of the same teams again. We had done so well to get promoted that year and we won some tight games in places we weren't expected to win. We beat Limerick down in Askeaton and followed that up by beating Fermanagh in Enniskillen, so it wasn't easy to get where we did but once things were changed up, it was very disheartening.

I'm not saying we were going to win everything around us but we had a good team and we had some really good players. We were playing the likes of Kerry and Armagh, and we were putting it up to them. We knew when we played Meath in 1986 that it would be a real test of where we were. Sean Boylan was in charge of them for a couple of years at that stage and he was starting to build something big and they were starting to make serious inroads. Nobody really expected us to put up much of a show against them. That was a top class Meath team, and they were tough. You were coming up against the likes of Mick Lyons, Joe Cassells, Brian Stafford… so we were really going to be up against it. Meath started well and were in front for most of the game. They were dominant but we were still managing to keep them in sight.

Once we brought it back to three points, I can remember we had chances and one chance might have even hit the post if I can remember correctly and, all of a sudden, we could have been level. For the last 20 minutes it was all Carlow and I can remember Mick Lyons dancing around the square trying to get the Meath lads going. We scored five points in-a-row and we had them under serious pressure. Meath had been the dominant team for 50 minutes but whatever happened for those last 20 minutes, we just took over. Once Meath got their goal – and that was their last score of the game – it just seemed to spark us into action and we were in control from then on.

When we were on top, I can remember every ball being kicked out and it didn't seem to matter where it was kicked out I just seemed to be under it – so I was sending the ball straight back in. The Meath lads were going frantic about it. It was those few silly wides when we were going well in that period which killed us and that was our downfall in the end. After our league promotion and then our performance against Kerry, that Meath game was probably the big game at that stage for us. We showed what we could do but, unfortunately, we didn't show it for long enough on the day.

Carlow had some great footballers around that time. Take Paddy Quirke. Paddy was as good as anybody that played the game… in both codes. The Molloy's from Rathvilly were good footballers. Tom Cullen at full-back was another. Tom probably didn't get the recognition he deserved but Tom was in Dublin at the time and he'd drive down to Carlow for training a couple of times a week. That was in the time before the motorway so a drive to Dublin back then was a lot harder than it is now, but it just showed the commitment. Lads wanted to play for Carlow and we had some top footballers. They had great dedication and I know if I had the same dedication as some of those lads I would have been a hell of a better player.

We had some good days in the Carlow jersey though. We might not have beaten Meath but we were very close. We ran Laois close then the following year in the Leinster Championship before we got revenge and actually beat them in Leinster in 1988 in Dr Cullen Park. That was a massive win for Carlow at the time and we haven't beaten Laois in the championship since. Laois still had pretty much the same team that had won the National League two years previous so they still had a very strong side, but we beat them with a goal near the end.

That Laois win meant we qualified for the quarter-final where we played

Dublin. I can't remember why now but that game was fixed for the June Bank Holiday Monday. It was the first championship game to be played on a Monday. It was a miserable day in Dr Cullen Park. It was absolutely soaking. I was marking Jim Ronayne. The referee was trying to start the game but myself and Jim were belting into one another. The ref had to have a word with both of us before he could throw in the ball and gave us both a warning. Now there was nothing in it really, just a bit of pushing and shoving but neither of us was giving in.

Once the referee turned his back we were back at it again, and at that stage he just decided to throw in the ball regardless and get it started. Noel McCaffrey was centre-back for Dublin that day and personally I thought he was the best player on the field. He didn't get the award though as I was chosen for it, and I still have the award at home. We may have been beaten by nine points but to still get the Man of the Match was nice. Anything like that is always a bonus.

After the game, we were all back at the hotel and we were listening back to the game and I can remember Jimmy Magee saying, 'I'm in the Carlow dressing-room there and I see Joe Dunne having a puff of a fag before he goes out on the field'. I'd say there was a few of us sharing the one cigarette before we went out!

I was probably better known for playing football for Carlow, but I was proud to play senior hurling for Carlow as well. I played a lot of underage hurling with Carlow Town, and played with Palatine then as well. I might not have been with them for long but I still ended up with a National League medal so that was another nice thing to look back on.

The International Rules series between Ireland and Australia was first played in 1984 over a three-game format. It was another great honour to be selected on that Irish squad. I was part of a Connacht team that played Australia in the lead-up and then I was selected to start in the very first Test between the countries. That game was played in Páirc Úi Chaoimh. We lost but won the second Test. We lost the series 2-1 in the end but it was a brilliant experience. At that time, nobody really knew what type of game it was, as it was the first year of it. I think that Australia were a lot stronger than what we were. In the following years things started to level up somewhat. It was great to be playing with players who were playing Division One football with their counties. Even just to see how they did things or to get in to their way of thinking. The big difference I found was just that they did things that little bit quicker than the counties in the lower divisions. We all did the same things but it was just speed that set them apart, I found, but it was a great insight to be involved with the top players in the country and see how they prepared. At the time I probably wasn't fit enough for that level and so I used to get up early every morning and run laps around a field that was just near my house. That was my way of getting up to that level.

It was different back then as regards fitness. Laps were still king. We would go to Carlow training and Vinny Harvey would be there with his trench coat and he'd say, 'Right lads… 10 laps!' There was a good chance a few of us would have been out the night before too so the laps weren't ideal recovery for that. Nowadays, I'd say laps are almost done away with.

I had played in a Railway Cup final for Leinster in 1983 and would have played with a lot of those lads on that team so by the time the International Rules came around I knew a lot of the players very well. Playing for Carlow, Leinster and then Ireland were all great experiences but I never dwelled on anything I achieved. After the game was over, I just moved on and focused on the next one.

Preparation back then was nothing like it is now. What we did was of its time and it was what teams did back then. The level of fitness, tactics and training that is there now is just crazy. The night before games I always believed in having a few pints. I never found it made a whole lot of difference. Now, having said, that there were times I went overboard as well. I remember myself and a teammate John 'Bonzo' McNally had been out the night before a game and on the way to the match the next day, a member of the management team brought us in a naggin of whiskey and a bottle of cider… trying to thaw us out!

Another time we travelled down to play Clare in a National League game. We went down the night before the game. A good few of us went to the nightclub, of course. 'Linda Martin and Chips' were playing at the disco. We had a great night in there anyway and once that was over, we all went into the lounge. Next thing 'Chips' came out after the show for a drink and before we knew it we were all sharing drinks and having a big sing-song. Linda Martin and the Carlow footballers!

Cyril Hughes went up then and got the guitar and he sang a song as well. Eventually, once everything had died down we all adjourned to our rooms and I'd say it must have been about 8am when we got to bed. We were supposed to play

Clare a few hours later and we weren't answering the door that morning so they had to go downstairs and get a key from reception to come up and wake myself and John McNally. We went to play the match anyway.

We had a kick-out at one stage and I can remember signalling to keep it away from my side and to kick it over to the other side where Paddy Quirke was. Paddy had only travelled down that morning so he was that bit fresher, whereas I could hardly see the ball, so they were at nothing sending it towards me. We had no water at all on the sideline so at one stage I went over to the Clare side looking for some water and a member of the Clare County Board handed me a bottle of water... or what I thought was water.

Keep in mind now that the same fella had been with us the night before when we were hanging out with 'Chips!' I stuck it down my gob anyway and God only knows how much I was after drinking... until I actually realised what it was... poitín! I think Carlow scored 0-2 that day, so that says it all really.

Many years ago, I was collecting an award up in Dublin. Martin Furlong from Offaly was going up with me as well to collect one also. I'd say between Martin and myself we must have drank two bottles of whiskey. I would have known all of those Offaly lads well having played with a lot of them for Leinster and then Ireland. I played against Walsh Island then in the club championship while playing for Tinryland. I got on well with all the Offaly lads and if I was picking someone as the greatest footballer I have ever seen play, it would be an Offaly man... Matt Connor. Matt was a fabulous footballer and he had a fantastic scoring record. He was a joy to watch.

I enjoyed myself off the pitch but I had plenty of great times on it too, and I was very lucky to have the career I did. Where else would you make friends for life like you would in the GAA? Even now, many years after I've finished playing I can still meet up with people from different counties after not seeing them for a long time and after a couple of minutes, it's like we were never apart. Before Covid struck, Bernard Flynn used to organise a charity golf event out in La Manga with a whole host of ex-GAA players. It used to be a fantastic few days away and all for a good cause. A few of us from Carlow went out to the event one year.

First night there and I couldn't get in to the room as I couldn't wake up Richie Moore, who was fast asleep inside in the bed. The next morning Michael Duignan came out of his room and I was asleep in the doorway. I was awoken to

Michael calling me, 'Tommy, are you alright in that doorway there?' That night then, we were all at the bar drinking and there was a massive sing-song going on. There were lads from nearly every county there and it was mighty craic. There was another group staying in the same hotel and they heard the racket we were making so they came down to see what was going on.

Who were the other bunch, only Roy Evans and Kenny Dalglish and a host of other Liverpool people who were also out there for a few days. Well they all joined in with the drinking and the singing and they had a great night as well.

Sure where else would you get it?

# JOHN BYRNE

**CARLOW 2-15** ★ **LONDON 3-10**
**All-Ireland SHC 'B' Final**
**Ruislip, London**
**JULY 12, 1992**

*John Byrne (back row, seventh from the left) is 20 years living in the United States, but made his mark at home before emigrating; particularly in the All-Ireland Hurling Championship in 1992.*

★ **CARLOW:** R Kielty; C Kealy, T English, B Lawler; J English, J Nevin, J Carey; B Hayden (1-0), P Brennan; D Doyle, M Mullins (0-5), J McDonald (0-1); P Murphy (0-1), **J Byrne (0-2)**, J Hayden (1-4). Subs: C Jordan (0-2) for Doyle.

★ **LONDON:** N Callaghy; P Butler, L Long, D McKenna (0-1); JJ Shields, J O'Donoghue, T Noonan; K Morrissey (0-2), F Moran; C Spain, A Wolfe, M McGrath (1-2); J Murphy (1-2), S O'Leary (0-1), P Lynch (1-2). Subs: N Daly for O'Donoghue, M Donoghue for Spain.

# THE ACTION

CARLOW QUALIFIED FOR an All-Ireland quarter-final glamour tie with Galway after they beat London to be crowned the All-Ireland 'B' champions. Carlow last won the title, then known as the Intermediate Championship, back in 1962 and exactly 30 years later they were back on top again.

Most people present would probably say that despite it finishing a two-point game, Carlow were the better team overall and thoroughly deserved this victory. At numerous stages Carlow were on the ropes and looked dead and buried, only to come back stronger each time; no doubt buoyed by the big Carlow crowd in attendance. This was a very good game of hurling throughout. It was close, tense and enthralling. London had a number of excellent stickmen and they gave the Carlow defence plenty to think about.

Carlow had their own masters too, however, and while everyone put in a massive shift, it is hard not to mention some of Carlow's shining lights in Tom English, Johnny Nevin and Joe Hayden. Tom English was awarded the Man of the Match, while Nevin was just his usual busy self. Joe Hayden with 1-4 to his name up front was on fire throughout. Ironically Hayden was being marked by one of London's better players, Paul Butler.

Ciaran Jordan's arrival into the game was of huge significance. Jordan was a fresh pair of legs and his two points were massive scores for Carlow. The last five minutes was when the real excitement came. London looked like they might be getting on top only for Jordan to drive over a monster point from midfield. London responded straightaway with a point from John Murphy, although supporters from both sides admitted that the score was wide. A draw looked likely. Not so however, as Mark Mullins converted a free before Jordan struck over another.

★★★★★

66

WINNING THE ALL-IRELAND 'B' championship was a massive high point in my career as back then the 'B' All-Ireland actually meant something. We won the 'Home' final after a replay against Westmeath, but to actually win the competition outright then afterwards, it was a special time no doubt. 1962 had been the previous time Carlow had won anything at championship level, when they won the intermediate competition so to do it exactly 30 years later was great. It brought great joy to Carlow at the time. I think that was typified by the crowds that welcomed the team home in Carlow town on the Monday. There were massive crowds in Shamrock Square that night.

The 'B' championship then was a very tough competition to win. Even though it was the second tier, you still had the likes of Carlow, Westmeath, London, Meath, Kerry and Kildare. We had been on a bit of a journey to get where we did. In 1991 we reached the 'Home' final of the competition where we lost out to Westmeath. That game had been played in Croke Park before the third game in the Dublin and Meath football saga that was going on that summer. When we went out onto the field that day there was probably already 30,000 in the stadium. It was an unbelievable atmosphere and by the time our game was coming to a close there was probably close to 60,000 there watching us.

A lot of the Dublin supporters were cheering for Carlow as well. I was playing corner-forward and I remember playing in to the Hill 16 end and hearing some Dub shouting, 'Go on John Byrne'. I was just thinking, *How the hell does he know me?* Obviously he got the name from the programme but I suppose I was still a little naive at that stage, but it's something that always sticks with me from that game.

Martin Fitzpatrick from Kilkenny was our manager at the time and he was a great man to have over us. He was a really good manager and I think he got the most out of that Carlow team for the time he was there. After that disappointing final loss against Westmeath, we were very determined going into 1992 that we finally had to win it. Not that it was going to be easy but with the players we had, we really felt we had to be pushing on. We beat Armagh away in the first round which meant we played Wicklow in the semi-final. That game was fixed for Croke Park so it was great to be back there again so soon. We beat Wicklow and as a result we qualified for the 'Home' final for the second year in-a-row and once again it would be Westmeath. I actually broke two fingers against Wicklow and I was absolutely gutted after as I knew I would miss the Westmeath game.

We played them in Tullamore and it ended in a draw. The replay was in Tullamore again and I was brought on in the second-half. Those two games were magic. Mark Mullins was outstanding. He was like our own Christy Ring… he was just unmarkable. Johnny Nevin was inspirational as usual. We had fantastic performances all over the field. Westmeath wanted to win that just as much as we did but the lads just pulled it out, and we got over the line 3-13 to 0-17. There were about 3,000 people in Tullamore that day and it was great to have a big Carlow support there.

Once again, a massive Carlow following made the journey over to Ruislip for the London game and add to that, there was a lot of Carlow people living in London so a lot of them were there as well to cheer us on. The game itself was very topsy turvy. The lead switched hands plenty of times. I had recovered sufficiently enough from the broken fingers to start at full-forward. Joe Hayden and Mark Mullins were on fire up front but we had star performers right throughout.

There was massive relief afterwards when we had finally done it. We were All-Ireland champions. What made it extra special for me was that I was captain that year. Having not collected any championship silverware since 1962, to then be captain of the next Carlow team that did win something… well that was special. Of course, we celebrated in London that night and had a great night there. We came back to Carlow the next day and there was a homecoming arranged for us at Shamrock Square. We had no idea of the crowds that were there. We were all taken aback by all the people that turned out to meet us. We probably thought there might be a few people there alright but nothing like what turned up.

One of the main reasons why the 'B' championship meant so much and was so sought after was that it gave the winners a back door entry to the Liam McCarthy. Our 'prize' for our win was a home quarter-final with a star-studded Galway. That was two weeks later, so by the time the celebrating had died down we didn't have much time to prepare. Believe it or not, going in to play Galway, we were very confident. We had come through a tough championship campaign and we really felt we could do something against Galway.

The training up to that point was excellent. Again Martin Fitzpatrick had us in great shape and he had us peaking at the right time. It's a great feeling when everybody is on the same page and all after the same goal. I can remember in the lead up to the game someone from Galway coming out and saying that they'd have no bother coming down to Dr Cullen Park. I think some of our lads maybe took that as a little bit patronising, in that they thought they'd beat us easy wherever we played them.

There were over 7,000 people in Dr Cullen Park to see that game. It was another massive crowd to play in front of and there was a great atmosphere. At half-time we were only four points down and Galway had gotten a goal just before the break from Joe Cooney, after a mix up in our defence which was a big blow to us. Galway pulled away a little in the second-half and won 4-19 to 3-9 in the end, but we put up a very good account of ourselves. Despite being on the losing side Mark Mullins gave one of the best performances I've ever seen. Mark was being marked by Galway great Tony Keady but he still ended up scoring 0-6 from play. I think he proved that to everybody, even more so then when he went and played senior hurling for Cork a few years later, and even went on to captain them.

I probably took the toughest belt of my career that day from Christy Helebert. I was given a poor pass from someone and it seemed to hang in the air for ages. I went for it anyway but Christy came in and hit me an unmerciful thump. It was out near the sideline and it was so hard I fell into the wire that was around the pitch. I was in bits afterwards, and sure I didn't know where I was at all.

It had been a great year for us and it wasn't long before 1993 came around and we were back in the Leinster Championship again and eager to impress. Kilkenny were the visitors to Dr Cullen Park… they beat us 5-19 to 0-16. There was another big crowd there but Kilkenny were just too good for us. That was a very strong team they had and they actually went on to win the All-Ireland later that year. I was up against Pat O'Neill that day… so no easy task. One thing that I can remember very clearly was before the game as we were making our way into the ground. A few of the players from both sides were walking in together and I can remember Willie Eustace, a big Myshall and Carlow man, turning to Kilkenny's Adrian Ronan and saying, 'Listen Adrian, take it easy on our lads today now will ya'. The two lads actually knew each other but I can remember Adrian firing back, 'Willie, I'm trying to make this team!' So in other words… it was a no!

My first encounter playing with Carlow was a rather sobering experience. I can remember it was a Sunday about 8.0 in the morning, maybe even earlier. There was a knock at the door so my mother answered and it was none other than our own Willie Eustace, and he was looking for me. I was only young then and working at the time, and Sunday morning was the only morning you'd get a bit of a lie in. Anyway I went to the door, still half-asleep. Willie just said, 'John don't think about it, just get your bag, get your hurl… come on'.

I got dressed, got the gear and hopped into the car. Ned Kavanagh was sitting in the front seat. We drive about a mile down the road and we picked up Mick Nolan, and after that we picked up Paddy Quirke. These were all legends and had all been playing for years. I was still only a teenager so I didn't say much. With the car now full, before I knew it we were on the dual-carriageway heading up north. I can't remember if it was Down or Derry we were playing but it was somewhere I had never been before anyway. We got there and my first thought was just, *What the f\*\*k am I doing here?* Surely Carlow had enough lads without needing to call me up. I played corner-forward and as the game was progressing it was getting more and more dirty.

Ned Kavanagh was playing corner-back and he was getting awful abuse from a fella in the stand. The more abuse he got the harder he was going for it on the field. After the game, Ned flung down the hurl and went over towards the stand and beckoned the lad down to see if they could sort their differences! The fella wasn't so keen by then so that was the end of it, but this was my introduction to senior county hurling. I was only a young lad and scared of my life!

My club Naomh Eoin were very strong at the time and they completed a six in-a-row of senior championships in the 90s. The funny thing at the time was that I played senior hurling for Carlow for two years before I was starting on the Myshall team. That was how strong the club was. The other side of that then was that it obviously showed that some of the good lads on the club team were not playing for Carlow when something like that was happening. It was a strange one though to start your career.

Throughout my career I had received many offers to go out to America and play hurling, New York in particular. At the time I was so involved with Carlow and then with the club after that, the timing was just never right. I was part of that six in-a-row side so it would have been hard to leave that behind. In 2002,

I was 32 and the factory I was working in had new owners so we were offered redundancy and at that stage I was thinking that maybe now was the perfect time to take the lads up on their offer and head over to New York for a holiday. I was only supposed to go out there for a few weeks, but a few days before I was due to leave I was asked by some of the lads from the Tipperary club if I would be willing to stick around for a bit longer. I would play with them and they'd help get me set up with a job and accommodation. I had nothing to lose so I said why not, I'd give it a shot at least and see how it goes.

I played two years with Tipperary and for someone that had played all of my hurling as a forward, for those two years I was played at centre-back and I have to say I absolutely loved it. I ended up marking Henry Shefflin at one stage in the 2003 championship final. Henry and Denis Byrne were both playing for Connecticut State. We had a very strong team ourselves which included John Carroll, Paul Curran and Eddie Brennan. It was nice to win a championship with Tipperary as they were very good to me when I was there. Afterwards I ended up moving to Boston and I got involved with the Wexford club while there and played with them. I met my wife in Boston and I've been here ever since. So much for only going over to America for a couple of weeks… I'm here nearly 20 years now!

I wasn't long in America when Naomh Eoin won the Senior Championship in 2003 and then another in '05. In 2003 they ran Birr to four points in the Leinster Club Championship and in '05 they only lost out to James Stephens by three points. I was getting settled in America then but definitely there were days through that era when I wished I was at home and involved with the lads. I have a good life over here now and I have my own family, but I always say no matter where you are in the world, home is home and your heart is always there. I try to stay connected with what's going on at home and I always try and follow everything that is going on in the GAA. I have to say though that the GAA community out in America is very much like back home with people looking out for one another. When my father passed away a number of years ago, there was a mass held for him in Boston and the church was packed, and that was a month after the funeral. So despite being out of Ireland, I find the GAA abroad is every bit as important as it is at home and people look out for each other just as much as they would anywhere else.

**99**

# RICHIE MOORE

**O' DONOVAN ROSSA (SKIBBEREEN) 1-7 ★ ÉIRE ÓG 0-8**
**All-Ireland Club SFC Final (Replay)**
**Gaelic Grounds, Limerick**
**MARCH 28, 1993**

*An agonising defeat in the 1993 All-Ireland club final replay hurt, but also propelled Éire Óg*
*(Richie Moore is second from the right in the front row) to further championship success at club*
*and provincial level.*

★ **ÉIRE ÓG:** J Kearns; J Wynne, **R Moore**, J Dooley; B Hayden (0-1), A Callinan, N
Fallon; G Ware (0-2), H Brennan; J Hayden (0-1), J Morrissey, T Nolan; J Murphy,
C Hayden, A Keating (0-4). Subs: D Moore for Nolan.

★ **O'DONOVAN ROSSA:** K O'Dwyer; J Evans, J O'Donovan, F McCarthy; G
O'Driscoll, A Davis, I Breen; D O'Driscoll, B O'Donovan; P Davis (1-2), J O'Driscoll
(0-1), D Driscoll; B Carmody, M McCarthy (0-4), N Murphy. Subs: M McCarthy for
G O'Driscoll.

# THE ACTION

ÉIRE ÓG'S DREAM of national glory was snatched from them with the quick shrill of a referee's whistle at the end of this absorbing club football final replay. With time almost up, O' Donovan Rossa were holding on to a slender two-point lead when Éire Óg's Joe Hayden sent in a free which went straight to the back of the net with the help of an Éire Óg hand on the way. The umpire signalled for a goal, but the referee overruled the man in white and decided not to allow the goal for what he judged as a square infringement. It was the cruellest way to lose for the Carlow champions, but there is a school of thought that they shouldn't have been in that position so late in the game as they hit five wides in succession in the second-half when they were on top. This game might not have been as memorable or as skilful as the drawn encounter but with the low scoring and closeness of the game, it nonetheless kept everyone on the edge of their seats until that frantic finish.

That goal may have been disallowed but the only goal of the game that did stand arrived in the 45th minute and it came from Pat Davis, who plunged a bobbing ball to the city end net. In fairness to Éire Óg, they didn't seem to flinch with this setback and outscored their rivals by a point from there until the end. With chances at a premium, both sides went in at the interval with 0-4 each on the scoreboard.

There was controversy surrounding that Davis goal too, as many felt that John Kearns was fouled in the action, while others suggested that there may have been a man in the square a little bit too early – but alas neither call was given and the goal stood. Anthony Keating and Brendan Hayden both pointed to reduce the deficit to the minimum but, unfortunately, this was followed up by three wides in the following four minutes, while Mick McCarthy pointed for the Cork side. With the game gone into injury time, Éire Óg were awarded a free. Joe Hayden took it and his effort landed perfectly underneath the crossbar. Darren Moore and Joe Murphy both went up for it and to the amazement of everybody the ball ended up in the net.

★ ★ ★ ★ ★

**"**

BY THE TIME the All-Ireland club final of 1993 came around, I was coming towards the tail end of my career. I was 39 at the time and I was still playing senior in both codes, football with Éire Óg and hurling with Carlow Town. Maybe, looking back now, it was a bit foolish but at the time you think you can do it, but once you get to that age the injuries become more frequent. In the 1992 county football championship, the start of the journey that would lead us to Croke Park, I pulled my hamstring two days before we played the first round.

We made it to the county final against Tinryland and I just made it back to fitness, although I didn't start. Tom Begley, who was playing full-back, did his cruciate ligament in that game and was taken off at half-time, so I got the call to go on in his place. At one point in the second-half when stretching for a ball, I tore the hamstring again and so Derek Wynne came in to replace me then; so we used three full-backs in the one game. That win over Tinryland was our first time to beat them in the county final, as they had beaten us in a few finals in the 70s and 80s.

After we won the Carlow championship, the journey continued and before we knew it we were in the Leinster final. Éire Óg had made its first Leinster final in 1980 but we lost out to Walterstown of Meath. On this occasion in 1992, we were up against Ballyroan of Laois and the club secured its first ever senior provincial crown. That game was actually played in early 1993 due to a frozen pitch in Newbridge the week before Christmas. I remember we had just got on the bus that day in Éire Óg, when we were told it was off.

There were big celebrations afterwards, of course, but once things calmed down in the New Year we had an All-Ireland semi-final to look forward too. We travelled up to Knockmore to take on the home side and after a tight struggle, we came out the right side to beat the Mayo champions and book our place in the All-Ireland club final on St Patrick's Day. Both Éire Óg and O'Donovan Rossa wore red so there had to be a change of colours for the final. We changed to the green of Leinster, while our Cork opponents wore the blue of Munster. The first day turned out to be a very good game and it ended up in a draw, 1-12 to 3-6 for us. With the game being played on St Patrick's Day, it was played on a Wednesday and the replay would be played 10 days later, the following Sunday week in the

Gaelic Grounds in Limerick. It was a poor day weather wise, so it wasn't going to be as high scoring as the drawn game. But it had much more controversy.

A friend of mine recently transferred the video of the game from old VHS tape to a USB for me and I watched it back. As the game was so long ago, it was kind of like watching a different game. I actually watched the game with my daughter. She would have been around four years old at the time of the game so this was her first time to see it and she couldn't get over the size of the crowd that turned up in Limerick. The first game really attracted the attention of everybody and first-time champions were going to be crowned no matter who won it, so a massive crowd made their way down to the Gaelic Grounds to watch the game.

The pitch itself was in very poor condition throughout. There was muck everywhere and everybody was falling around. Even the linesman running up and down the sideline was getting destroyed and slipping around. The state of the pitch and the bad weather meant there was never going to be many scores given up and no team was going to run away with it. The sides went in at the break level at 0-4 apiece, which just shows how much of a dog fight it was.

Towards the end of the game, we thought we had snatched it when a free from Joe Hayden went straight to the net but the referee blew his whistle and said it was a square ball. We thought we had it won for a second only to have it taken back from us just as quick. It was pure madness. It was a rollercoaster of emotions for both sets of players. I was playing full-back so when this was happening at the other end of the field, it was hard for us at that end to see what was going on or what exactly had happened. The thing was, when the ball hit the net, one of the umpires went for his flag straight away to signal the goal, but the referee still overruled him.

That was bad enough, but to rub salt into the wounds, the only goal of the game, which had come about 15 minutes before, could just as easily been ruled out for a square infringement as they looked to have had a man in the square but the referee seemed to think that one was okay and it stood. Once the game was over, it wasn't until that night that we got to see the replay of the goal, as the game was shown again on TV; it was only then did we see what had happened and got to see what all the controversy was about.

It's easy to look back now on the controversy of both goals, but again I think we had enough of ball on the day and we kicked enough wides and dropped enough balls in to the goalie's hands that we probably should never have been in that position in the first place but sometimes these things just happen in sport. We didn't take those chances and we were made to pay in the end.

When we won that Leinster Championship in 1992, little did anyone realise the journey that the club would go on from there. By the end of the 90s, Éire Óg had won five Leinster Senior Championships and reached another All-Ireland final in 1996. I've often thought about it; had we won the All-Ireland title the first time we might never have gotten to another Leinster final again. Look at Baltinglass around the same time, they won one Leinster championship but they also won the All-Ireland.

After the disappointment of that final defeat, a few months later we were back in Carlow Championship action and in the middle of that I hurt my back and I decided then that it was time to call it quits and, as it happened, I ended up being out for two years with it before it felt anyway right. It was a simple twist and it was a bit sore later that night but I thought nothing more of it. The following night I went up training with the hurlers and there was a lad who I'd normally beat by a few yards doing sprints, but he was beating me with ease on this particular night so I knew something was wrong when I wasn't able to give my best. The following day was the start of eight weeks of being on my back, 24 hours a day, which was followed by 72-hour epidural spine injections to try and release the trapped nerves. It was pain I wouldn't wish on anyone.

I did come back afterwards and play junior football and hurling, but as regards playing senior, that was the end for me. By that stage I wasn't far off 40 and was still playing senior dual club so I had done well really. Playing dual club was great but I was lucky enough to be playing dual county as well for a long number of years. I played senior football for Carlow for almost 15 seasons while playing with the senior hurlers for the best part of a decade. While there wasn't any major success in either code and there were plenty of bad days, we also had some great days too and there were days we went out and showed that we could be as good as any team when we put our mind to it.

There is no denying it, that there was great fun had off the field as well. There was one year we played a National League game against Clare in Ennis. We were out of the running for promotion at that stage so it had been agreed with management that we could go out the night before. Some of the team didn't want to go out, so they organised two buses to bring lads down; one the night before the game and one the day of the game. We were staying in the West County Hotel in Ennis. We met Linda Martin who was at a dance there while we also took in a 21st, and a wedding. Tommy Dwyer even managed to swap his gold ear ring with a total stranger at the bar!

I remember when we went up to play Fermanagh in Irvinestown. We actually achieved promotion that time. I was out injured with my hamstring at the time but I was brought along to all the games regardless. The Troubles were rife at the time in the north so we knew we wouldn't be getting any post-game drinks afterwards. We were staying in a hotel in Dundalk before the game; so the hotel manager agreed with the bar owner across the road to open up for us before the game so we could get some takeaway drinks to have on the journey back from Irvinestown, back to Dundalk where we would be having a meal. After we had finished up, it was all back onto the bus, and straight in to the cans. We stopped in Drogheda then, but it was about 10pm at this stage. I decided then to ring a friend of mine, Skates Keating, who ran a pub in Dublin. We got to Stoneybatter eventually and had a few drinks there. Around 3.30 in the morning we got a visit from the guards, as they had seen two lads being carried out! Thankfully, they showed some leniency once we left immediately.

Carlow had some great footballers around that time and we took playing for Carlow very seriously, and we were all honoured to wear the jersey. Anyone that put on the jersey took great pride in it. Playing for your county is the highest honour and while we had a laugh off the field, at the same time we gave it everything once we went out there. I first played senior hurling for Carlow Town at 16 and played senior football for Éire Óg as a 17-year-old in 1971, in a first round championship replay defeat to Tinryland. The full-back line that time was Tommy Corcoran, Cran Hogan and Seamus Fitzpatrick, so I was never going to get a look in there. The night before the game I was at a dance and was told by an Éire Óg supporter, who was in the know, to 'Go home… you never know what might happen tomorrow'. I thought there was no chance I was getting in to that full-back line. What I didn't know at the time was that Cran Hogan had cried off with bad ankles, so I got the nod to start. Little did I know that I'd get nearly 22 years playing senior and get to appear in an All-Ireland club final. After I finished up playing I still stayed involved and in 1996 when the club reached its second All-Ireland final, I was a selector.

One of my favourite memories from that time was in early 1994 when the club sent the team and mentors away on a holiday to the Canary Islands as an appreciation of our achievements in reaching the All-Ireland final. At the time little did anyone realise that the club would win a second Leinster Championship in 1993 against Erin's Isle of Dublin, so what was supposed to be a relaxing holiday actually wound up as a training holiday for the upcoming All-Ireland semi-final against Castlebar Mitchels! Still, a great time was had and it was a nice gesture from the club. I was very lucky to be involved in 16 senior football finals, successful in 12, while in hurling I played in five finals and was successful in four of those. There were so many of my former Carlow teammates, some who even played for Leinster and who were so much better than me, but they never got the chance to win a senior championship, so I know how lucky I was.

One of the reasons I was able to stay playing at the top for so long was that I had a great woman behind me in my wife, Joan. Whenever people are talking about Éire Óg and the Moore connection comes into the conversation, she always says that she has more Éire Óg blood than me. Her father Tom Haughney and her uncles all played for the club in the 1950s and 60s before any of the Moore's ever came on the scene. As players get older and you have children it can be difficult to combine everything and still keep playing but my wife was Éire Óg through and through, so that definitely made it that bit easier going out to training every night. She has always been a great GAA woman. I'll always remember one of the older lads in the club years ago commenting, 'You'll always know Richie Moore is playing. He might be playing s***e but he'll always have a clean pair of shorts'. I'd say that was a fair statement!

# SEAN KAVANAGH

**LAOIS 2-11 ★ CARLOW 1-13**
**Leinster SFC Quarter-Final**
**O'Moore Park, Portlaoise**
**JUNE 18, 1995**

*Carlow losing to Laois twice in the championship in 1995 was an historic event for the GAA, and the regret, and excitement, of that summer lived on with Sean Kavanagh (in action here against Down in the All-Ireland qualifiers almost 10 years later).*

★ **CARLOW:** J Kearns; J Murphy, J Wynne, J Dooley; W Quinlan (0-1), H Brennan, B Hayden; **S Kavanagh (0-2)**, G Ware (0-1); N Doyle (0-2), J Nevin (0-3), A Keating (1-2); A Bowe, C Hayden, J Hayden (0-2). Subs: J Morrissey for C Hayden, J Reid for Keating.

★ **LAOIS:** E Burke; A Phelan, M Dempsey, T Conroy; E Delaney, T Lawlor, A Lacey; T Maher (0-1), G Doyle; T Dunne, PJ Dempsey, M Lawlor; M O'Brien (0-2), D Delaney (2-5), L Turley (0-2). Subs: H Emerson for PJ Dempsey, T Smith for Lacey, M Turley (0-1) for Dunne.

# THE ACTION

LAOIS USED UP all of their luck getting out of this game against their local rivals Carlow. It was a shame it had to end the way it did with a disputed point at the end and all the controversy that followed. That 'point' came with the sides level as time was almost up. Laois substitute Michael Turley, not long on the field, attempted to kick the winner – which the replay would show later had clearly gone wide – and with the officials giving the score, Carlow were behind. Carlow did have a chance almost straightaway, but James Reid rushed his effort and the ball went wide.

Laois goalkeeper Emmet Burke was the busier of the two netminders in the first-half as he pulled off two vital saves, the first from Sean Kavanagh, while Joe Murphy followed up with another effort shortly after. Willie Quinlan also had another great goal chance just before the interval but his shot went screaming over the bar. Any visions of an easy Laois victory were quickly quashed as Carlow had early scores on the board through Anthony Keating, Johnny Nevin, Noel Doyle and Sean Kavanagh all in the first seven minutes. Laois did eventually get into their stride and got their act together with a number of points, while Damien Delaney scored their goal which left it 1-8 to 0-11 at half-time. When Anthony Keating scored an early Carlow goal just after the restart, there were real signs that we were set for a shock.

Arguably, the turning point in the game came when Laois were awarded a penalty. Delaney stepped up but his kick was excellently saved by John Kearns, only for Delaney to react quickly to knock home the rebound. In the final dozen minutes there was to be only one 'score' and that was Turley's final effort. Carlow were very busy and industrious during this period but for all their hard work they only had one effort for a score which was a wide from Brendan Hayden. At that stage a draw looked on the cards until that final frantic finish.

★★★★★

66

IF I AM being honest, I would probably say that game against Laois didn't define my career as such or anything, but I picked it out because it was a massive game for Carlow and, I suppose, all the controversy that came afterwards and how it finished up on the day. Carlow would have a poor enough record against Laois but going in to that game in 1995 we knew we had a great chance. We had won the All-Ireland SFC 'B' championship in late 1994 so that was a big boost. At that time the league started before Christmas so we would have had games week on week between both competitions. We were probably a little more focused on the 'B' championship than the league and that showed in the results as it was a mixed bag and we were out of the running in the league after Christmas; but regardless, winning the All-Ireland 'B' was a big thing back then. When the New Year came around we never got going at all during the league. Maybe it was the comedown after the success of winning the 'B' but we were a little flat for whatever reason.

The league ended with a whimper and there were poor turnouts near the end. Despite this, we actually had a very good run-in to the Laois game. There was a big gap between the end of the league and the championship, but we had a good seven or eight weeks of hard training and we were confident going into it. We were totally focused on Laois. We had no preliminary round draw that year so the game was a straight quarter-final.

There was an extra interest going in to the game in that Bobby Miller was over us. Bobby was a proud Laois man, but there were no divided loyalties that day. In fairness to Bobby, he was fully behind us and fully focused on beating Laois and he probably had the inside track on them as well. Bobby had been over Éire Óg for a number of years and had a lot of success there so he knew the Carlow scene quite well. As for the day itself, it was absolutely roasting. There was talk of supporters fainting in the stands and on up the bank.

Both teams had spells in the first-half where they were on top. It was hard to play in that heat but we were giving as good as we got. We were going up against a Division One team and holding our own. There was a massive crowd at the game as well and between everything it just felt one of those proper championship days and I was delighted to be a part of it.

I was working in Lapple in Carlow town at the time and there was good craic with the Graiguecullen and Killeshin lads in the lead up to the game. I was young and very fit at the time and I held my own against Laois. I was marking Tony 'Barney' Maher and we had a great battle. Garvan Ware was a good partner at midfield too; we worked well together.

We got a great boost early in the second-half when Anthony Keating scored a goal. It might have been early in the second-half but people were genuinely thinking then that a shock was on the cards. The rest of the game was close throughout with never a big margin between the sides at any stage even though Laois scored a second goal midway through the half with Damien Delaney again goaling. Going in to the last few minutes it was looking likely to end in a draw but there was still time for a last play, and that controversial moment.

Laois worked the ball up field and it was given out to Michael Turley, who had only come into the game as a substitute. Michael's kick for a point was given as a score. I was out around the middle of the field so I didn't have the best view, but I could tell by the reaction of the players around that area and the supporters behind the goal, that something wasn't right. There were no camera phones or anything around at that time so we probably didn't get to see it until that night on *The Sunday Game* where they slowed it down – and it was clear then that it was wide. Between *The Sunday Game* and local radio, they both were talking about it so we knew there was going to be more to come of it.

A lot had happened in those couple of minutes and once the whistle went, it was clear that the players weren't happy. The thing about it is that we had no grounds for a re-fixture. Once the game was over and the ref sent in his report and the score, then there was nothing we could do. It was similar to the Leinster football final in 2010 and the whole controversy there between Meath and Louth. The only way that was going to be replayed was if Meath offered it and it was the same thing in our situation.

All the footage on TV had showed it was clearly wide and in fairness to Laois they offered to play the game again the following Sunday in Portlaoise. Laois were given some kind of Fair Play award from the GAA that Sunday then for allowing the game to be replayed.

Word came through on the Tuesday I think that the game was on again for that weekend. I had heard that a few boys were still in the pub on Tuesday when they found out but I definitely wasn't. Maybe the Monday alright, but not the Tuesday! I think our first training session back lads still were still a little bit unsure what was going on. The game was on, but the whole thing happened so quickly that there was probably a little bit of confusion still. As the week went on then we definitely got more focused and were fully intent on giving another big performance. In fairness to Laois, it was a good thing they did by offering to replay the game but our record against them was poor and maybe they felt a little bit that they should be beating Carlow anyway, so maybe they were happy enough to play it again.

To be fair as well, that was a very good Laois team around that time. They had reached the semi-final of the National League that year and once they eventually got over us the second day they were beaten by Dublin in the Leinster semi-final – that was the day Jason Sherlock scored the goal after losing his boot. Dublin went on to win the All-Ireland that year so Laois weren't that far off. Despite that, we were still confident once again going into the second day.

That day was very similar to the first day. We were back in Portlaoise and once again there was nothing in it. No matter what division Laois were in over the years, Carlow always put it up to them. We might not have beaten them often, but we were always capable of a performance against them. Sometimes when two close neighbours like that go at it, form can go out the window. Laois scored a goal through Mick Lawlor and from there they kind of had that cushion for the rest of the game, and they won by that goal in the end. We had put in two very good performances against a top team but, at the end of the day, we still had nothing to show.

You'd be thinking different things after. I remember thinking that if we had gotten a draw the first day and got the replay back to Dr Cullen Park, would we have had a better chance? Of course, you'll never know, but it's only natural to have the 'what ifs' in your head. There were no qualifiers at that time either and I think if they were around they would have really helped Carlow as we had a strong side that could have gone on a run and built on those Laois performances. There was definitely a lull there afterwards. We all went back to our clubs then ahead of the county championship but there was definitely a comedown and it probably took a while to get over it.

By the time we were back in with Carlow again for the following season, it was still pretty much the same panel of players and we were eager to push on going into 1996. We had two big championship victories over Wexford and Wicklow, and it looked like we had turned a corner and were following up on our championship performances against Laois the previous year.

That was until we ran into Meath in Croke Park. Ahead of that game, there was talk that Carlow could actually beat Meath. We had come off the back of two championship wins and there was genuine hope that we could pull it off. Ultimately, we never performed on the day and were totally outclassed and Meath would finish out the year as All-Ireland champions. We were just blown out of the water by a great team, beaten 0-24 to 0-6. Meath were just way ahead of us in almost every sector. Physicality, fitness, football… whatever, it didn't matter what way, we just couldn't keep up.

After 1997, Bobby Miller stepped down and things started to slip a little after that. Bobby had great stability there with the players he had and the set-up he had created and when he left it was a big blow and probably set us back a little. Between his involvement between Éire Óg and then Carlow he put in a good long spell in the county, but we were still all sorry to see him go. I've played under a lot of Carlow managers throughout my career. I made my senior debut under Alan Larkin in 1991 and went all the way through until 2005. There were plenty of highs and as many lows during my career but I loved playing for Carlow.

In 2005 I had played in the National League but by the time the championship came around I had finished up. After the league, I felt that I wasn't enjoying it as much anymore and I also felt that the legs were starting to go at that level, so it was hard. I didn't want to hang on just for the sake of it so I called it a day with Carlow mid-season, although I did play on with Rathvilly for many more years after.

I enjoyed my time with Carlow. If I didn't enjoy it then I wouldn't have done it year after year. There were plenty of bad times, of course. Times when you mightn't be playing well or maybe certain times numbers mightn't be great at training but you kept going. You try to do your best yourself and to keep up your side of the bargain as best you can. You want to play at the highest level you can and that is senior county football and that is what I wanted to do growing up. It was because of Carlow that I ended up getting the call to play for Leinster. I have two Railway Cup medals at home, and while I didn't get on the field for any of them, it was still a massive honour to be involved and to get to train and play with some of the best footballers around. Even to be asked to play with Leinster was an honour.

I remember we'd train for Leinster once a week up in Kildangan Stud of all places. I'd head up on a Wednesday night and we'd do our bit up there. I have to say it was really enjoyable. I always felt that I held my own against anyone I was up against and never felt I was out of my depth.

# STEPHEN BAMBRICK

### OLD LEIGHLIN 1-10 ★ PALATINE 0-11
### Carlow SFC Final
### Dr Cullen Park, Carlow
### SEPTEMBER 7, 1997

*Old Leighlin's first senior football championship win in 1997 topped everything else in Stephen Bambrick's (fifth from the right, front row) busy career.*

★ **OLD LEIGHLIN: S Bambrick**; N Sheehy, N Bambrick, K Hayden; M Jordan, T Connolly, S McClean; R McGrath (0-1), N Jordan (0-1); J Hayden (0-1), Benji O'Brien (0-1), S Hayden (0-1); M Roche, J Nevin (0-3), B Lawler (1-1). Subs: J Carey (0-1) for Roche.

★ **PALATINE:** T Hickey; M Nolan, B Farrell, A Hosey; P O'Dwyer, P Cunningham, P Mullins; M Brennan, J Byrne; L Cullen, M Kelly, B Gordon (0-2); P Reid (0-1), John Reid (0-2), James Reid (0-5). Subs: J Kelly for P Reid, B Kelly (0-1) for M Kelly, K Fitzharris for Cullen.

# THE ACTION

COUNTY STAR JOHNNY Nevin carried the main hopes of his side while also holding the greatest source of fear for Palatine and after the game he was the name on everybody's lips as he kicked three points and won the Man of the match award. There was great rejoicing among Carlow people as Johnny had finally won a senior football championship medal.

Palatine, who hadn't won the SFC since 1952, were 0-4 to 0-3 ahead after 14 minutes, mainly due to county man James Reid, but this was the only time they led in the match – and that lead lasted only five minutes. Once Nevin fielded a weak kick out and pointed to level things, followed by an excellent point from play by Niall Jordan, Palatine were always struggling to get back on terms, and Old Leighlin led by 0-7 to 0-4 at the interval.

At the start of the second-half, Palatine introduced John Kelly and he proceeded to make such an impact that it begged the question why he was not in from the start. The No 26, a teacher based in Saudi Arabia, restored Palatine's broken midfield superiority, making a very positive contribution, both in his fielding and distribution. A 37th minute James Reid point cut the lead back to two points, 0-8 to 0-6. However, a goal was always going to have a major bearing on this game and it fell to Old Leighlin in the 44th minute. A Palatine defender carelessly put the ball out over the sideline and Benji O'Brien's subsequent lineball went across the face of goal, where it was fielded and crashed to the net superbly all in one movement by Brian Lawler.

After a Pal point from Reid, the same player, after outflanking the Old Leighlin defence, was in on goal and looked certain to raise a green flag, but goalkeeper Stephen Bambrick read his intentions well and saved. Barry Gordon did point from play from the same movement, which provided some compensation to leave only a goal between the sides. With just five minutes left, a John Reid point from play cut Old Leighlin's lead to just one. They were unlucky however not to go ahead as midfielder Micko Brennan hit the post. With the game entering injury time, Johnny Nevin converted a close range free.

★★★★★

**"**

I DON'T THINK anybody in Old Leighlin, Carlow or beyond could have expected what unfolded in Dr Cullen Park on the first Sunday of September 1997. As a club, we had only opened our grounds earlier that year, and here we were now in our first SFC final. As my late father Stephen said, 'A little old village above in the butt of The Ridge'. That senior appearance was only a year on from a narrow first round Intermediate Championship win over our parish rivals Leighlinbridge, which culminated in meeting an up-and-coming O'Hanrahans in the final.

In that Intermediate final, we were caught by an early Pa Kavanagh goal after indecision in our defence, and he very nearly added a second shortly after, but I didn't buy the dummy he was selling on the edge of the square!

A seventeen-year-old John Hayden it was who netted the vital goal for us that day. That O' Hanrahans team would have their day though. They won the intermediate the following year and followed up with four senior championships and a Leinster club title, but this was our day. It finished 1-9 to 1-7 and I remember bawling my eyes out the next morning. You never forget your first adult championship medal for your club. A SHC medal with Naomh Brid followed later that year for around seven or eight of us – the opposite of 1994, when we lost both the IFC and SHC finals.

Old Leighlin had actually done back-to-back titles before. The 1974 JFC was captured before the intermediate title followed only 12 months later. That junior win was the club's first ever championship win and my father later penned the song *The Boys in Blue* (which he sang at the drop of a hat) after that win.

The late Pat Foley, and Noel Bambrick were our first and regular countymen at this stage, with Pat being a next-door neighbour and Noel my first cousin. This was probably the start of my obsession with the GAA from an early age. Unfortunately, Pat died in a car accident on December 19, 1979. I was in third class at the time and I will never forget hearing the news. Pat was a frequent visitor to our house. I still have the cloth from the Subbuteo soccer game he helped me set up! Another great neighbour and Pat's close friend Luke Meaney was my lift to many matches for the years to come. The question asked when 1997 did pan out the way it did was, if Pat was still around where would he have been playing or would we have had SFC honours earlier.

When we reached the senior final in 1997, a good few lads had county final experience behind them, just not the senior football final. We had lost the SHC final with Parnells in 1994, before we won it with newly formed Naomh Brid in 1996. As well as that, five lads out of the 16 used against Palatine had won an All-Ireland SHC 'B' medal with Carlow in 1992, including one Johnny Nevin, so we all had plenty of big game experience. Tom 'Doc' Hughes, a passionate Ballinabranna man was over Old Leighlin then. Doc would talk all day where GAA and horses were concerned. His line was, 'Old Leighlin have never lost a senior final!'

The first group game in 1997 saw us up against our other parish rivals Ballinabranna. I remember that game for a different reason. The game was on a Saturday evening and I had a driving lesson that morning. The lessons were not going well... brutal in fact. 'Stephen you may cancel the test next Thursday, as you haven't a hope of passing.' Not what you want to hear from your instructor, but I wasn't cancelling. We won the game 1-8 to 1-4. Their goal, I wasn't happy conceding. That evening we had the 'afters' of a wedding to attend.

Our intermediate winning captain from the previous year, Pakie Geoghegan got married earlier that day so we went out to that after the game. I had maybe two, three pints at most... and I'd never be rowdy with drink. I'd be more likely to be asleep in a corner somewhere but a fella got lippy with me and, with the day I had, between conceding the goal and the driving lessons, I just had enough. I grabbed him by the neck... and next thing I'm brought out of the wedding. But, to cut a long story short, the driving test wasn't cancelled but was actually passed, so it all turned out alright in the end!

Growing up, I was obsessed with the GAA. I even called our dog 'Kerry' after the great team of the 70s and 80s. Our neighbours, the Jordans had a good size garden joining the local quarry. They had a set of goalposts as well. I would spend a lot of time over there with my good friend Niall (we were born 23 days apart), his younger brother Michael, along with the Sheehy brothers, Philip and Frank. That's where we would play soccer, football, hurling for many hours, honing our skills. Niall and Michael's uncle Joe Walshe had won a couple of Senior Championships with Tinryland and played with Carlow for many years, and seeing Joe was as near as any of us thought we'd get to winning one, if we were to be brutally honest. Although our headmaster and juvenile hurling coach Eddie O'Sullivan would have instilled in us that giving up was never an option, and nothing was impossible. A Minor hurling 'A' and 'B' in 1987 – a never done before or since double - and subsequent under-21 hurling championships in 1988 and '90 were proof of his philosophy

In 1997 we had three games in eight days. Why exactly I can't remember now, but we had to play them anyway. The third game was against Naomh Eoin and we had to win it to go through to the semi-final – following a win and loss to Tinryland and Clonmore respectively in our previous two games. We had a lot of injuries with the heavy fixture load. I was secretary of the club at the time and a couple of us went out to county chairman Jim English's house to see about a change. Niall Jordan was in England for work around then and he was planning to come home for the match but we still didn't know where we stood. The county board stood firm though and no change was granted. Niall came home and helped us to only the second semi-final victory in our history. Michael Jordan took a goal-bound Ger Byrne shot off the line to beat Rathvilly and seal our place in a first ever final following a great team performance.

The late Paul Donaghy visited Stone Developments for a preview in *The Nationalist* the week leading into the game, and Ned Sheehy (who for the Doc's liking gave Paul too much material), Seamus McClean, Benji O'Brien and yours truly were all there. A young John Hayden, who was working there for the summer, was also present. There was a follow up the week after the final with a brilliant photo taken at the Big Tree for the *Nationalist* again – with my father, and his brothers Bill, Davy and Jim. Billy Forde, and Matt, Patsy and Patrick Carey were also in the picture with the Conlon Cup pride of place. Patrick and Patsy having travelled home from America for the final for which Palatine were favourites. My mother's brother Jack had passed away in August and his month's mind was the Friday before the game. Uncle Jim and my father were in rare form after a few pints in Ballinkillen Community Centre. They, like many who had done work for the club, played, and then supplied players to the club over the years, were like kids waiting for Christmas morning to arrive!

Our opponents Palatine wouldn't have been on our radar other than they beat us in the 1985 intermediate final. They too reached the senior final in their first year up and players like Tom Hickey, Micko Brennan and Pat Reid were still in tow looking for that senior medal -1952 was their last win with former Meath player and Carlow manager Liam Hayes's father Jim prominent. If there's a better feeling than coming up the tunnel in Dr Cullen Park for your club's first county final and representing your village, it could only be bettered by winning it. Seven of our starting team all lived on the one stretch of road.

'Stay focused in the parade', the Doc had told us. *Amhran Na bhfiann* was played and away we went defending the Cannery end in the first-half. I caught an early ball under the crossbar, which was settling for me as the noise on county final day is deafening. It's like no other day; every ball is life and death.

County finals can be cagey affairs and, ideally, I think you need a spread of scorers instead of depending on one or two to do it, and it was John Hayden who had the honour of being our first ever scorer in a senior final. We went in with a three-point interval lead and with six different scorers, and that meant we were right in it, but facing a strong enough breeze in the second-half. James Reid was their main scoring threat but, overall as a team, we were just to a man playing slightly better, although John Kelly's introduction changed that – his work in Saudi Arabia denying him a starting position. I saved a James Reid effort shortly after; the ball ended up under me somehow. Brian Kelly whizzed one wide also, and it was a nervy last 10 minutes with nothing more than a score in it. Lads were asking the umpires what's left, whereas I was covering my ears. I didn't want any distractions. It was fitting that Johnny Nevin should kick our last score.

We won the next two kickouts and Pat Ahern's final whistle sparked wild celebrations and I looked up… and the scoreboard… it read… Old Leighlin 1-10, Palatine 0-11… in big yellow writing. Holy God! From 8 to 15, and throw in sub John Carey… all bar one scored from play. It was a monumental effort. Tom Connolly went where no Old Leighlin man had gone before, up the steps of the Lennon Stand to collect the Conlon Cup. My first memory of reaching the dressing-room after was seeing a teary-eyed Willie Bambrick, Niall's father. It showed what it meant to all in our community. The *Irish Independent* on Monday had county final reports up and down the country. We were now no different than a Nemo Rangers or a Rathnew. *We were county champions!*

The village was rocking, and the quarry lorry was rocking too… bringing us to the

Big Tree in the village. Carey's had a shed converted which was later christened Club Heifer for the spillover crowd. The video of the game landed on Monday evening, with the few who did make work in the quarry rejoining the celebrations. The late Seanie Brennan from Tinryland, along with Willie Quinlan and Willie's former manager for club and county, the late Bobby Millar, also joined us on the Sunday. It was the biggest crowd in the village since St Lazerian and 1,500 monks resided in the village many moons ago! It was mad stuff entirely for the week.

The Leinster Club Championship meant Parnell Park and a star-studded Erin's Isle. Mick Deegan, Johnny and Keith Barr, Charlie Redmond awaited. Straight in at the deep end. A big change from going to Navan and Longford on sessions following Éire Óg! We had runs on the Barrow track to improve our fitness and a couple of league games too. We knew this was going to be a big test but just how big was soon all too apparent as the game was over after 10 minutes. Robbie Boyle and Niall Crossan blitzed us in a 5-22 to 0-5 defeat. It was a different level to anything we'd faced before. They were on a different path to us with a Leinster and All-Ireland their objective.

After we beat Palatine in 1997, they eventually got over the line in 2006; ironically over a Doc Hughes trained Kildavin/Clonegal side. Old Leighlin reached another senior final then in 2003, when I captained, but we were beaten by O'Hanrahan's after a replay. I didn't have to wait long to captain a winning team, however, as in 2004 I climbed the steps in Dr Cullen Park as Naomh Brid won the Senior Hurling Championship. After I had retired then the footballers won three senior championships in 2010, '11 and '13 which ensured that being on the terrace wasn't all that bad!

# PAT COADY

## ST MULLINS 2-15 ★ NAOMH EOIN 1-9
### Carlow SHC Final
### Dr Cullen Park, Carlow
### OCTOBER 12, 1997

*Pat Coady is presented with his Christy Ring Cup 'Hurling Champion 15' award by GAA president Sean Kelly in 2005, and (inset) in action against Offaly in the NHL Division 2 final in 2005.*

★ **ST MULLINS:** R Kielthy; E McDonald, T Doyle, C Byrne; R Dreelan, S O'Shea, A Ralph; D Kavanagh, M Ryan (0-2); D Doyle (2-3), **P Coady (0-7)**, J McDonald; P Murphy (0-2), J Cahill (0-1), S Gahan. Subs: M Murphy for Cahill.

★ **NAOMH EOIN:** TJ Foley; N Kavanagh, P Jordan, P Keogh; M Minchin, K Nolan, D Tracey; A Curry, R Foley (0-1); B Murphy (1-1), Mick Slye (0-5), Michaél Slye(0-1); C Jordan (0-1), D Murphy, J Byrne. Subs: D Slye for Curry, A Keogh for Tracey, J Slye for Nolan.

# THE ACTION

UNDERDOGS ST MULLINS stunned favourites Naomh Eoin to take their first SHC title since 1989 after this comprehensive victory. Naomh Eoin have proved to be a bogey side for St Mullins over the previous decade or so but two goals from David Doyle saw St Mullins win with ease. St Mullins were in charge from start to finish and they had star performers all over the field. Young Thomas Doyle at full-back had an excellent game, especially on such a big name as Des Murphy. Centre-forward Pat Coady chipped in with 0-7 over the hour. These were just two standout performances, but in truth St Mullins were on top right throughout the game in every position.

It was St Mullins who were on the board first and two early scores from Coady got rid of any early nerves there may have been. They led 0-8 to 0-6 at half-time. The second-half was 10 minutes old when the pendulum firmly started to seriously swing in St Mullins favour. David Doyle struck a ground shot which went through a body of defenders and past TJ Foley in the Naomh Eoin goal. Pat Coady, Michael Ryan and Doyle all tacked on points and, all of a sudden, they had an eight point lead.

At this stage, Naomh Eoin looked a beaten docket. They were finding it hard to gain any clean possession and any time they did get it, they were hunted down in packs by a ravenous St Mullins side that clearly smelled blood. With less than 10 minutes to go, everyone knew it was St Mullins' day when Coady nailed a sideline cut from about 60 metres out. There was still more drama to come. With seven minutes left, Brian Murphy scored a late goal for Naomh Eoin but almost immediately at the other end David Doyle drove a bullet of a shot to the back of the net to grab his second green flag of the day. With the final whistle came wild celebrations from the St Mullins players and supporters alike as the premier hurling title in the county was back in green and white again.

★★★★★

66

I CAN CLEARLY remember the first senior county final I played in. I was only a young 18-year-old and I was marking the great Ned Kavanagh of Naomh Eoin, who at that stage had a long successful career behind him for both club and county in both codes. I was raw, and Ned hurled me up a stick that day and I was taken off shortly after half-time.

Later on in my career, I wore contact lenses but, at that time, I would have still worn my glasses under my helmet. At one stage in the first-half I got a belt under a high ball and one of the lenses popped out of the glasses and I didn't know where I was. I couldn't see a thing... I was all over the place. I think I was better off wearing no glasses at all than going around with one good eye and one bad eye, because you just can't see anything. Between everything, I was pure raw and also had little experience, but you learn when you're hurling against the likes of Naomh Eoin.

St Mullins had lost a few finals to Naomh Eoin in the early 90s so they really were a bogey team for us. In 1993, they beat us after a replay. I was still only about 18 and I remember walking out of the dressing-room, obviously disappointed after losing, but county secretary Tommy O'Neill, who has since passed away, handed me a letter on the way out, inviting me to join the Carlow senior hurling panel. I went out to the car to see my mother and father and I was like a lad who had just won 10 county finals, but again, it just shows the naivety of youth.

We lost another county final in 1996, this time falling to Naomh Bríd but we had beaten Naomh Eoin in the semi-final in Bagenalstown. Beating the Miseal men was a big monkey off our back and the general consensus was the final was ours to lose, but lose it is what we did. Johnny Nevin gave his customary Man of the Match county final performance for Naomh Bríd but they deserved it and we didn't back up our semi-final win with the same level of performance in the final. We were of course disappointed to lose that game but when the dust had settled we were eager to push on then going into 1997.

Jim O'Connell and his management team had decided to stay on for 1997 and we were all delighted they were sticking around. We learned a lot from the previous year and we sailed our way through the championship. We had been beaten in enough finals and we were sick of it. Going into 1997, lads just said that this was it, we were going to put the foot down now.

We qualified for the semi-final quickly enough and along the way we beat the champions of the previous year, Naomh Bríd which put down a big marker for us. We beat Carlow Town in the semi final to qualify for our second final in-a-row… and waiting for us there were our old friends from Miseal. The final itself started off like any county final. It was tetchy and tense. We were playing well but not as well as we'd have liked, but at half-time we held a slender 0-8 to 0-6 lead. Naomh Eoin always had a reputation for being big tough men, well able to hurl of course but they were always known as big hardy men. By that stage though, we had a few big lads ourselves and we just weren't going to take a backward step that day. We were able to hold our own physically with Miseal and once we were able to show that, then I think maybe they thought that it wasn't going to be the same old story with them brushing us aside in finals. It's funny the way things work out sometimes.

David Doyle was a little bit older than the rest of us and had suffered a lot more against Miseal in county finals than some of the younger lads. David scored 2-3 in the final, but that was normal for David. He was a goal machine. Whenever he got the ball he only had goals on his mind and thankfully he got two that day. They got a goal from Brian Murphy near the end to put a bit of respectability on the score board but almost straightaway David got another goal to put some gloss on it. We knocked over a couple of extra points and at that stage we were firmly in charge. Near the end of the game we were awarded a lineball and I went over to take it. I struck it sweetly and it went straight over the bar. I remember raising my arms once that went over and looking up to the sky, as I firmly believed we were going to win it at that stage.

I will never forget the feeling when the final whistle went. People were going wild and all the supporters came onto the field. We had all the emotions. We were all delighted to be county champions, of course. There was massive relief there too that we had finally gotten over the one side we just always struggled against on the big days. Any one that plays sport knows that when that monkey is off your back then the shackles are gone and there is no limit from then on to what you can achieve. After that 1997 win, we went on to win the championship again '99, 2000 and '02, and we actually beat Naomh Eoin in all three of those finals.

We celebrated that county final win as much as any team could. We eventually got back to the field and we had a Leinster Championship campaign to prepare for. We travelled up to play the Louth champions Naomh Moninne in the first round and we won the game comfortably enough. The bus journey home from Dundalk to St Mullins must have been the longest bus journey ever as there were a couple of stops on the way home that evening for refreshments and plenty of toilet breaks!

That win set us up for a quarter final clash with Dublin champions O'Tooles in Dr Cullen Park. Kilkenny's Eamon Morrissey and James 'Shiner' Brennan were both playing for O'Tooles at the time and they scored a fair chunk of their scores against us that day in Carlow as our Leinster adventure came to an end. Declan Kavanagh, Richard Dreelan and I would nearly always have travelled to matches together. Many nights, even before important championship games, the three of us would have a few pints. Maybe we'd go in to Graiguenamanagh or somewhere, but wherever we'd go, we would have a pint or two and I'm sure we probably went for one the night before that O'Tooles game. The first 20 minutes of that game we were all over them but then for the second-half we couldn't keep it up and we just ran out of steam. I remember walking off the field and thinking to myself that there was a lesson to be learned and I wouldn't be drinking the night before a game again.

As an aside to that story, we actually played O'Tooles again in the 2002 Leinster Club Championship, again in Dr Cullen Park. Before the game, our manager Tommy Buggy got John Wynne in to have a chat with us. John would have been on those successful Éire Óg football teams of the 1990s and he also won an All-Ireland SFC 'B' with Carlow. John was a prison officer in Portlaoise, so he and Tommy knew each other through work. We sat in the dressing-rooms in Carlow Town hurling club, next to Dr Cullen Park. After we were finished, we were all standing around outside chatting, while at the same time we noticed O'Tooles were just finishing up their warm up on the hurling club pitch. They were coming down to Carlow to win and nothing else. We could see that.

As they were walking down from the pitch I said to the boys that we'll play along now and pretend to be real aul culchies who had no interest in the game. Just as the O'Tooles lads were walking past us, I shouted over to Eugene McDonald,

'Hey Mac, are my boots in the back of your car? Jaysus I don't know where I left them after training on Tuesday night'. Now, I don't know if that made any difference, but maybe one of them heard it. They were champions of Dublin and they all had the fancy boots and socks pulled up to the knees, whereas we were just the lads from the country who had no chance. We tore into them anyway and we ended up beating them. That win was probably one of the first big victories for a Carlow team in the Leinster Club Hurling Championship. It was a massive difference walking off the field that day against O'Tooles than five years earlier against the same opposition.

I had great days playing with club and county in my career. Picking a game of my life was not easy. I settled on that 1997 win but there were plenty of other special days too. One that sticks out in my head from over the years was neither a club nor county game, but a college game from 1994. I was playing with St Pat's, Drumcondra and we were playing in the third tier of colleges hurling at the time. I think it is called the Fergal Maher Cup nowadays. Most of our lads were from places like Donegal, Mayo, Leitrim and Roscommon, for example. They were all football men and most of them had never held a hurl before. The few of us that could hurl, our instruction to our footballers on the team was to get down over the ball, hold your arse over it and wait for someone who can hurl to come in and bail you out. Great advice!

We qualified for the final against Mary I from Limerick and we got the train down to the game. Éamonn Cregan was in charge of Mary I at the time. There was an awful deluge of rain leading up to the match and it continued then for the match itself. I remember we got a lineball during the first-half and I was going to take it. I had the ball all set and atop a lovely piece of grass to hit it. I was just about to strike it, only didn't Cregan come in and drive the ball into the ground and in to the muck. I stopped then, just as I was about to strike the ball and stood back and re-set the ball again. I don't know what stopped me from just pulling on Cregan there and then, but I managed to stay calm.

Once I did actually get to strike it, it sailed straight over the bar and that was probably a better way to answer him back than anything else. From the resulting puck out, I got possession. The ball just landed dead on my hurl. I took off and ended up scoring a goal, so in the space of a couple of minutes that was a four point turnaround in what was a very low scoring game played in awful conditions.

Ultimately, I picked the 1997 county final as it was my first senior county championship. The ones in between were special too of course but my final one was also very satisfactory, if a little unexpected.

In 2010, I came out of retirement for one last shot at glory. I had actually retired in 2007 after the county final. We had played Naomh Bríd in the semi-final that year and right at the start of the second-half from the throw in I got a belt on my right hand. It was pure accidental but I ended up breaking a bone in my hand. We had the county final the following weekend. During the week, I met a doctor who I knew. I met him on the morning of the county final and he said to me, 'Pat, I'll fix your finger so that if a horse bit it, you won't feel it'. Anyway, he put two needles in my hand and I could feel nothing. He then taped my damaged finger to the one beside it so when I moved my hand the finger would go with it.

I was able to play the match anyway, but with about 10 minutes to go the anaesthetic wore off and the pain started to come back in the finger. We were beaten in the final that day and afterwards I had no choice but to retire as the finger was in bits and I had done awful damage to the soft tissue. In the next two years I had three or four operations on the finger and it had started to straighten out a small bit. In the meantime over the winter, I had been talking to a few of the lads in the club and they were saying how they had just got a new trainer, Jim Doyle, ahead of the 2010 season. St Mullins had just come off the back of an awful season where they didn't even qualify for the semi-finals so the club wasn't going well at all. The word was that all players were going to receive letters about going back to training. I was talking to the club chairman John Joe Murphy and even though I was an ex player at this stage, I suggested to him that maybe a letter could be sent my way?!

The letter arrived anyway shortly after and I spent a bit of time contemplating it, and I had a chat with my wife too. If I was going back we had to be sure, as there were plenty of risks attached. Obviously the finger was the biggest factor and how it would hold up in the heat of championship. As well as that, I hadn't held a hurl for well over two years, but I said I'd go back and train and give it a go anyway and see what happened.

I went back when the time came around, as the finger wasn't too bad at that stage. Since then, it has actually gotten worse and is fully bent in now. At the time the occupational therapist in Waterford had made me a mould for the finger so I would strap it on every night before I went to bed and that kept the finger straight during the night time, so it wasn't too bad by the time each game came around. 2010 ended up being a fairytale ending as we won the county championship, defeating Mount Leinster Rangers in the final. I got the Man of the Match award too which was nice, so as comebacks go it couldn't have gone any better.

# WILLIE QUINLAN

**ÉIRE ÓG 1-11 ★ KILMACUD CROKES 0-11**
Leinster Club SFC FINAL 1998 (Second Replay)
St Conleth's Park, Newbridge
JANUARY 31, 1999

*Willie Quinlan celebrates after scoring his side's first goal during the Leinster Club Championship final second replay against Kilmacud Crokes in Newbridge.*

★ **ÉIRE ÓG:** J Kearns; B Hayden, A Corcoran, J Dooley; J Murphy (0-1), P Doyle, A Callinan; T Nolan, J Morrissey (0-2); B Carbery (0-2), G Ware, K Haughney; **W Quinlan (1-1)**, L Turley (0-1), A Keating (0-4). Subs: P Kingston for Haughney, H Brennan for Nolan, J Hayden for Carbery.

★ **KILMACUD CROKES:** M Pender; C O'Dwyer, C Deegan (0-1), C Cleary; J O'Callaghan, J Magee (0-1), R Leahy; J Costello (0-2), M Leahy; P Ward, M Dillon, C Redmond; R Cosgrove (0-1), R Brennan (0-3), M O'Keeffe (0-3). Subs: C Kelleher for Redmond.

# THE ACTION

A FIRST-HALF OF almost flawless football put Éire Óg firmly on their way to a fifth Leinster club football title of the 90s as they finally overcame the challenge of Kilmacud Crokes at the third attempt. The opening thirty minutes saw the Carlow side open up a 1-8 to 0-3 lead and while they had to withstand a strong second-half comeback from Kilmacud, the remaining 10 minutes left no doubt about the hunger of these Éire Óg boys.

Éire Óg were never headed in the game and traded early points before the game's only goal in the fifth minute. Tom Nolan took a line ball towards the town goal. Jody Morrissey got the deftest of touches as backs and forwards rose highest to claim the ball before it landed in the hands of Willie Quinlan, and he sent a shot to the bottom corner of Mick Pender's goal.

Key to the win was midfield supremacy where Jody Morrissey and Garvan Ware were well on top and this stranglehold was only broken when Crokes sent Conor Deegan out there to try and curb their influence later in the game. That the midfield was winning this battle was key further up the field as the movement of the Éire Óg forwards was out of the top drawer, with Willie Quinlan, Leo Turley and Anthony 'Muckle' Keating in particular creating gaping holes in the opposition defence. Crokes did try right up to the finish and a brace of points from Robbie Brennan and John Costello closed the gap but they just couldn't break through the Éire Óg defence to find that all important goal.

Jody Morrissey was the Man of the Match and it was his partnership with Ware that supplied so much good ball to the forwards in that first-half blitz. Alan Callinan put in a huge shift all day and was very effective in curbing the influence of his marker. Joe Murphy also had a huge game at the back. Up front, Willie Quinlan with 1-1 and Anthony Keating with 0-4 were once again showing how much they love the big day out.

★ ★ ★ ★ ★

**"**

I'VE BEEN PART of some great teams over the years between Éire Óg and Carlow, but for sheer drama and excitement it could only be one game for me. During the 90s the club won five Leinster senior club titles which was phenomenal but when we reached the 1998 final against Kilmacud Crokes, it went to three games, meaning there was no winner until the end of January 1999.

The first game obviously ended up in a draw and I actually broke two ribs in that game. I remember going to my doctor after the match and he told me to go and see him again on the Thursday. He told me he'd give me an injection and see if I'd be able to train on my own. Thursday came, and he gave me the injection, so I went over the road and trained on my own in Carlow College but it didn't work. I trained for about 20 minutes and it was a disaster. I could barely walk after it.... could barely get up off the ground, so that was disappointing but the ribs were just too bad to chance it.

For the second game, I was still in pain and I actually got another injection, but this was just to go and watch the match, never mind play. I was probably the happiest man coming out of Tullamore that day as I knew there would be a good chance I would be available again for the next day. The second replay then, the third game, was bringing us both to Newbridge.

We got off to a great start and kicked a couple of early points through Anthony Keating, while I chipped in with one myself also. The goal was the big moment in the game. We got a lineball and Tom Nolan was going to take it. It was sent in and Jody Morrissey got a little flick to the ball. Everyone went up for the ball and, for some reason, my man stepped out four or five yards. I stayed and the ball just came to me. I turned and just smashed it in to the right side of the goalkeeper. We seemed to push on even further after the goal and we tagged on an extra couple of points, and we had a good lead at half-time. They came back strongly at us in the second-half and narrowed the gap back to two points at one stage but when they got a point, we'd go down and kick one at the other end. In fairness, they kept coming back but they just couldn't get past us on the day.

Rather than being one game that sticks out. To me, it was the whole episode that stands out. Three games between two great teams. That second game in Tullamore was played in torrential rain. At the end, I think the referee was looking to play extra-time but looking at it, between the awful weather and the tough physical slog the players had put in, both teams were out on their feet at that stage.

It was probably the right decision because it would have been a terrible way to lose it in extra-time because one score probably would have won it, such were the conditions. There was a fantastic buzz and a great build up to all our club games back in the 90s. Even at the time, I don't know if we realised what we had done. Winning five Leinster club titles in seven years and reaching two All-Ireland senior club finals. Unfortunate that we didn't win one, but we had a great run. We had some great games over the years and beat some top teams.

I'll always remember the day we finally beat Kilmacud. It's funny the things that come back to you. I remember a ball was kicked in to me. I turned and stuck it over the bar and the camera went on to me, and I had a big smile on my face and I just remember thinking that we're not going to lose here today. We always felt that way though. Even though we'd be playing teams from Dublin and other traditionally stronger counties, we always felt we would win. We played Dublin teams five times in the Leinster Championships over those years and we were never beaten in any of them. We just always seemed to get the upper hand on them.

Once we won our first Leinster in 1992, the confidence just started to grow. Bobby Miller was with us at the time and he really turned our club around. We won a three in-a-row of county championships from 1987 to '89 and we were beaten in the first round of the Leinster club every single time. It just seemed to be a fitness thing. Teams just always seemed to be fitter than us but when Bobby came along, he changed all that. From then on, it was all fitness, fitness… fitness. We won so many games in the last five or 10 minutes through fitness that we probably would have lost previously to that, so when Bobby came in at the start of the 90s, he changed our training regime and our mindset as well. Bobby actually won a couple of Leinster Championships with us and he left Éire Óg then to take over the Carlow senior team.

In 1994, under Bobby, Carlow won the All-Ireland SFC 'B' title and I think there were 11 Éire Óg men starting, and Jody Morrissey came on as a sub as well. In 1995 we played Laois in two games. Laois offering a replay to us after one of their points was actually shown to be wide later on and we lost a close game the second day out. I remember being out drinking on the Monday in Lennon's bar and Ber Hennessy coming in to tell us that we were playing Laois again that weekend, and that we were going to be training that night. Everybody just scattered straightaway. We all went home and had a bite to eat… and back up to Dr Cullen Park that night for a light session.

I think back then, in the 90s that players enjoyed both sides of it a bit more. You enjoyed your football, but you enjoyed the social side of it as well. Back then with Carlow, we probably would have been out maybe three times a week and one of those was often a challenge game. Looking at it nowadays, it seems to be a seven-day week thing for players between football, gym sessions, video analysis or whatever else there is. Even the likes of Carlow and other Division Four teams, they're still nearly at it all week as well. It doesn't matter the level, the commitment levels are totally different now.

In 1996, we were going well. We thought we were going well anyway. Carlow beat Wexford and Wicklow in the championship but then we ran into Meath in Croke Park and they beat us 0-24 to 0-6. It was men against boys. Meath had the likes of Darren Fay, Graham Geraghty and Trevor Giles coming on the scene and they just blew us away. Meath went on to win the All-Ireland that year. I remember Martin O'Connell was playing corner back for Meath and everybody was saying he was past it… that his best days were behind him. That day, I just could not get away from him. He was still so big and strong. He was a real Meath player, just so tough. Despite that setback, it was great to still be working with Bobby Miller, despite the different set up between club and county.

Bobby, who sadly passed away in 2006, changed the club for the better and even when he left for the Carlow job, we continued to be successful in Carlow and Leinster. John Courtney won a Leinster Championship with us and so too did Pat Critchley.

After that third Kilmacud game, we didn't have long to celebrate as we were due to play Crossmaglen Rangers in the All-Ireland semi-final just a few weeks later, due to the Leinster Championship running on so late. We celebrated on the Sunday night, and probably the Monday too, before we were back training on the Tuesday night. Those Tuesday night training sessions were probably the hardest sessions we used to do. The Monday after a game would often turn in to an all-day drinking session but, no matter what, we always turned up for training on the Tuesday night.

We played Crossmaglen up in Navan and they beat us by a few points. Despite us being Carlow and Leinster champions at the time, that year was probably the last great hurrah for a lot of lads as a good few finished up playing at the same time not long after. Normally, when lads stop playing senior, they might drop down and play a little bit of intermediate or junior. We probably had eight or nine lads who just stopped playing at around 30 or 31 years of age but at the same time, a lot of us had played an awful amount of football over a short period of time. I think a lot of lads stopped around the same time and it would be seven years until we won another county championship.

After that, I suppose it was a transition period for Éire Óg and we didn't win a Senior Championship again until 2005. I finished up playing senior when I was 42. I played a bit of intermediate then and at 45 won a Junior Championship. I probably ended up playing a little too long but, at the same time, I enjoyed every minute of it. I played my first senior league game for Éire Óg in 1984 and the following year I made my Senior Championship debut but we were beaten by Naomh Eoin.

We did the three in-a-row from 1986 to '88 and I played on with the senior club side until 2008. We beat Palatine after a replay in the county final and we reached the Leinster Championship semi-final, but we were well beaten by Rhode. I came on that day in Dr Cullen Park and, looking back, I probably shouldn't have. I remember going for a ball in the second-half and the head will tell you you'll make it but the body was saying something else. Just as I was about to gather the ball, out of nowhere one of the Rhode lads came and gathered the ball and knocked me clean out in the process. It was at that moment then I said to myself, that it's probably time to step away from playing senior and maybe do my few years at intermediate and junior before stepping away all together.

# JOHNNY KAVANAGH

**WESTMEATH 2-10 ★ CARLOW 1-8**
**Leinster SFC Preliminary Round**
**Dr Cullen Park, Carlow**
**MAY 9, 1999**

*Johnny Kavanagh in action in the Leinster Championship in 2000 and (inset) one year earlier he gets his marching orders on his county debut against Westmeath.*

★ **WESTMEATH:** A Lennon; D Brady, R Casey, D Murphy; A Lyons, D Mitchell, K Ryan; R O'Carroll, J Cooney; D Healy, P Conway, S Colleary; G Heavin (0-9), M Flanagan (2-0), K Lyons. Subs: M Staunton (0-1) for Colleary, D Dolan for Ryan, E Casey for Healy.

★ **CARLOW:** J Brennan; B Farrell, A Corden, P O'Dwyer; J Murphy, K Walker, **J Kavanagh**; G Ware (1-0), J Morrissey (0-3); N Doyle (0-1), S Kavanagh, W Quinlan; M Dowling (0-3), J Nevin (0-1), P Kavanagh. Subs: J Byrne for O'Dwyer, P Kingston for Dowling, M Carpenter for P Kavanagh.

# THE ACTION

THE FOOTBALL CHAMPIONSHIP started off in farcical circumstances as Carlow and Westmeath were the first teams to feel the full effects of the new yellow and red card rules brought in by the GAA. Six players were sent off in all – four from Carlow and two from Westmeath, and this incensed supporters of both sides in the attendance of 3,000. The fact that the game was played in such poor weather didn't help either with players from both sides falling and slipping. Before all the cards were flashed, the game itself actually got off to a flying start as first Carlow's Garvan Ware took a sideline ball which seemed to go all the way to the back of the net without a touch. It didn't take Westmeath long to get one back, however, as after a mix up in the Carlow defence, Martin Flanagan was on hand to fire home. Westmeath kicked on from here and a number of points from Ger Heavin had Westmeath in the lead.

Westmeath never led by more than two points in the first-half but that could have been even more as Heavin's penalty was expertly saved by John Brennan. Carlow's Johnny Kavanagh was the first man to see red. Kavanagh, on his senior championship debut only lasted 17 minutes as by that stage he had picked up his second yellow card. Brian Farrell and Kenny Lyons both were sent to the line in the first-half also. The second-half was not long on when what probably seemed to be the harshest sending off of them all, as Carlow centre-back Ken Walker was sent off for a second yellow card – and this was probably the turning point in the game.

Westmeath had snuck ahead at this point, but there was to be more drama as first Sean Kavanagh and then Rory O'Connell were sent off, which meant Carlow were down to 11 men while Westmeath were down to 13. Amazingly, despite this, Carlow actually went ahead with points from Jody Morrissey and Noel Doyle. However, this could not last as the numerical disadvantage was just too much and Heavin put the away side back in front. With time almost up, the final nail was put in Carlow's coffin as full-forward Martin Flanagan scored his, and Westmeath's second goal.

★★★★★

66

MOST PEOPLE WILL remember their championship debut as something fondly to look back on but, unfortunately, my championship debut for the Carlow senior footballers will be remembered alright, but for all the wrong reasons. I had been in training with the footballers before when I was around 18 or 19, but for different reasons it took until 1999 to make my championship debut. Cyril Hughes was our manager at the time and I was grateful to him for giving me my chance and naturally when someone puts their trust in you like that, then you want to pay them back as much as possible. It had been a long time since a Leighlinbridge man had played Senior Championship football for Carlow, so everybody was in at it.

The day itself was wet and miserable, and it was not going to make for a great game of football. As well as that, it was the first game of the championship and the new red and yellow card system was being introduced and, of course, Carlow and Westmeath were the first two teams this new system was being 'trialled' on. Niall Barrett from Cork was the referee and he had to deal with the new rules and go on what he was told. What happened during the game then could only be described as farcical as six players were given red cards, four from Carlow and two from Westmeath. I don't know how many yellows were flashed on top of that, but there were plenty of those too.

I was the first to go and I lasted the grand total of 17 minutes! I didn't even get a kick of the ball before I was gone; I think I got one hand-pass and that was it. I can remember the first yellow card… it was for a slight jersey tug on Damien Healy. A free against maybe, but it was a bit early in the game to be flashing a yellow for something like that. The second yellow then was even worse. I remember being out around the middle of the field waiting for the kickout and there was just a little jostling with my opponent, both just trying to get first to the kickout. Next thing, the ref comes up, the Westmeath man gets a yellow, I get a yellow… and was quickly followed by a red. I just couldn't believe it – I was absolutely stunned. I don't think I had been sent off before that day and I didn't even know where to go or what to do. I was sent off once or twice after that alright, but that day was the first and it was such a shock.

I was embarrassed more than anything. I went over to the dugout and never said a word to anyone… I just sat there. I felt bad, but as the day went on we quickly realised it wouldn't all be about my red card as five more were to follow me to the line. It just seemed like any time anybody was touched then there was a card. The bad weather didn't help either with lads slipping everywhere but it just turned in to a pure farce by the end of it.

At the time, I probably had a little resentment to the referee as I just felt hard done by. I don't mind getting sent off if you deserve it but there was nothing in it, just a little jostling which goes on all the time and, all of a sudden, my day was done. To be fair to Niall Barrett, he was probably thrown in at the deep end too. We were not given much information in the lead up to the game about the new card system, only that the first foul would be a tick and your name would go in the book but, as it transpired, nearly every foul, even for the simplest thing, seemed to be a yellow and in a lot of cases, was followed by a red.

The match was all over the papers the following day and there were meetings held that week and we actually got a replay out of it as Leinster Council were in favour of it being replayed. However, Westmeath appealed that decision and they won, which meant just as quickly as we got the replay, it was taken away from us again. Westmeath argued that it was the same rules for them on the day as it was for us and I suppose they had a point. We actually went back training on the Tuesday night and I think there was a meeting going on the same night. By the time training was over, word had filtered through that the replay was off and we were told to go home. To make matters worse then, they changed the rules afterwards for the rest of the championship and relaxed the use of cards a little which was a little hard to take as well as it showed that they knew what had happened in our game was wrong. Sometimes the smaller counties never get those breaks and the fact that these new rules were only used first for Carlow and Westmeath in championship was proof of that.

The amazing thing was that despite being down to 11 players coming down the final stretch, we still led with not long to go only for Westmeath to catch us in the final few minutes, so it was still a great effort by the lads who were still out there and hadn't been sent off! In the aftermath, it turns out my red card, along with that of Ken Walker were rescinded, not that that made any difference but it actually made it a little worse in a way as it proved that what happened on the day did not warrant any cards. Sean Kavanagh and Bryan Farrell had their red cards upheld.

That might have been my Senior Football Championship debut but, by that stage, I had been playing senior hurling for Carlow for a number of years. Being a dual player was a lot more common in those days and was probably easier to combine both as, for a start, there was no back door and so there wasn't as many games. The National League used to start before Christmas as well at that time and it was rare, if ever, that football and hurling games would clash on the same weekend. If we had a football game any weekend, then we would probably train a little bit more with the footballers that week and the same with the hurlers. Any manager I played under during those years were all understanding of the dual player and they all worked together which was a huge help.

One such occasion games did kind of clash though was in 2000. Both the Leinster Football and Hurling Championships started off with round robin games that year. Carlow played games against Wicklow, Wexford and Longford in the football championship, while the hurlers faced Dublin, Laois and Westmeath. Myself and Johnny Nevin played six championship games that year across both codes.

I used to swap jerseys after every game and poor Tommy O' Neill, God rest him, used to go mad at me after every game for giving the jerseys away!

The first weekend was fairly hectic to start off with. The hurlers played Dublin in Dr Cullen Park on a lovely Saturday evening and we just came up short on the night, losing by a single point. It was a hard loss to take as Dublin were massive favourites to beat us and to come so close to pulling off a major shock, it would have been massive for Carlow.

At the time, I had an aunt of mine, Claire, who has since passed away, working in the Holy Angels day cay care centre in Carlow. Claire was a great GAA woman, and as they had a hydrotherapy pool in the centre, she managed to get both of us in there after the game, just to maybe help with the soreness and have us a bit fresher for the football the next day.

The following day, again a really warm day, Johnny and I headed to Aughrim and both started again for the footballers against Wicklow. It was a really busy few weeks but very enjoyable at the same time. Being a dual player, you could be training four or five nights a week but for us at the time it was just the norm to be doing it. We lost to Laois in the hurling then, before beating Westmeath, a game which doubled up as a league game. In the football then, unfortunately we followed up the Wicklow loss with further defeats against Wexford and Longford. I started corner-back against Longford and managed to score 1-1.

The footballers won the O'Byrne Cup in 2002. Pat Roe was in charge that time and we had come off the back of a successful championship run in 2001 under Pat where we had played five championship games and so to carry that form in to 2002 and beat Wicklow in an O'Byrne Cup final was a special day – and to do it in Dr Cullen Park as well made it even better. We beat Laois in the semi-final in Portarlington and that was the last time Carlow have beaten Laois in a competitive game.

That O'Byrne Cup win was massive for Carlow at the time but, unfortunately, we didn't carry through afterwards as results in the league campaign were poor enough. We were beaten by Westmeath in the Leinster Championship and a week later then we lost our full-back and team captain Andrew Corden in a tragic accident. Of course, that cast a huge cloud not just over the team but the whole county in general, I think. We were due to play Laois in the qualifiers in Dr Cullen Park and we didn't even know if we would fulfil the fixture, but the players met and decided that Andrew probably would not have wanted the game to be cancelled and so we decided to go ahead and play. It wasn't ideal preparation of course but as players we felt the right call was to play although I'd say none of us were in the right frame of mind going out that day. The No 3 jersey was hung up in the dressing-room before the game and we all wore black armbands going out, but realistically we were probably never going to win that game.

Pat Roe stood down after that then after two seasons and Mick 'Mickser' Condon came in. Mickser lasted two years and that second season, 2004 was as up and down as you could get. We reached the semi-final of the O'Byrne Cup where we beat a very strong Dublin team on the way and were unlucky to lose out to Páidí Ó Sé's Westmeath in the semi-final. Things seemed to be going good but league results were poor, although we did start off with a win over Monaghan; but by the time we played Donegal in the last game in Ballyshannon, the wheels had fallen off the wagon.

The hotel we stayed in for that trip to Donegal, the Holyrood Hotel, was owned by Brian McEniff and he knew what he was up to, I'm sure. There was a nightclub there and the music was loud and he knew it would be a distraction, and it was. We were told by management we could have a couple of pints the night before the game but it was never going to be just a couple and, of course, it turned into an all-night session. The management team there at the time all enjoyed a bit of craic as well and after a while nobody was going back to the room and especially when we had nobody to tell us to go back. That was the last game of the league and promotion was well gone for us at that stage. Still and all, we were playing for our county and nobody wants to go out and get hammered but with preparation like the night before it was never going to end well and Donegal beat us out the gate. Not long after that, Mickser Condon and his management team were gone and nobody knew where to go from there.

Johnny Nevin and Brendan Hayden took over the training for a few weeks before Luke Dempsey came in as the manager. Luke really was a breath of fresh air and everything was positive with him. Luke only had a few weeks with us and we beat Longford in the championship, a game nobody expected us to win before rattling Laois the next day out. Laois were the reigning Leinster champions at the time and to have them come to Dr Cullen Park where the place was absolutely heaving, and the sun beating down was great, and it would have been unthinkable just a few weeks before hand. Down beat us in the qualifiers then but we had played well enough and, as I said, considering where we were a short while before I'm sure most people would have been happy with how the season panned out performance-wise. Most of us were sick of moral victories at that stage. I think everybody expected Luke Dempsey to stay on afterwards but for whatever reason it didn't happen and Luke actually ended up taking over Longford instead.

We might not have held on to Luke, but we did get Liam Hayes instead. Liam was well known as a top midfielder through his time with Meath and we were excited about it. Liam was probably looking towards the future with Carlow and a few of the older lads such as Johnny Nevin and myself were let go from the panel, while Sean Kavanagh left in the middle of the season too. We missed the league that year but we were called back in for the championship so Johnny and I went back in and, of course, we were only too delighted to do so. At that stage I was 35 so I knew my days were numbered in a Carlow jersey, so I wasn't going to turn down an invitation. As it turns out that was my last season playing for Carlow in both senior hurling and football. To be fair it was probably time to leave anyway by then as I had been playing for Carlow since the early 90s.

I loved playing for Carlow. I wouldn't have done it for so long otherwise. I just loved playing in general. Even now I'd still love to be playing. My last game of football was in 2020 playing with Leighlinbridge in the Junior 'C' Championship and I was a couple of months shy of my fiftieth birthday. I didn't get on too bad considering either. I'm working in Mountjoy as a prison officer and so I'd be on the treadmill most days when I get a chance there, so I always like to maintain some level of fitness. I'd still love to be togging out for the club but when you're working and living in Dublin and doing shift work it's not always easy to stay involved.

# NIALL ENGLISH

**O'HANRAHANS 1-7 ★ NA FIANNA 1-5**
**Leinster Club SFC Final**
**O'Moore Park, Portlaoise**
**DECEMBER 3, 2000**

*Niall English lifts the Sean McCabe Cup after O'Hanrahans defeated Na Fianna in the Leinster Club Football Championship final in O'Moore Park.*

★ **O'HANRAHANS:** J Brennan; B English, A Corden, **N English**; B Hannon, K Walker, K Kavanagh; P Nolan, A Bowe; G Walker, P Kavanagh (0-4), D Bermingham (0-2); B Walker (1-1), A Kavanagh, S Farrell. Subs: B Quigley for Farrell.

★ **NA FIANNA:** S Gray; N O'Murchu, B McManus, T Lynch; S Connell (0-1), N Clancy, S McGlinchey; S Forde, K McGeeney; M Galvin (0-2), D Farrell, A Shearer (1-0); I Foley(0-1), J Sherlock, D Mackin. Subs: P McCarthy for McManus, K Donnelly (0-1) for Forde, D Keegan for Foley.

# THE ACTION

O'HANRAHANS ARE THE High Kings of Leinster. The 'Blues' have now joined their town counterparts Éire Óg on the Leinster roll of honour, and they did it the hard way too. Highly fancied Dublin kingpins Na Fianna were expected to easily win this final but club football in the depths of winter is a different animal and there are no doubts as to which team played all the football on the day – and that was the Carlow side. Na Fianna went in to this game as defending Leinster champions and going for two in-a-row. They also had a team stacked with county players such as Dessie Farrell, Jason Sherlock, Senan Connell, Mick Galvin and Armagh's Kieran McGeeney to name a few.

O'Hanrahans had plenty of talent on board too in what was a team with more than half the starters still under-21. Na Fianna played with the wind in the first-half but still only went in at the break leading by 0-4 to 0-2. The fitness of the O'Hanrahans side was also very obvious to all watching, and they came out in the second-half and, aided by the wind, went on to score 1-5 without reply. David Bermingham and Pa Kavanagh scored early points, before Bermingham pointed again from a similar distance out. Pa Kavanagh then put over a pair of frees before the game's defining moment. A long clearance out was directed to Brian Walker and the No. 13 made no mistake when he drove the ball to the back of the net. From two points down, the Blues were now six points up, but that was to be their last score of the game. Mick Galvin responded with a point before O'Hanrahans were made to sweat when Aaron Shearer goaled to leave two between the teams.

Similar to the O'Hanrahans goal, however, the Na Fianna score was also their last of the game. From here on in, the Carlow side defended like true champions and each ball that came in was sent straight back out. At the other end of the field, the eventual winners hit five wides in eight minutes to create more tension. With time almost up, it was O'Hanrahans who were still playing all the football. When the final whistle went there was pandemonium and great scenes all around as O'Hanrahans were now the second team from Ireland's second smallest county to call themselves Leinster's finest.

★★★★★

66

TO WIN A Leinster Senior Club Championship was the pinnacle for the club in its history. At that stage we were in the middle of a three in-a-row of Carlow Senior Championships, 1999-2001. The previous Senior Championship win by the club before 1999 was in 1961 – so 38 years was a long time to be waiting for a club with such a long and proud history. What made it even more significant at the time was the age profile of the team. When we beat Na Fianna in that Leinster final, we had eight under-21s on the starting team and most of those lads had also played in the 1999 final when we won our first county senior final beating Éire Óg.

Éire Óg had won their fifth Leinster Championship earlier that season, so it just proved how competitive club football was in Carlow at the time. The 90s were a good time for the O'Hanrahans club at underage level. The club had won back to back Minor Championships in 1995 and '96 and followed that up with four Under-21 Championships in a row (1997-2000).

Breffni Hannon, Brian Walker, Alan Bowe, my brother Vincent and I were the oldest on the senior team. We would like to think that the blend of experience with the successful minor and 21s teams formed the right balance over those years. Looking back now, it was a great period in the club's history, and there was great club spirit and a fantastic buzz around the club. The achievements created a lifelong bond between players, families, supporters and everyone involved in the club.

In the middle of all those underage titles, we also won the Intermediate Championship in 1997 and it's crazy to think within just three years we would go from Carlow intermediate champions to Leinster senior club champions. What a journey. We had very good footballers but there was a physical and mental maturity to the lads that were coming through. Lads like Pa, Ken and Anthony Kavanagh, Ken Walker, Philip Nolan, John Brennan and Andrew Corden were all very good footballers, but all tough competitive operators too.

To win a championship you obviously need a lot of different ingredients, everyone striving for a common 'target', talented, committed footballers, determination to succeed, and self-belief. It is significant commitment to get to the top and to sustain it over a number of years. Andrews's loss was huge. It was tragic and broke our hearts; it left a void, as he was someone we could not replace.

Andrew was and still is so highly regarded; he had it all and we could have played him anywhere on the field. He had his whole life ahead of him.

JJ Lambert was manager in 1998 and we were beaten by Rathvilly in the senior semi-final in our first year up from intermediate. JJ believed the club needed an experienced outside manager to take this group of players to the next level and reach their potential. In late 1998, JJ and John McDermott approached Mick Dempsey to manage the club's senior team and whilst Mick had been approached by numerous other clubs he was impressed by their professionalism, but acknowledged he knew little about the O'Hanrahans club. Reflecting now, I think the lads challenged Mick in different ways to what he was used to in previous management jobs. We had a few characters that required Mick's man-management skills, but soon enough the training started. The success we had at senior level may not have come without Michael Dempsey. There was always talent within our club, but Mick brought the discipline and training that we needed to be successful at senior. While Mick was the manager, he had a great team with him; Noel Richardson, JJ Lambert and Anthony Kavanagh Snr all played a massive part in the success of that period. Korky as physio kept the lads on the field when we needed them.

I was a few years older than most of the lads and some of us had lost two senior hurling finals with Carlow Town in the 90s, so there was additional experience there for the 1999 football final. While I was growing up, the club was really struggling to get juvenile mentors over teams. It was only when people like Brian Dunne, Barry Rock, Brendan Walker, David Walker and Anthony Kavanagh started to get involved at underage that the club consistently fielded teams at underage grades. My father John was a big influence on me, and others like Paddy and Ciss Carpenter, and Martin Doogue were always supporting and assisting the club.

Despite 1999 being this team's first Senior Championship win, we were still eager to see how we would compete in Leinster. We were handed a tough opener away to Kildare champions Sarsfields. We lost by a point and as much as we were disappointed, we knew we had a serious chance to compete at that level. Thankfully, we didn't have long to wait to get back again as we put back-to-back Carlow championships together the following year beating Éire Óg again in the

2000 final. Our first Leinster club game out was a home clash against Dicksboro from Kilkenny. We were probably expected to win that game easy but on a day with awful conditions they hit us for two early goals and after 10 minutes they led by 2-1 to no score. From there on we slowly got to grips with the challenge. Dicksboro didn't score in the second-half and we won by eight points in the end, 2-10 to 2-2. Michael Dempsey was over his own club St Joseph's as well as O'Hanrahans and whilst we won the Carlow championship that year, they won the Laois championship as well. The same day we played Dicksboro, St Joseph's were playing Abbeylara up in Longford, so Michael had to make a call which match he would attend. He went up to Longford as maybe he thought that we'd have enough to get over the Kilkenny side; that he didn't need to be there. We did enough to go through to the next round while St Joseph's were beaten by a point.

We played the Westmeath champions Coralstown/Kinnegad in the quarter-final and if we thought the weather was bad against Dicksboro, this was even worse. A lot of games were called off around the country that day but our game went ahead. At half-time, Kinnegad were well on top and they had built up a big lead. We were eight points down. The bad weather continued for the second-half but we started to claw it back, bit by bit. Pa Kavanagh had a great game and he ended with 1-6 to his name. It was a good comeback from us and we got out of it with a draw with the replay set for Mullingar the following Saturday.

Mark Carpenter was on fire early on the second day out and kicked a few early points. At the same time, he was getting plenty of off the ball attention and he ended up getting sent-off and with his suspension then, he ended up missing both the semi-final and final. Gavin Walker got some very important scores, including a goal from a penalty. There was nothing between the teams throughout and once again it finished in a draw, although this time there would be extra-time. At that stage, we had to reshuffle the pack a little bit as Andrew Corden was unavailable for extra-time. Andrew's brother was getting married in Spain and JJ Lambert had organised for a helicopter, with Peter Connors to take Andrew from Mullingar straight to Dublin airport. With the game finishing level, Andrew had a flight to catch so he left at the end of normal time and missed the extra-time. My brother Vincent came in for Andrew and in the end, we scraped through by a point.

Those two tight games and the period of extra-time definitely stood to us as we headed into a semi-final clash with Kildare champions Moorefield. Winning tight games and coming from behind started to become a habit, and created great self-belief within the squad. It was another wet and windy day but nothing like our first two outings. We were playing against the wind in the second-half and were two points down with about five minutes still to play. We kicked the last three scores of the game to win by a point, with the winner coming from Brian Walker from a fantastic effort which he judged perfectly into the wind.

That Na Fianna team had many household names and county stars. They had also been in the All-Ireland final in Croke Park only that March, where they were beaten by Crossmaglen Rangers. They had Jason Sherlock, Dessie Farrell, Senan Connell, Mick Galvin, as well as Armagh's Kieran McGeeney. They actually had three of the starting forwards on the 1995 All-Ireland winning Dublin team in Sherlock, Farrell and Galvin.

I picked up a leg injury in the semi-final, but the pain didn't manifest until the post-match meal. It must have been the adrenaline, but it was fine for the final. On the day, we managed to deal with their 'big guns' fairly well. This was down to an excellent man marking job on Jason Sherlock by Andrew Corden. Ken Walker did a similar job with Dessie Farrell. Everyone played their part; it was a massive squad effort. In my opinion, no O'Hanrahans man lost their personal battle that day.

We had played some great football in the first-half but we went in at the break behind by 0-4 to 0-2. We were happy enough at that stage, as they had played with the wind and we felt we had contained them well enough. We came out in the second-half and scored 1-5 without reply to go six points up. Brian Walker's goal was effectively the winning of the game. Brian had scored two goals in the county final, and he kicked the winner in the semi-final against Moorefield – and now he had scored probably the most famous goal in the club's history. That was to be our last score though and Na Fianna came back at us with 1-1 and similar to us, their goal was also to be their last score. Blues men defended with our lives throughout, but especially towards the end. Anytime they came near us, we just smothered them up. There are a few standout moments from the day. I remember Andrew Corden and Jason Sherlock both going for a ball at one stage in the corner under the stand side but in their efforts they both slipped. Sherlock was still on the grass but Andrew was the first to get up and, instead of going down on the ball, at sprint pace he just jabbed it up with his toe to his hand and away he went. It was just a stand-out memory for me, of a young player who was at the top of his game and showing that skill against another one of the top players around at the time.

Afterwards, there were tears of joy and singing from lifelong O'Hanrahans supporters and family members; everyone was in the dressing room… media, supporters, family… everyone was there and in fairness to Na Fianna, they were very gracious in defeat. On a personal level, I was delighted to be named Leinster Senior Club Player of the Year. A lone piper led us off the bus from Shamrock Square and down Barrack Street to Carpenters. The celebrations were in Carpenters and all across Carlow.

We knew though that we had another big game coming up the following February so as much as we celebrated, Mick still had us training away over the Christmas. We had a training weekend down in Wexford over the Christmas and we met with Liam Griffin, who spoke with such passion and reminded us that you might not get another chance of an All-Ireland – how right he was.

Our All-Ireland semi-final pitted us against competition kingpins Nemo Rangers. Of course, they had a massive tradition in the club championship, having won it six times up to that point. We got off to a great start through an early goal from Anthony Kavanagh but Nemo were in control for the remainder of the half, and they were five points up at the break. We improved in the second-half and outscored them but we came up short by two points in the end, 0-12 to 1-7. I'd say if you were to ask any of the lads about that day, that they'd all tell you that we didn't do ourselves justice. I think we lost momentum, and the 10-week break between games didn't help us; we would love to have played two weeks after the Leinster final. Look, we ran them close, losing by two points, but it was hugely disappointing and there is definitely a bit of regret there; but all in all, it was a fantastic journey. To be captain of that team was just the icing on the cake.

We won the county championship again later that year to complete a three in-a-row but were beaten by a point by Sarsfields in Leinster for the second time in three years. In 2003, I had the honour of captaining the team again; we won our fourth championship in five years but were beaten by Arles/Kilcruise by a point in the Leinster Championship.

If someone had told us, that we would win four Senior Championships in five years and a Leinster Championship on top of that, you'd have said what planet are you on? The standard of club football in Carlow at that time was very high. Éire Óg had won five Leinster Championships in the 90s and we actually got to the level where we beat them in a county final. To be fair to Éire Óg, with all the success they had, they raised the bar and if anyone was going to beat them then they'd have to get up to that level as Éire Óg weren't going to drop their standards.

Whilst I had success playing football, I would say that football was probably my second sport. Hurling was the number one for me growing up. I think I was probably around 12 years of age when I first played hurling for Carlow and played all the way up to senior level, where I played with them for nine years in the National League and Leinster Championship. My brothers Vinny, Barry and Karol have all hurled with Carlow up through the grades as well.

Carlow had won the All-Ireland 'B' championship in 1992 and I was brought on to the panel the following year. Hurling was big in the family – my Uncle Jim English won three All-Irelands with Wexford and was captain of the team that won in 1956. Jim later went on to be chairman of the Carlow County Board and it was a great twist when he actually presented me with the Conlon Cup in 2000 and '03 as captain of those championship winning teams.

# JOHN McGRATH

### SLIGO 2-14 ★ CARLOW 2-7
### All-Ireland SFC Qualifiers Round 2
### Dr Cullen Park, Carlow
### JUNE 23, 2001

*John McGrath goes highest to field against Sligo in Dr Cullen Park, in Carlow's historic fifth championship match in 2001.*

★ **SLIGO:** J Curran; P Gallagher, N Carew, B Phillips; P Doohan, M Langan, P Naughton (0-1); P Durcan, K Quinn; S Davey (1-0), P Taylor (0-4), E O'Hara (0-1); D Sloyan (1-2), J McPartland (0-1), G McGowan (0-4). Subs: D McGarty (0-1) for Taylor, K Killeen for Davey, K O'Neill for McGowan, R Keane for Naughton, N Maguire for Phillips.

★ **CARLOW:** P. McGrath; John Hickey, B Farrell, V Fleming; S O'Brien, J Byrne, C Kelly; A Bowe, S Kavanagh (0-2), J Nevin (0-1), W Quinlan (0-3), J McGrath(2-0); J Kavanagh, M Carpenter, B Kelly (0-1). Subs: E McGarry for J Kavanagh, M Drea for C Kelly, James Hickey for Bowe, J Hughes for B Kelly, P O'Dwyer for John Hickey.

## THE ACTION

CARLOW SENIOR FOOTBALLERS' fairytale season finally came to an end with this defeat to Sligo. This was Carlow's fifth championship game of the season and the most the senior team had played since 1944. Carlow had defeated Wicklow after a replay in Leinster before being beaten by Kildare in Croke Park. A first round qualifier victory over Waterford followed, before Sligo finally brought the Carlow dream to an end.

Sligo held an 0-8 to 0-3 lead at half-time, but it could have been closer as Mark Carpenter hit the post, while Willie Quinlan missed a couple of frees. In truth, Sligo were the better team from start to finish and despite a late Carlow rally they never looked like losing this game. Carlow only scored one point from play in the first 45 minutes. The first goal of the game arrived when Sligo were already in a commanding 0-12 to 0-2 lead – Sean Davey giving Paudge McGrath no chance with his shot. Seven minutes later the ball was in McGrath's net again and this time it was Dessie Sloyan who scored after good work from Dara McGarty and Eamonn O'Hara.

Carlow sensed Sligo had taken their foot off the pedal a little at that stage and then decided to finish with some sense of pride. Midfielder Sean Kavanagh, who had a very good game, pointed before John McGrath scored two goals in the last seven minutes. The first goal was finished by McGrath after good work by James Hickey and Mark Carpenter, while the second was finished to the net after a high ball was sent in, with McGrath injuring himself in the process.

To be fair, the Carlow forwards tried hard but things just did not seem to fall for them. McGrath finished with two goals to his name but the Clonmore man caught a few nice balls too and can be pleased with his day. Sligo emptied the bench in the second half and this is probably why their intensity dropped so much, although each sub who came in also looked sharp and were all very eager to get some much needed game time as bigger tests lay ahead.

★★★★★

66

PLAYING FOR CARLOW, we weren't winning trophies every year or anything, but I enjoyed it. And it is always a proud day when you pull on the county jersey! It is fair to say during my time with Carlow we did have a little bit of success. I was lucky to be playing in 2001, when the county had its longest championship run since 1944.

We played Sligo in the second round of the qualifiers in Dr Cullen Park. From my own point of view, I felt I played well on the night and ended up scoring two goals. As a team, unfortunately, we just didn't seem to perform to the same level as we had done in our previous games. It was a Saturday evening in Carlow and a really nice warm evening to go with it. There was a huge crowd at it and it made for a great atmosphere. It was a perfect evening for football. That was a really good Sligo team at the time, as they went on to beat Kildare in the next round after they beat us, before they ran into Dublin. They had the likes of Paul Taylor, Sean Davey, Eamonn O'Hara, Dessie Sloyan… to name but a few, so they had a lot of really good footballers.

We had had a really good campaign up to that Sligo game. Pat Roe was in charge and we had been drawn against Wicklow in the first round of the Leinster Championship. I started that day but I went over on my ankle when the ball was thrown in and I had to come off at half-time as I ended up tearing ligaments in my ankle. The game ended in a draw in Newbridge and the replay was back there again the following week, but I wasn't going to be back for that and as disappointed as I was that I couldn't play, that disappointment quickly turned to joy when we came out the right side of a tight tense struggle by a single point – which meant I'd have a chance of getting back for the next round. One thing I remember from watching that replay from the sideline is my brother Paudge in the goal catching a high ball over the crossbar from a Wicklow free that could have put them ahead. It's funny the things you remember as the years go by.

That next day out was a quarter-final date with Kildare in Croke Park. I didn't start but I came on at half-time and we definitely had them rattled, especially when we got the goal through Willie Quinlan which brought us right back in to it. But Kildare just kicked a few extra points towards the end to see them through. I came on at wing forward but was moved out to midfield shortly after. I remember going over to pick up Niall Buckley and he just shouldered me straight in to the chest. *This is real senior championship football here now and I better get used to it*, I told myself!

Another thing I can remember from that day was early on where Willie Quinlan hit Glenn Ryan a great shoulder. For a small man, Willie had great power and that early hit gave everyone a great lift. Yeah we lost that game by five points in the end but Kildare were Leinster champions at the time, and we gave a great account of ourselves. 2001 was the first year of the qualifiers and so, after the Kildare game, we were delighted to have another game in the championship. We were drawn against Waterford and we beat them down in Dungarvan, which then set us up for the clash with Sligo.

That night had extra significance for me as well, with Paudge in the goal. I had been in and out of the team that year but Paudge had been in goal for all of the championship. I had played on the same teams as Paudge all the way up with our club Clonmore and it's always nice to share the same field with your brother, but to do it at county level made it even better. I was working in Maynooth at the time and Paudge was working in Dublin, so he'd collect me and we'd head to training together. It was a proud time for both of us to be playing together for Carlow but a particular proud time for Clonmore. Peter Kiernan and John Connolly from the club were involved around that time as well, so to have four men from the same small country club was a great achievement.

For a small country club to have four lads around the panel gave the club an identity, I suppose in a way, and although we never won anything we were competitive in the Senior Championship, reaching the knockout stages on a number of occasions.

A few months before that Sligo game our mother had unfortunately passed away. She was only 48 at the time and we were devastated. It's amazing what sport can do too, as even though we were all grieving, playing football kind of helped us to cope with it, even if only for a little while at a time. There's a lot to be said for sport during times like that and the fact that the both of us were involved meant that we could kind of rely on each other. My mother Norah always said myself and Paudge were the best players on the pitch, even if we had played a shocker. Our father Mick was always our biggest fan but also our worst critic, always demanding a bit more. It must be his stubborn Galway/Mayo roots! The appetite that dad still has for the game, and for Carlow GAA in particular is incredible.

It's a shame that, for whatever reason, we never got going that night against Sligo until it was too late. We were well behind at half-time and I can remember Pat Roe going mad in the dressing-room at the break.

He told us to forget about the big crowd that was there to see us and to just remember back to the previous games where we had played so well, and to try and draw on some of that for the second-half. We all knew we could play better than that but Sligo had already raced out of the traps and they had a comfortable lead, which they could kind of hold onto for the remainder of the game. All of Sligo's forwards scored, while we were struggling to even get the ball up to our forwards. Midway through the second-half we finally started to play a little but, in truth, the game was well and truly gone by then and we lost by seven points in the end. On a personal level it was nice to score the two goals in the second-half and I caught a few balls out around the middle also, but it was disappointing not to lose as such but in the way we lost, in that we knew we had so much more in us that we just never showed on the night.

We were disappointed to be out of course, but when we reflected on it, we had had a great season playing five championship games. There was a great buzz around the county that summer because of it. Around that time, Éire Óg and O'Hanrahans would have been very strong but I think they only had maybe two lads each on the panel. During Pat Roe's time, there was a great mix of clubs; no club was dominating the squad and a lot of clubs had a representation on it. I'm not saying we had a great run due to that, because you want the best players in the team no matter what club they're from, but I'm just making the point that there was a bigger spread that year than other years.

Pat had a simple but effective way of playing football. He always wanted to let the ball do the work, as no man could run faster than the ball! He also had us really fit at the time, and that was a big thing with Pat… he wanted us all to be flying fit. I can remember him threatening to tie my leg one night at training if I did one more solo! He didn't want to be slowing down the game at all; it was give it and go, and keep the ball moving fast. He wanted everything fast.

I was an average enough player but Pat definitely made me into a better player as he had belief in me, and once a player has belief and is confident then it's amazing what it can do for your game. I thoroughly enjoyed my time playing under Pat. We were beaten by Sligo that June and we were back together only a couple of months later then ahead of 2002. The O'Byrne Cup had games pre-Christmas that year so we had an early start and come January then we actually won the competition. Considering it had been so long since Carlow had won anything, it was great to be part of that team. We had some tough games on the way to the final and even the final itself was a great occasion… Carlow and Wicklow in an O'Byrne Cup final in front of a big crowd in Dr Cullen Park, it was a great time to be involved.

Obviously then, we had massive aspirations going into the league a few weeks later but unfortunately our good form seemed to desert us from then on, as we finished second bottom in the league. Things didn't improve for the championship either as we were beaten by Westmeath in Leinster, and then we went down to Laois at home in the qualifiers. In between those games we lost our team captain Andrew Corden to a tragic accident and we were in no fit state for football after that. Andrew was a lovely fella and a very good footballer. His death rocked the panel, and football was the last thing on a lot of lads minds after that.

I was first called into the Carlow senior panel in the mid-90s under Bobby Miller. I think it was more a case of making up the numbers for training but I never got any league or championship games under Bobby. I played a few practice games alright, but never competitively. Paddy Morrissey came in afterwards and that didn't go well at all. Paddy didn't even know my name and that wasn't good, so I was never going to last too long there. Cyril Hughes came in then and I suppose as a Carlow man he knew the lay of the land. Cyril was in charge when we played Westmeath in the championship in 1999 on the day that will be remembered for the red card fiasco that followed. By the time of that game I had left the squad, as I wasn't named in the championship panel for that game. I had just started a new job up in Maynooth at the time too and I wasn't prepared to just be an outside member of the panel. I suppose I was young and very naïve, but that's youth for you really, in that you don't see the bigger picture.

In fairness, Cyril called me in again for the following season and I was happy to accept that invitation and to rejoin the panel. The one thing about a county like Carlow is that managers only ever stay for maybe two years. After Pat Roe stepped aside after two relatively successful years you could say I didn't stay around much longer. I played under Mick Condon in 2003 and in to '04 before I decided to step away. We were beaten by London in the league in 2004 but a few nights before the game I was told I would be starting which was grand. The day of the game then we were doing our warm-up and I was told I wouldn't be starting after all which was a major come down.

During the game then I must have spent half the time warming up on the sideline, but I never got the call to go on and we lost in the end by a point. I remember having a conversation with Mick afterwards and he basically said I wasn't in his plans anymore, so I left the panel then. As it happens, Mick Condon didn't last too long after me either as he left mid-season and Luke Dempsey came in instead. Carlow beat Longford in the championship and ran Laois close in the summer, but while it would have been nice to have been out there I had probably made peace with the decision by then.

Look, I will be the first to admit I wasn't the most natural player in the world. I wouldn't be a lad to be turning a game on its head with a moment of genius, but I had good workrate and a good pair of hands – but I wasn't looking in and thinking that I should have been out there playing instead of this fella or that fella. I knew every lad that was there by then was as good or better than me, so I was happy with my decision, although I would have liked for it to end a bit better. A few weeks later, in July 2004, I tore my cruciate ligament playing with the club so that put an end to any thoughts I might have ever had about going back.

That was the end of my county career, but I had come a long way since I was first picked for Carlow at under-16 level. The highlight at underage was probably in 1994 when we qualified to meet Dublin in the Minor Championship in Croke Park. We were beaten on the day but the experience and training that year was brilliant and it really got me hooked, in that I just wanted more. I spent two years playing midfield for the under-21s then, but playing minor and under-21 doesn't always mean that you'll progress straight to the senior side. It takes a lot of hard work and good performances at club level to make the step up. Thankfully, I got the chance to do it and I'm happy to be able to say that I did.

That cruciate injury was a big blow but I was out for a similar long period a few years later, as in 2007 I broke my leg playing a club game so that was another long spell out. Those two injuries were major setbacks but, thankfully, I've been pretty much injury free since and I am still playing with the junior team in Clonmore and still enjoying it. I think if I stopped playing I'd miss it too much, so I'll keep playing for as long as I can and see where that takes me

# DES SHAW

**NAOMH BRÍD 3-8 ★ NAOMH EOIN 1-7**
**Carlow U-21 HC Final**
**Dr Cullen Park, Carlow**
**NOVEMBER 22, 2003**

*Des Shaw in action for Carlow against Kerry in the Christy Ring Cup, but despite his decade-long career in the county jersey he remembers an under-21 game with Naomh Bríd as the 'Game of his Life'.*

★ **NAOMH BRÍD:** J Kane; A Dermody, G Hickey, D Nolan; W Minchin, **D Shaw**, S Watchorn; A Brennan (0-1), B Nolan; C McNally, B Sheehan, H Kelly (0-2); M Brennan (1-5), P Kelly (2-0), B McNally. Subs: J Sheehan for C McNally, C Smyth for B Sheehan, D Sheehan for P Kelly.

★ **NAOMH EOIN:** P Foley; M Murphy, C Nolan, Andrew Quirke; JJ O'Brien, S Kavanagh, T Minchin; S Smithers, P Quirke; B O'Brien, J Quirke (0-1), Alan Quirke (0-5); B Murphy (1-0), E Spruhan (0-1), B Mullins. Subs: S Curry for Smithers, K Foley for B O'Brien.

# THE ACTION

GOALS FROM MARK Brennan and a brace from Paddy Kelly were the difference as Naomh Bríd claimed this under-21 hurling title with a comprehensive win. With 28 minutes gone in the game and Naomh Bríd leading 0-3 to 0-2, the first goal of the game arrived. A long clearance from team captain Des Shaw was caught by Mark Brennan and the corner-forward made tracks for goal. Brennan's kicked attempt for goal was brilliantly saved by Naomh Eoin goalkeeper Pat Foley. The cheers from their supporters didn't last long however as from the rebound Paddy Kelly sent a first time ground shot to the back of the net. From the resulting puck out, wing back Sean Watchorn caught the high ball and sent it straight back into the danger area, the breaking ball again falling to Kelly and, again, Kelly with a ground shot raised his second green flag of the afternoon. Both sides were reduced to 14 players midway through the first-half with Martin Murphy and Bernard McNally receiving their marching orders after both players clashed over near the sideline.

Those goals gave Naomh Bríd a 2-4 to 0-3 interval lead, but four unanswered points from Naomh Eoin after the restart cut the deficit to 2-4 to 0-7 with 12 minutes of the second-half played. It could have been even closer were it not for a missed penalty by Brian Murphy. Hughie Kelly scored a point to stop the momentum of the men from Miseal and his side got the clinching score in the 19th minute. Alan Brennan sent a long dropping ball in towards the Naomh Eoin goalmouth. The ball was cleared, but only as far as Barry Sheehan and his ground pull across goal found his teammate Mark Brennan who made no mistake from close range to rattle the net.

Naomh Bríd were led by the excellent Des Shaw, the winning captain a rock from centre-back and it was Shaw along with his wing backs Willie Minchin and Carlow minor Sean Watchorn who cleared their lines and supplied the forwards with plenty of ball.

★★★★★

66

AT MY AGE group, when we were coming up through the underage grades, we were always known to have a few nice tidy hurlers in our ranks. Mark Brennan, Sean Watchorn, lads like that... great players. All the way up though, we never won an 'A' championship. We won a couple of 'B' titles alright but as regards the big ones, I suppose we were kind of starved for success and we really wanted to win an 'A' championship. A lot of lads on Naomh Bríd teams were playing for Carlow and doing well there, and a lot of us had some success playing schools with De La Salle Bagenalstown, so it wasn't like we had never won anything, but with the club we just never managed the big ones. I actually had an under-21 'A' medal already as we won the championship in 1999. I was goalkeeper that year, but I was only 15 then so it was well above my age group and at the time, being so young, I didn't appreciate it. When we won it in 2003, I was playing out the field and I was playing senior for Carlow at the time, so it definitely meant that bit more.

I was captain then too, and I suppose I had ambitions of being one of the leaders on the team. Only 12 months previous, in 2002, Naomh Bríd actually reached the final of the Minor 'A' Championship but we were narrowly beaten by Carlow Town. That Carlow Town team had won every 'A' championship from under-12 all the way up, so they were red hot favourites going into that final.

In that minor final, I was marking Ruairi Dunbar. I played senior for Carlow with Ruairi so I was used to marking him in training. He was a brilliant player. Good striker of the ball and deadly from open play and from frees. He got a good few frees that day and I think he got one point from play, so I felt that despite losing, that I had done well on him. Afterwards, Ruairi was awarded the Man of the Match and I remember standing on the pitch after, looking up at that. There is a great quote from the Michael Jordan documentary, *The Last Dance*, where he says 'And I took that personally'. I had that moment after that minor final. That was definite motivation for me to win an 'A' championship the following year. Looking back now, in hindsight, Ruairi was probably deserving of the award. He was their main man and was lethal from frees, but on the day I thought I stifled him.

With only a handful of hurling clubs in Carlow, we were sure to meet again soon and the following year we did end up meeting Carlow Town, this time in the semi-final of the Under 21 Championship… and I was due to mark Ruairi again. I was a man possessed that day to win. We ended up beating Carlow Town and made it through to the final.

I was very lucky in 2003, in that Seamus Brennan, our manager, named me captain. That was a huge responsibility and a huge honour for me because I was only 19 and there were a couple of older lads who it would have been their last year at that age level, who I thought might get it. But at the same time, I was delighted to accept it. Over the years I had been captain of a couple of teams, but this was the first time being captain where you genuinely believed that you could go all the way and actually win something.

Being captain too, I felt I needed to put in a little bit of ground work and I recruited a few lads who hadn't hurled in a few years. Hughie Kelly hadn't played hurling since he was around 14, but he came back that year. Hughie, along with Ger Hickey, were massive additions to have back with us, so things felt good.

Going into that final, we had a good few lads playing who had played in the Minor final loss the year before so we were all so determined to win that Under 21 title. Again though, we went into the final as underdogs. We were playing Naomh Eoin and they had won the Senior Championship only a couple of weeks before hand before they rattled Offaly kingpins Birr in the Leinster Club Championship. They had a good few of that senior side playing on the Under 21 team so they were warm favourites to add the Under 21 Championship to the senior title. Because Naomh Eoin had won the senior and they had a couple of games in the Leinster Club, we had to wait until they were knocked out of that and as we had played our semi-final a good few weeks before hand, we were hanging around for a while for the final to be played. Waiting in the long grass if you like!

It was tough in a way to keep training as no one knew when the final was likely to be played the further Naomh Eoin went in the championship. We were still ready though and we knew all the Miseal lads anyway as a lot of us were playing for Carlow together, so we knew what we were facing into that day.

Naomh Eoin might have been big favourites but we weren't a bad team either and a lot of our lads went on to win a couple of Senior Hurling Championships in the years that followed so we felt that we were as good as anyone, despite what everyone else might have been saying.

Eventually, the final day came. The game was played at the end of November and when you are playing winter hurling you know what you're going to get. The pitch was heavy. It was scrappy, conditions were poor. It wasn't the best conditions for a good game of hurling so it was going to be a tough game, very physical. It was going to be a war of attrition, and you couldn't ask for better opponents for all those attributes than Naomh Eoin. Over the years that was probably their strength. Being big strong men who brought the physicality, but who were also able to hurl.

I can remember a few strange things going on even before the game as regards selection. Firstly, Seamus Brennan named Mark Brennan at corner-forward which no one expected. Mark normally played at centre-forward and he was our main man up front. I think the thought process was to avoid Naomh Eoin's No 6 Shane Kavanagh. Mark and Shane were two of the best hurlers in the county and if they were marking each other I think the two lads would just end up cancelling each other out.

The dubious task of getting that job of trying to curb Shane fell to Barry Sheehan. Unfortunately, Barry passed away a few years later in a tragic accident, but if Barry was here today he'd probably tell you that he wasn't the most cultural hurler in the world but he was there to work hard and to try and stifle Shane as best he could. The second strange one was Paddy Kelly. Paddy was normally a defender and in the two games in the run up to that final, he had played beside me in the half-back line and now, here he was picked to play in the full-forward line. Paddy wasn't the tallest, but he was well built and he was as strong as anything. We were all scratching our heads at these decisions. Of course, it's easy to say now in hindsight that they worked because we won, but had we not, then it would have been a different story.

Early on in the game, it was point for point, real tit for tat. We were holding our own and I can still remember the first goal, it gave us a great boost. I caught a long clearance and I sent a high ball into Mark Brennan and typical Mark, he caught it and turned for goal. His shot was brilliantly saved by Pat Foley. The rebound spilled out though and, lo and behold, who was there to drive it to the back of the net only Paddy Kelly. From the resulting puck out, the ball was caught by Sean Watchorn and a little similar to the first goal, the ball was sent into the square again. As time goes on the details become a little hazy, but what

I do remember was the end result and that from the goalmouth scramble, it was Paddy Kelly once again who drove the ball low and hard to the back of the net.

If you read the reports from after the game, he was being called the 'Bilboa Bomber' but I don't think the name lasted too long as I don't think Paddy ever scored a goal again after that day!

Those two goals gave us a bit of a lead then and with it being winter hurling and being a slow game it kind of gave us a little bit of a cushion to defend more. We defended with our lives from then on and the game tended to be very scrappy with a lot of frees given out, so it wasn't pretty to watch.

The expected second-half comeback from Naomh Eoin didn't take long to start as right from the throw in they came at us with everything. They came to within three points of us and anyone who has ever played sport knows that when the momentum is going against you, then it is very hard to turn it around. From my own point of view, as centre-back, I just tried to hold the middle as much as possible. We tried to keep the defensive unit as solid as we could and hopefully not concede any goals because if we did then we were in real trouble. Of course, that was easier said than done because for most of the game I was marking man mountain, John Quirke. In a way I was lucky in that I was just coming off my first season playing senior hurling for Carlow and most nights in training I was marking another man mountain, and clubmate of John's, in Des Murphy. So as a young 19-year-old marking big Des every night, I was learning how to deal with the big men all the time. As I was that bit smaller, it was hard for me to take them on physically so it was all about trying to out hurl them instead.

Thankfully, we managed to get a couple of points to stem the tide after that onslaught and this was quickly followed by our third goal from the stick of Mark Brennan which gave us a nice cushion once again, and despite Naomh Eoin getting a goal themselves late on we had enough of a lead built up by then which we were all so desperate to cling onto and ultimately we did.

We had not been winning any 'A' championships up to that point and yet when we won that under-21 title, it was the start of something special as we went to win another one two years later, while two Senior Championships arrived in 2004 and 2008.

I think the fact that so many of the under-21 lads were young and hungry; it fed into the senior team. Already on the senior team you had a good few lads who I suppose were well into the middle of their career. Lads like Johnny Nevin, Niall Bambrick, Stephen Bambrick, Johnny Kavanagh, who had all won the Senior Championship in 1996. Those lads all knew how to win but they hadn't got back there since. The older fellas probably fed off the younger lads coming into the team and with all those factors combined, the club had massive hunger, and ambition to win another Senior Championship.

We actually ended up winning another under-21 championship in 2005, so you had the likes of Declan Kelly, Cathal Coughlan and James Kane coming through from that team into the senior set up, so there was plenty of talent there, and hunger. I think those two Senior Championship winning teams was proof of what we had in the club at that time and those under-21 successes were a great feeder in the years that followed.

That year was an extra special year for me, really. I was just out of minor and I was straight into playing senior hurling for Carlow. We had won the All-Ireland Minor 'B' Championship with Carlow in 2002 and a few of us from that team were asked to go straight in with the seniors the following year. I remember going up to play my first game with Carlow. We played Maynooth in a challenge game. I played corner-back and it went well so I ended up staying there for over 10 years then after that. In 2003, my first year with the seniors, we went up to Navan and beat Meath in the Leinster Championship. Kilkenny's Michael Walsh was in charge then and it was a great win as we were big underdogs going into that game. It was the start of a long career playing in the Carlow senior jersey and I enjoyed every minute of it.

# JOHNNY NEVIN

**CARLOW 4-15 ★ LONGFORD 1-16**
**Leinster SFC First Round**
**O'Connor Park, Tullamore**
**MAY 9, 2004**

*Johnny Nevin in action for Carlow in 2004 against Laois, the summer in which the county rose from the ashes to defeat Longford in the Leinster Championship.*

★ **CARLOW:** J Clarke; B Farrell, S O'Brien, C McCarthy; K Walker, J Hayden (0-1), J Byrne (0-1); M Brennan, T Walsh (0-1); P Hickey (1-1), **J Nevin (0-2)**, M Carpenter (1-1); S Rea (2-3), S Kavanagh (0-3), B Carbery (0-1). Subs: B English for Walker, B Kelly (0-1) for Carbery, W Power for Brennan.

★ **LONGFORD:** G Tonra; D Ledwith, C Conefrey, S Carroll; E Ledwith, D Hanniffy, A O'Connor; L Keenan (0-1), T Smullen (0-1); P O'Hara, J Kenny, P Barden (0-4); J Martin (1-1), N Sheridan (0-3), P Davis (0-6). Subs: S Lynch for Kenny, M Lennon for Martin, M Kelly for Lynch.

## THE ACTION

CARLOW DID A modern-day Phoenix when rising from the ashes of a disappointing National League campaign and management controversy, when they recorded a rare, and very welcome Leinster SFC win in Tullamore. The standard of football was far from level one, but that memory will be submerged in the euphoria of a win the bookmakers quoted as mission impossible. The opening half was tense, ending 0-7 each after the teams were level four times. The contest was finely balanced for 62 minutes, but what transpired in the final eight will go down in Carlow folklore, with the ball resting in the Longford rigging three times. There were few signs of the hectic climax as Longford cut a six-point deficit back to a single point between the 42nd and 62nd minute.

Carlow had blitzed Longford just after the break also, hitting what must have been the quickest 1-4 in living memory. The score that settled Carlow down was a fisted Mark Carpenter green flag after he beat the goalkeeper in an aerial duel, after great industry from Sean Kavanagh, Simon Rea and the ageless Johnny Nevin. Carlow needed that cushion too as in the ninth minute of the second-half, Jamsie Martin crashed home a goal for Longford. Carlow could never put more than two points between the teams for the remainder of the half; that was until Patrick Hickey raised the biggest Carlow cheer of the day when he goaled.

The icing was well and truly put on the cake when corner-forward Simon Rea twice beat Gavin Tonra in the Longford goal in the final minutes; his second, and Carlow's fourth, a well struck penalty. The final whistle was greeted with massive celebrations by both players and supporters as with new management only in place a few weeks after mid-season controversy, this win was not expected by anybody.

★ ★ ★ ★ ★

66

THE YEAR 2004 is a year that will stand out for me for a few reasons. We had a good O'Byrne Cup run, followed by a mixed enough league campaign. We followed it up with an unexpected championship victory over Longford and then taking on Laois, the Leinster champions in our own backyard. So once again, we mixed the good with the bad.

It was a turbulent year all the same though. Before the championship started, we had been managed by Mick 'Mickser' Condon, who was in his second year in charge. After a few uninspiring performances and things just not seeming as they should be, the players decided something needed to be done. The following week at training, the players had a vote. The end result was that the players voted for change, and just like that… Mickser was gone. Things hadn't felt right for a long time and a lot of players were questioning things. No matter what way you look at it, when players vote to get rid of a manager, it's a very brave thing to do because straightaway you're putting yourself under incredible pressure to perform. If you get rid of a manager and then don't back it up with results, then you can look very foolish.

The National League was a mixed bag as usual for us. However, when we went up to play Donegal in our last league game in Ballyshannon, the wheels had well and truly fallen off. We were beaten 3-15 to 0-5 and I think after that, the players had kind of said that look, we need a change here. That everything needed to change. As well as that, after we finished up our league campaign with that Donegal hammering, there would have been plenty of rumours around of people going out drinking the night before that game, so that just added to it.

Not long after Mickser stepped away, the county board came to Brendan Hayden (Junior) and myself and asked us to do the training for the next couple of weeks, until they found someone to take on the role full time. We were happy to do this but after a couple of weeks, Luke Dempsey was unveiled as the new man in. It was a breath of fresh air. Luke was a big name and he brought a great enthusiasm to the set up. I have to say there was a little bit of relief when he came in too, as it meant I could step back from training the lads and I could now concentrate fully on playing, and focus on that ahead of the championship. I was happy to help out with the training at the time but it is hard to concentrate on your own game as well when you're trying to keep everybody else happy and make sure training is done right. Once Luke came in, I was able to give my own game the full attention it deserved.

Training went well and on the day we gave a great performance to not just win, but win well in the end. That win was massive because we were under huge pressure from everybody outside the camp. Everybody was waiting for us to fall after getting rid of the manager and if we did lose that game then it would have been very hard for us to come back from that and no manager would have wanted to touch us then.

We were massive underdogs going in to play Longford. Earlier that year, they had caused their own massive shock when they beat Kerry in the National League in Pearse Park, so they were overwhelming favourites going to Tullamore to play us. Longford had a lot of good footballers with them at that time too. The likes of Paul Barden, Niall Sheridan and Padraig Davis… they were all good footballers.

From where we were coming from, that was a standout game for me. A stand out performance as well which was even better. The wheels might have fallen off up in Ballyshannon but we hadn't a bad year overall really up to that point. As was normal for Carlow then, we mixed the good with the bad.

The year started off great for us. We beat Wicklow in the O'Byrne cup and the following week, in Dr Cullen Park again, we beat Dublin. That was probably one of the best performances we ever put together. It wasn't a weakened Dublin selection either. They had the likes of Stephen Cluxton, Jason Sherlock, Ciaran Whelan, Paddy Christie, Shane Ryan, Brian Cullen, Senan Connell and more top lads playing. So, to beat them by a point in front of our own fans was something else. In later years in the O'Byrne Cup, Dublin might put out a third team or maybe even their under-21 team sometimes, but that was a near full strength Dublin team that day.

The semi-final then brought us to Cusack Park in Mullingar to face Westmeath. Páidí Ó Sé had just taken charge there at that stage so there was a big buzz around him and around Westmeath in general. There was a big crowd in Mullingar that day. We played well in patches but were unlucky to lose out by a single point. Westmeath lost that O'Byrne final to Meath, but Páidí had bigger fish to fry and just a few months later they were celebrating a first ever Leinster Championship title.

We might have missed out on an O'Byrne Cup final appearance but still, we were happy with how we were going. We started the league off with a bang then. We had Monaghan down in Dr Cullen Park and we beat them by two points. That was a huge win to start off the campaign. Unfortunately, we didn't back up that opening day performance and we had three successive losses against Roscommon, Offaly and Leitrim. We went down to Clare after that and beat them in their own backyard; a big win, but we were out of the promotion race by then. Despite that win in Ennis, the league petered out from there and when London came to Carlow, they beat us on a miserable day. We finished up our campaign then with that trip up to Donegal where we were well beaten and I suppose the arse had well and truly fallen out of it by then.

There was probably a little bit too much socialising on some away trips. At that point the players made a decision, so we were putting ourselves under massive pressure. I think we answered those questions a few weeks later when the Longford game came around and each man put in a huge performance. No one expected us to win that day but we knew ourselves we had to win or else what we did would have been for nothing. We had to back it up. There were no two ways about it.

After beating Longford, our prize was a home game against Mick O Dwyer's Laois in the quarter-final. They were the current Leinster champions and there was always a big rivalry between both sides. It was played on a roasting hot Sunday and Dr Cullen Park was absolutely packed. We scored an early goal through Brian Kelly to give us a great lift and, overall, we put up a good performance but in the end Laois had just that little bit too much and they won by five points. They made it back to the Leinster final again, but were beaten by Westmeath after a replay.

We played Down in the qualifiers and we were four points up early on, but Down ended up beating us by six points in the end; they had that bit of class about them in fairness. Looking back, it was a strange one when Mickser stepped down in the middle of the year because the same thing happened to the hurlers during that year too with Michael Walsh stepping down halfway through the season and Eoin Garvey coming in. It was a crazy few weeks for Carlow teams.

The 1994 All-Ireland SFC 'B' final against Westmeath, in Tullamore also, as well as the All-Ireland SHC 'B' win over London in 1992 were big games that stick out in my mind. All massive games and big results for Carlow GAA but that Longford one stands out just because what happened before and where we had come from. They're just a couple of standout games that you'd remember, but then at the same time there'd be an awful amount of games over the years that you wouldn't want to remember either for different reasons.

After that Down game in the qualifiers, everyone expected Luke Dempsey to stay on full time with Carlow and that was probably what he was hinting at as well at the time. Unfortunately, that didn't come to pass and he ended up taking the Longford job instead. I think he said it was the travelling up and down was too much to take it on full time. He did come back to Carlow again in 2009 and ended up staying for four years but ,look, maybe it just didn't suit him at that moment to take it up. It was unfortunate he didn't stay on that first time though because there was the making of a good team and it would have been a bit of continuity into the following season. Liam Hayes came in then ahead of 2005 and, once again, the league was all over the place. In the championship then we played Wexford up in Croke Park and I think we were beaten by five points after a very slow start where we conceded three early goals. We managed to bring it back at one stage in the game, but Wexford just kicked on near the end, although once we got going, we did perform quite well.

We beat Offaly at home then in a cracking game in Dr Cullen Park in the qualifiers before we were well beaten by Limerick the following week. Wexford and Limerick then were only coming into their prime and they were both very strong and both had long spells playing in Division One of the league.

Carlow had some fantastic footballers back then. As good as anywhere, but for different reasons we just never seemed to get a good run going for long enough. You'll always have good days and bad days though and definitely that day in Tullamore was a good day.

# SIMON REA
## (& MARK CARPENTER)

**CARLOW 0-14 ★ OFFALY 1-10**
**All-Ireland SFC Qualifiers, Round One**
**Dr Cullen Park, Carlow**
**JUNE 18, 2005**

*Simon Rea had his shooting boots on against Offaly in 2005, when Carlow surprised the Faithful County in the All-Ireland qualifiers.*

★ **CARLOW:** J Brennan; C McCarthy (0-1), L Murphy, P Cashin; J Hayden, W Power, R Sinnott; P Walsh, T Walsh; B Carbery (0-1), J Byrne, P Hickey; **S Rea (0-8), M Carpenter (0-2)**, B Kelly (0-2). Subs: J Kehoe for Power, P Kelly for Sinnott, R Walker for Hickey, K Pender for B Kelly.

★ **OFFALY:** P Kelly; C Daly, C Evans, S Brady; J Keane, S Sullivan, K Slattery; C McManus, A McNamee; J Reynolds (0-1), M Daly (0-1), N Coughlan (0-1); N McNamee (1-6), P Kellaghan, C Quinn. Subs: J Coughlan (0-1) for M Daly, T Deehan for Kellaghan.

# THE ACTION

MARK CARPENTER WAS the Carlow hero after this Qualifier clash, with the full-forward scoring the winning point with almost 39 minutes gone in the second-half. Carpenter received the ball out near the sideline before slipping away from his marker and shooting an outrageous score from underneath the stand. Carlow should never have been in that position in the first place, however, depending on a last minute winner, as they were five points up with 65 minutes on the clock before Offaly managed to get back level.

Carlow were dealt a massive blow after only five minutes when centre-back Willie Power was stretchered off with a suspected broken leg. After a lengthy delay, the game restarted and Carlow seemed to have an early grip on proceedings with Simon Rea kicking over three early frees, all from out near the sideline, while Niall McNamee was equally on form for Offaly from placed balls. It took Carlow until the 23rd minute to score from play and it was fitting that Simon Rea was the man to get it. Indeed, Rea was Carlow's lone scorer for the first-half when Carlow led by 0-7 to 0-4.

Carlow should have been out of sight at the start of the second-half and it was Rea again who had the opportunity. The half was only a minute old when the corner-forward bore down on goal, but his shot came back off the base of the upright. Points were swapped by both sides, before three frees from Niall McNamee had Offaly level and, all of a sudden, the momentum looked to be with the away side. Credit to Carlow though they came back and two points from Brian Kelly, and one from Brian Carbery restored Carlow's three-point lead. Simon Rea then scored from play and when Cormac McCarthy came all the way up from corner-back to score a huge booming point it gave Carlow a five-point lead.

James Coughlan and another from McNamee brought it back to three, before Offaly were awarded a penalty when Carlow goalkeeper John Brennan fouled Thomas Deehan. McNamee buried the penalty to make it a draw game as the clocked ticked into injury time. Amazingly there was more drama to come as Carlow mustered one last attack up the field and the ball fell to Carpenter. His winning point meant a first championship win over Offaly in 63 years.

★ ★ ★ ★ ★

66

BEATING OFFALY IN championship football was probably one of my most memorable days, if not the most memorable in a Carlow jersey. Prior to that Offaly game, we had played Wexford in the Leinster Championship in Croke Park. That was a funny old game in that Wexford hit us for three early goals and after 15 minutes it might have been something like 3-2 to 0-3 – and those early goals looked to have given Wexford the platform to go on and win well.

In fairness, we battled on in the second-half and brought it back level at one stage. We ran out of steam near the end, however, and Wexford ended running out winners by 3-12 to 2-10. We might have lost against Wexford but we were happy enough that we didn't throw in the towel with those early goals and that we stayed battling away in the second-half. Of course, we were disappointed we didn't get over the line against Wexford but we went down fighting.

We drew Offaly in the qualifiers and we were reasonably confident going in after our performance in Croke Park. Our manager at the time was Liam Hayes, and Liam was a great man for getting players up for a match. I think Liam probably brought his whole business acumen to being a manager. He was very organised, a very good planner and he was an excellent speaker. That was the one thing that I really found out while working with him. He had a way with words, but it was the way he said things, not just what he said. He had a really good way of instilling confidence in players.

I think that Offaly were coming down to Carlow expecting to beat us. I always think about tradition in the GAA and how big a part it has to play. Obviously, Offaly have a huge tradition in both codes. They probably would have looked down on us as we didn't have as strong a tradition as them and so they were fully expecting a win that day, I have no doubt. Some teams are nearly beaten before they go out because of who they're playing, the same way some teams have already won before they've taken the field. Because of tradition, we weren't supposed to beat Offaly. They had been beaten by Laois by two points in the Leinster Championship. That was an excellent Laois team, so when Offaly were drawn with Carlow, we weren't given much of a chance. All the pressure and expectation was on them. We were under no pressure and that definitely played into our hands. I always knew that that group of players were capable of putting in a massive performance and well capable of taking a good scalp. It was just a case of what Carlow team would turn up on any given day, but we definitely had the players.

We did our warm-up that day in the Carlow Town hurling club grounds, right beside Dr Cullen Park. I always like to get in a good bit of practice with the frees but there was a bit of a wind and I probably started the frees too far out to begin with. I was striking them well but they weren't all going over. Come to the game then, and one of the first frees I got was a difficult enough one to start. Out near the far touchline and there was still bit of a wind going across towards the tunnel. There's always a thing in my head when I'm kicking frees, and that is to start well. If you start well and your eye is in, then you're away with it. Luckily enough that first free went over. It wasn't an easy one to start with but the fact it went over meant the confidence was up straightaway.

One of my memories from that game is that both defences seemed to be on top with the majority of scores coming from frees. We had a slight edge around midfield with Patrick and Thomas Walsh both playing really well, but overall the defenders were on top throughout. I scored a few frees in the first-half and even though they were all on my side, they were all difficult. They were all testers. I scored them all though and all that came from that first difficult free as once that went over I felt the rest would follow suit. Its funny looking back to the warm-up where none of them were going over and then during the game every free I took was going over, so it's mad the way things work out sometimes.

I always felt that as the main free-taker that you had to put in the extra work. Either turning up early before training or else staying behind late afterwards, but I always felt it was my responsibility to put in that extra time and to go the extra mile. If I wasn't going well, there were other free-takers on the field who would have taken them on so it was up to me to keep sharp and to put in the extra hours. Thankfully, the free-taking went well for me that day and I managed to kick a couple from play too. The longer the game went on then, we knew the more of a chance we had. We won most of the breaks around the field, any loose dirty ball, lads just threw themselves on it in an effort to gain possession. We retired at half-time with a three point lead.

We had a chance to really put some daylight between ourselves right at the start of the second-half as we had a great goal chance. I think it was Brian Kelly who put me through one-on-one with Padraig Kelly in the Offaly goal. Just at the crucial time, the ball seemed to get away from me, but I still managed to get a little toe poke on it. But the ball came back off the bottom of the post. That would have put us well on the road to victory and it was a massive let off for Offaly. We didn't let that disappointment deter us though and for the remainder of the half we kept our three or four points in front for the most part and even stretched it out to five at one stage.

In the midst of all the madness in that second-half, it's often forgotten is that our corner-back Cormac McCarthy came up to kick a massive score. It was equally as good as Mark Carpenter's point to win it. I can remember roaring at Cormac and telling him not to shoot. Next thing, he kicks an absolute boomer of a point. I've seen Cormac kicking enough football over the years for Éire Óg and Carlow training and when he kicks a point like that, you know it's your day.

We still had that five-point lead with about five minutes of normal time remaining. Offaly kicked a few frees and then they were awarded a penalty which Niall McNamee duly dispatched and that goal brought it level. It looked like it was going to extra-time,but we had one last attack and the ball was worked out to Mark Carpenter who from a similar position to Cormac McCarthy's earlier point kicked over a massive score. Mark was a fabulous footballer and I'd seen him do similar things like that before, so when the ball was worked out to him, I knew it was the right person who had the ball at that late stage of the game. I was more pleased to see Mark with the ball at that moment than Cormac McCarthy coming up!

The buzz afterwards was just unreal. I think the fact that we probably had the game won and then all of a sudden it looked like we had it lost, and then to come back again and win it with the last kick of the game… emotions were all over the place. One of the first things I did after the game was to go over to their midfielder Ciaran McManus. He was down on his knees and was inconsolable. I remember shaking hands with him and him looking up at me. I could tell he was in shock. I got to know Ciaran as we both played Railway Cup together with Leinster. He was a real nice fella but the shock on his face in that moment is definitely something that stands out for me in the moments after the final whistle

I remember getting back to the dressing-room afterwards and I'll never forget the silence in the Offaly room. Even the players walking off the field afterwards, they could barely get their heads up to look at anybody. They were all in shock. That win for Carlow was the first time we had beaten Offaly in championship football since 1942 so you could understand they were expecting to win but we were under no pressure that day, where as everything was on Offaly to just turn up and win.

We had beaten Longford in Tullamore the year before in the championship when Luke Dempsey came in at short notice and that was a great win, but the fact the Offaly game was in Carlow and to see so many Carlow people there, that was special. I remember the bar was open next door in the hurling club and being in there and getting pats on the back and all the congratulations. There was elation. Championship wins for Carlow over that 10-year period where I was involved were few and far between, so when you do get days like that you kind of have to enjoy them, and enjoy them we did.

The sad thing then was that after such a high, we were brought back down to earth two weeks later where we were so flat against Limerick. That was very disappointing. We were drawn at home for another Saturday evening clash and this time it was live on TV. We were dealt a massive blow going into that game with the news that Thomas Walsh had suffered a fractured cheekbone and would miss out. Thomas was a fantastic midfielder and was outstanding against Offaly, so we were always going to feel his loss.

We went into that Limerick game thinking that we had a great chance and that we'd give it a right good go. Funnily enough, the expectation was now on us to perform. Maybe looking back now, it might be easy to say that we got too caught up in it all. The high of the Offaly game, plus the TV cameras coming down, but whatever it was we just fell flat again. One thing I remember is we just never met Limerick's physicality, whereas against Offaly we did and again that was disappointing. They beat us 2-15 to 0-7 and it was definitely as one-sided as the score line suggests.

That Carlow panel from Liam Hayes' era was probably the closest we had in a long time to having all the best players available. Liam stepped down after the 2006 campaign having done two years in charge and I was disappointed he didn't stay on again, as I felt he could have gotten more out of us, but it certainly wasn't an easy job for him. Liam was a businessman so he had his own things going on. I liked working under Liam though. He brought a bit of organisation and structure to the set up and we all liked him as a person as well as a manager.

I know it's always hard to compare different eras, but if you were to look at that Carlow team and compare it to the Carlow team under Turlough O'Brien in recent years, it's interesting. On paper, the team from the 00s probably had six scoring forwards, or at least each forward was the main scorer for their club, whereas in recent times the majority of Carlow scores are coming from Paul Broderick as he has definitely been Carlow's main marksman. The difference though is that the current team's commitment levels are through the roof and I've seen it first-hand having been asked in as a selector in recent years.

Going back, we might have had more scoring forwards back then but the other side of that is that commitment levels probably let a lot of lads down back then and despite having very strong teams on paper and indeed on the field of play, we never seemed to get it together for a long period of time and more often than not, we seemed to underperform.

Looking back at that era, you'd have to ask did we get enough out of ourselves? Did we all fully commit to it from a training point of view? I definitely think that squad of players should have achieved more and there was more in each of us but for whatever reason things never worked out. Back then, even after league games, most of the team would have gone out for a few pints. The social aspect was a big part of it. We had a good few lads who enjoyed their few jars but once they went out on the field and performed you didn't mind, but at the same time, as I've said, I do think that group of players from the mid-00s did definitely underachieve. We were very inconsistent as a team. We beat Longford in 2004 in what was a huge win but we lost our following two championship games. After we beat Offaly in 2005 we were sky high then going into the Limerick game we just never showed up. We beat Wicklow in 2006, but then were beaten by Laois in Leinster and Meath in the qualifiers. We never seemed to be able to back up one big championship win with another.

Nowadays, I'm not saying lads don't enjoy it, but the level of preparation that goes into being a county player now… it's nearly seven days a week. I do think it's important for lads to let off some steam every now and then, as it can't always be the pressure cooker for lads.

**99**

# MARK CARPENTER

*Mark Carpenter on one of his trademark speedy runs for Carlow in 2004.*

"

I WAS UNDECIDED for a while on what was the 'Game of my Life'. I was going to pick numerous different games between club, county and even winning a Railway Cup for Leinster out in Boston. In the end, I decided on the Offaly game mainly for the way it ended. That probably wasn't the best game I ever played for Carlow but, at the time, that team had turned a corner and were playing a nice brand of football. It was really enjoyable and I was kind of at an age where I was mature enough to play that kind of football, and I could do things that I probably couldn't do a few years before hand. That year was probably one of the most enjoyable years of football I had playing with Carlow.

Liam Hayes was our manager in 2005 and '06. Before Liam came in I wouldn't have known much about him but I quickly figured out his pedigree. Liam's father

Jim was from Carlow and had played senior football for the county, so Liam had those home ties to the county. The players all seemed to row in behind the manager as they could all see he was doing it for the betterment of Carlow and genuinely wanted to progress the team. When you talked to Liam you could tell that he had a caring for the players, and really wanted to improve things. In previous years with Carlow I always found that the starting 15 for championship games would always have six or seven debutants and it's very hard to build any momentum in a team when that happens every year. I think going into that season we had a good mix of youth and experience, and we seemed to have more of a settled team. There was also a nice bond between the players and the management group, which wouldn't always be there.

The National League that year was pretty much the same as usual for Carlow. We mixed some good performances with some not so good, but we were nowhere near promotion. By the time the championship came around we were confident enough though. The mood had picked up and things were going well in training.

We played Wexford in Croke Park and were beaten by five points. One of the key moments from that game was that our half-back Richie Sinnott was sent-off, harshly in my opinion and that had a massive bearing on the game. We were disappointed to lose but it was a really good performance and we were starting to believe that maybe we were actually a little better than we had been over the previous few years, and we definitely looked to be progressing.

When we drew Offaly in the qualifiers at home, we looked at it as a good draw. It was a game we thought we could win, although Offaly probably saw it as a good draw too. The fact was, however, that Carlow hadn't beaten Offaly in championship since the 40s, so our record against them was very poor. On a personal note, I can remember the team watching the video of the Offaly versus Laois game in the Leinster Championship a couple of weeks previous. Conor Evans, the Offaly full-back was outstanding that day as Offaly only lost out to an excellent Laois team by two points. I was playing full-forward at the time so I knew I'd be coming up against him. We came out of that meeting after watching that game and I can remember a few lads saying to me I'd better be bringing my A-game as Conor would be tough! Even more so after that meeting we had, but there was definitely pressure to perform the next day. It was good because all the pressure was coming from the group themselves and we knew there was a performance coming.

The build-up coming into the Offaly game was really good. I felt good and I think all the lads did too. It was a good day for championship and there was a real buzz around. Offaly and Waterford were playing after our game in the hurling championship so there was a massive crowd in Dr Cullen Park for the double-header. The Offaly midfield pairing of Ciaran McManus and Alan McNamee were very highly rated then but both Patrick and Thomas Walsh were well on top throughout. The two Walsh's together were a formidable partnership on their day.

The game was close for most of the first-half. The one major incident I remember from that first half was our centre-back Willie Power breaking his leg very early on, so there was a big hold up from that. Come the second-half then, we seemed to step it up a little and were really outperforming Offaly. We were five points up with only a couple of minutes left and at that stage you just couldn't see us losing. We were playing really well and were well on top. Then within a couple of kick-outs Offaly hit us for a quick 1-2 and, all of a sudden… we're level. At that point you're thinking, *Oh here we go again.* It looked like all our hard work was about to come undone.

Play carried on afterwards and the ball was worked up to me out near the sideline underneath the stand. Over all the years, it's one of the only scores I got where I can remember the whole build up. In that moment I didn't get much time to think about what I was going to do. I just needed to create a yard or two of space, put the boot through it and I managed to get off my kick. Once it left my boot I could see it was going straight over. If I was to do that kick again 10 times over I'd probably miss it each time. The day that was in it though and all that was at stake, plus the fact I was playing well, meant I was always going to go for it. I had all the range of emotions in such a short space of time. We looked home and dry, only then to look like we might actually lose it and, from there, to go and kick the winning score! It was probably the only time in my career I kicked the winning score in a championship match at that level.

Once the game was over the place went wild. I didn't really get to enjoy the moment or partake in much of the celebrations, however, as I had a funeral to attend. We have a family run business where we have an off licence, a bar and a funeral home. I had to dash back to the dressing-room after the game and then hop straight into the car and head for home. I grabbed a quick shower and put on the suit and headed over. On my way home after the match, I remember driving down Tullow Street in town and seeing some people who were coming from the match, all in their jerseys and all celebrating. It was a little surreal, to have gone from such a high to having to organise a funeral, all in the space of a very short time.

We were paired at home to Limerick in the next round and, in hindsight now, I think maybe we might have got a little ahead of ourselves. As much as we were playing well together, a lot of us were still young and naive. That Limerick game was on a Saturday evening in Dr Cullen Park, the same as the Offaly game and again there was a good buzz going into it. The RTE cameras were there to capture it this time which just added to the buzz. In the end we just didn't perform against Limerick. Carlow were unlucky in a way to run into Wexford and Limerick that year as both sides would normally be teams that Carlow would look at and always fancy their chances of beating either. It was just bad timing that when we played them together that both Wexford and Limerick were both among the top teams in the country and both had played Division One football.

We were eager to push on then going into 2006 but, once again, we mixed the good with the bad in the league. It was only in recent times that Carlow really started to take the league seriously and started to see results. I think in general the league is taken more serious now by all teams. Back then, we probably didn't take it as serious as we should have but, realistically, the league is where the likes of Carlow are going to be making progress. By the time championship came around in 2006, once again we pulled a big performance out of the bag as we hammered Wicklow down in Wexford Park, but we followed that up with a below par performance against Laois in O'Moore Park.

Consistency was probably the biggest problem during my time with Carlow. We had some great results over the years but we could never string enough good performances together to go on any kind of a run. We had such a high turnover of players in Carlow most years that we could never really find a settled team, so that was part of our downfall. I think the two years we had under Liam Hayes was probably the most settled panel, certainly in my time with Carlow anyway, but again it didn't last long and lads would be coming and going again soon after. I know from a player's point of view, it's disappointing if you're coming in to play and straightaway you see you're missing four or five players from the previous year. It's very disheartening.

My main commitment around that time was with work and when you have a family business it's always a little bit easier to get time off to go training or to play a game, so I never had any doubts about playing for Carlow. My mother Ciss was a big GAA person herself and she'd actually have a couple of Railway Cup medals playing camogie for Leinster. She'd go to all the games as well, and my father Paddy would have played for Carlow for years too, so the GAA was big in the family anyway. It was never pushed on me, but at the same time you always want to follow the tradition in your family.

I made my senior debut for Carlow in 1998. I couldn't make the Carlow minors the year before and here I was being called up to the senior team a year later. I remember working in the off-licence and Brendan Hayden Senior calling in and asking me would I go up and train with the senior footballers. Paddy Morrissey was manger at the time and I said I'd go in and see what happened. We played Westmeath in the Leinster Championship up in Mullingar and although we lost, I scored a goal. Despite that though, I knew deep down I wasn't anywhere near the standard required for that level just yet. I probably wouldn't have admitted it at the time but I knew it.

I probably had more bad days than good playing for Carlow but, looking back, I don't look at the results as such really. There were a few good days for sure and they were all brilliant. I enjoyed spending so much time with my friends over the years playing football. At the time I was training and playing, I probably wouldn't have said that but when you're in the middle of it you don't appreciate it as much. That only comes much later. We were all part of something and were all part of a journey of trying to get somewhere. Whether it was positive or negative through results each week, we were all part of it together. I remember being in the pub one Christmas a few years ago and meeting Joe Byrne and Thomas Walsh. Thomas is out in America now but it was like we had just picked up from our last training session and we had never been apart. We'd talk back about old games we played or just the craic we used to have, and just bring up old stories. I think that's the important part of the GAA. I really enjoyed my time with Carlow. It's never something I'd look back and think, *Jeez you could have been doing something else.*

I was lucky enough to play Railway Cup football with Leinster in my career and to actually win a medal with them. I was part of the team that won it outright in 2006, scoring 1-2 in the final against Connacht. That game was played out in

Boston so we were all flown out by the GAA and it was a great trip, and there were a couple of great sessions with all the players after that game. We had played Ulster in the semi-final and I can remember thinking early on that I wasn't out of my depth and that I was well able for it. I was marking Francie Bellew. Francie had won an All-Ireland medal with Armagh and was an All Star. I'd often see him on the TV and think, *Jesus he's big, he can't be that quick.* I would have always fancied myself as being as fast as anyone but I remember the first ball that came in and sure enough he was as quick as me! At another stage during the game I ended up on Barry Owens of Fermanagh, another man with All Stars. I'd say there were only about 20 people looking at that game that night which was a real shame, but it was a huge honour for me to play for Leinster.

Sometimes, I often wonder in Carlow if we had put more pressure on ourselves over the years maybe we might have gotten more out of it on the pitch but, looking back, I wouldn't change a thing. Yes we would have liked to win a bit more, but the group that was there were all good lads. We had some great days out and followed them up with some great nights afterwards. It was a great way to spend such a large part of your life doing something that you love. All of our spare time was about getting ourselves fit and healthy to play football at the top level. Plenty of lads might talk about it, but we were all doing it. It was a great time in my life.

# RUAIRI DUNBAR

**WICKLOW 2-8** ★ **CARLOW 1-11**
**Christy Ring Cup**
**Pearse Park, Arklow**
**JUNE 3, 2006**

*Ruairi Dunbar makes one of his trademark strikes for goal, against Laois in 2010.*

★ **WICKLOW:** J Driver; MJ O'Neill, G Keogh, G Bermingham; B Stones, T McGrath (0-1), MA O'Neill; J O'Neill, G Doran (0-1); E Dunne, J Murphy, T Doyle; A O'Brien (0-1), E Furlong, J Keogh (1-4). Subs: D Hyland (0-1) for Doyle, C Kavanagh for Dunne, D Moran (1-0) for Furlong, N Driver for G Keogh.

★ **CARLOW:** F Foley; A Gaule, T Doyle, D Shaw; E Coady, S Kavanagh, L Kenny; A Brennan, C Hughes (0-1); **R Dunbar (0-4)**, R Foley, D Roberts (1-1); P Kehoe (0-1), D Murphy, B Lawler (0-1). Subs: P Coady (0-2) for Murphy, B Cox (0-1) for E Coady, J Waters for Lawler.

## THE ACTION

WICKLOW AND CARLOW fought out a tough round one game in the Christy Ring Cup and, at the end of the game, the points were shared. Carlow were coming off the back of a good Ring campaign the previous year and would have expected to win this, but at the same time games between these two counties are always close and this was no exception.

Throughout this gripping encounter, the sides were level seven times. Carlow were forced to play the last 20 minutes with 14 men after their star forward and ace free taker Ruairi Dunbar was sent off on a straight red card. Wicklow held a one-point lead at half-time, ahead by 1-4 to 0-6, and another goal from Dennis Moran looked like it would set them up for a memorable victory. But Damien Roberts bagged a goal back for Carlow, before substitute Barry Cox fired over the equalising point for the away side.

Carlow were big favourites coming in to this game but Wicklow were up for the fight and deserved a draw. Carlow kept going to the end and Cox's late score to draw the game was thoroughly deserved.

There is no doubt that Carlow were badly hampered by the dismissal of Dunbar as he was Carlow's best forward up to that point and the forwards just didn't seem to be moving as well without him in their side. Still Carlow kept plugging away and despite being down to 14 players, still managed to come away with a share of the spoils.

★★★★★

66

WHEN I WAS asked to pick a game of my life, straight away I had my mind made up. It wasn't a game we won, or even the best game I played, but it stands out for many different reasons. It's funny that the game I picked was a game where I was sent off but the result of that had an effect on me afterwards. Even the date is ingrained in my head. I couldn't remember the dates for the majority of games I played in over the years, but I never forget that date.

Every year when June 3 comes around, it always brings me back to that game. Before that game I was fairly easy going and after that game and the sending off – not even just the sending off but the whole circus that went with it – I was a lot crankier, both on and off the field. I always believed hurling was going to be my safety net and that the game would always look after me, but I lost trust in people in the game a little after that day. I suppose a lot of this was down to my obsession with hurling, which was instilled in me by my father Paul, a Wexford man that raised me on stories of the Rackards and Wexford hurling.

2006 was the second year of the new Christy Ring Cup which had been brought in to help the Tier Two counties and it was a great competition for the likes of Carlow. Games between Carlow and Wicklow were always close back around then and this game was no different.

I had started the game really well and was happy enough with how I was going. The game was tight and I think Wicklow led by a point at half-time. I had scored 0-4 before being sent off, but I felt I was going really well at the time and felt on top of my game. I was on the frees that day and they were going well for me. I'd been taking frees my entire career from underage and I loved taking them. Pat Coady wasn't starting that day and so, any time I went to take a free all the Wicklow lads were calling me Pat Coady! It was harmless stuff really, just trying to put me off. It didn't bother me and I just took it as a compliment instead and I find stuff like that just spurs you on. I remember getting a point at one stage and flicking the ball over a lad's head and sending it over the bar. You get those games every now and then where things just seem to be going for you and that day in Arklow felt like one of them.

At one stage in the second-half, myself and one of the Wicklow players were both tussling for a ball and as the ball broke away, he made that classic move of grabbing my hurl under his arm. I was going the opposite direction, so I just yanked the hurl out from under his arm. There was nothing in it and I thought nothing more of it. Of course, the linesman there didn't think so. The referee actually saw what happened and he never said a word, but a few seconds later the play was brought back as the linesman called him over and he said what he thought he had seen. The referee explained that I was seen striking and I had to go. The fact that the Wicklow player went down holding himself didn't help matters either. However, I must state that I'm not saying he was diving, he was a very talented and competitive hurler.

A couple of days later I rang the player in question to tell him there was no malice in it and to ask if he'd help with the appeal. He was very decent and said he would help, although his words to me were, 'Don't worry about it, you didn't actually hit me at all, I just went down'. Whether he was saying it to make me feel better or if true, I don't know. As if I wasn't annoyed enough already... I was fit to explode then!

We were then talking to the Wicklow back-room lads and they were both going to write a letter which I believe was supposed to state that I caused no damage or harm to the player. What they actually did write was that I had, 'caused lacerations and grazing to the skin' and then they finished their letter with how they thought I did deserve a one-month suspension, but that three months was too severe! With all that against me going into the appeal, I was never going to get off.

The suspension that followed was a bit of a joke. It was the only time I had ever been suspended in my career. We appealed it, as I felt I was hard done by. We went through the appeal process and I went up to Croke Park with Eddie Byrne and he spoke really well for me and my case. I was only 19 at the time and I was up in Croke Park, and with several lads all at the other side of the table, it can be daunting for a young lad. I remember Enda Muldoon was up there the same night, as he was having his case heard for a disciplinary issue also. There was a delegate there from Down and it looked like he had the casting vote, or some clout, as he held up the referee's report and the statement from Wicklow.

To be honest, he seemed like the only one interested in what I was saying when defending myself. So, I left the room and came back in when called and was informed that the ban was upheld. I lost my appeal and was given a three-month suspension.

The thing is Enda Muldoon was only given a one-month ban. He retaliated after he was struck in the privates which was on video and, to be fair, I think that's a normal reaction! However, it was still a striking offence, but video helped his cause. What really went against me, and it was the same for most of the other lower-level counties, was video evidence. Nowadays most counties will have someone recording their games but it wasn't as common then, and with no evidence to actually look at, it was only the referee's report against my word and, ultimately, I lost.

How I actually found out about the suspension initially was that I was at home eating my breakfast and it came on the news on the radio. I wasn't told by anyone from the county board or from Croke Park. I got no official word from anybody and if I hadn't heard it on the radio then, I often wonder how long more it would have been until I was told about it. As if I wasn't annoyed enough about it already then that made it 10 times worse. Three months suspended might not sound like a lot in the grander scheme of things, but it depends what way it falls. You could get three months during the winter and not miss a single game back then, whereas with my situation my three months were at the start of the summer which meant I wouldn't be allowed back to play hurling until the start of September. So, my whole summer was ruined.

It wasn't like I was allowed to train either. Suspension meant exactly that, in that I wasn't even allowed to train with the team. I wasn't allowed to train with the club or even play challenge matches. At the start, I would go to Carlow training just in my street clothes, but after a while I even stopped doing that. Of course, it would happen that when I was suspended for the whole summer that Carlow went all the way to the Christy Ring final in Croke Park. The manager Eoin Garvey insisted that I travel up with the panel on the day, in fairness to him, and if you look at the team photo from that day I have an awful scowl on me!

I can remember my first game back at the start of September. I was playing for my club Carlow Town against Mount Leinster Rangers in the county Senior Championship and we lost out in a high scoring contest. To say I was like a man possessed would be an understatement. Pat Kehoe was the ref and I remember him welcoming me back and I grunted something back at him. I just had all this energy built up in me over the summer and I knew that day what I was going out to do. I was just a different man on the pitch from then on. I probably had a bit of a chip on my shoulder after Wicklow too. I think I got a point from the throw in, and I even got one over my head at one stage, but I was just so glad to be back and so was going to make the most of it. I might have ended up with about 2-6 or something but I played really well and it felt really good to be back. I definitely brought more aggression to my game. I was putting in more shoulders and getting more involved physically than I might have had before.

It didn't matter if I was playing for club, county or college, I just went out with a different mentality from that day on. It was kind of 'Me against the World' kind of thing. Now that might sound a little bit extreme, but that's just how I felt at the time and I realised that no one was going to look out for you. I just went out and played the game a different way from then on. I wouldn't say I was a dirty player but I definitely used my physicality a bit more.

I walked away from the county set up when I was around 26 and that's something I've regretted since, but I just had so much hurling done at that stage and so many injuries. I was still training really hard but, at the same time, didn't feel like I was getting as much out of myself as I should have been. Looking back now, maybe I was burnt out as I was just hurling all the time for such a long time. Between everything, I decided to take a step back in early 2012 after a Walsh Cup game. At the end of that year, I moved up to Dublin and I also transferred up there to play with St Brigid's. After Kevin Ryan left, John Meyler came in and he invited me back on the panel, and I was delighted to go back in although the gap away from the set up affected me and I found it hard to get back up to speed for different reasons.

One of the things that John did early on was to get all of the players' hearts screened and the results of my test were irregular, so I had to go for follow up tests afterwards. The result was that they found I had an enlarged heart and I had to stop playing sport for about four months. This was just to see if there would be any change if I wasn't doing any physical sport and to see if it was possibly down to over-training. I was also just so tired at the time, just always shattered. I also have a condition called Hashimoto's disease which affects the thyroid and that was also impacting me greatly and was only diagnosed in September 2014... so I had a lot going on.

After the few months off and taking the tablets, I felt really good again but by the time 2014 came around, I was living, working and playing in Dublin and I just couldn't give the commitment at that stage to go back in again, as much as I wanted to. I also got married and our daughter was born in 2015, so even more so then, I couldn't justify giving the commitment that an inter-county player needs to give at that stage of my life. Even though I got back in there under John Meyler, I do regret walking away in 2012, and the older I get and the more I look back, I probably should have talked a little more about things rather than throwing the toys out of the pram, as I felt that period when I stepped away, I was hurling really well, but totally exhausted.

I first came into the Carlow senior hurling panel in 2005. It was my first year out of minor and I was straight into the senior set up under Eoin Garvey. It is a massive jump from playing minor and then straight to senior, even at club level, never mind inter county. Luckily for me, the likes of Pat Coady, Des Shaw, Johnny Nevin and many others on the panel were a big help in getting me settled in and getting rid of any nerves I might have had. I wasn't long on the panel when we flew over to London for a league game. It was my first time on a plane, and on the Saturday night a good few of the lads went out for a few drinks. I was only young and just so excited to be involved, so I decided to stay away from the bright lights. Instead, I went to the cinema along with Pat Coady and Barry Cox; we went to see the film Hide and Seek starring Robert De Niro. I remember sitting in the cinema thinking, *This is mad, I'm sitting here with a Carlow legend like Pat and tomorrow I'll be hurling with him.*

We won that game comfortably enough but I ended up going off early as I broke a couple of ribs. I didn't know that at the time though and it wasn't until I got home that I was prompted by my mother Grainne to go for an x-ray. That was just a sign of things to come though as regards injuries. I even put out an AC joint once putting on a jacket… that will just show you how jinxed I was!

I was lucky enough during my time with Carlow that I did have some success. In that first year with the senior team in 2005, we famously beat Offaly in the league and we reached the Division Two league final. I was also part of two Christy Ring Cup winning teams, while beating Laois in the qualifiers was another massive day for Carlow hurling.

That first Christy Ring Cup win in 2008 was something special. Obviously, I had missed the 2006 final against Antrim due to that suspension so it was great to be able to get back there and to actually play in a final. The final was taken out of Croke Park the week before the game and was eventually fixed for Tullamore. We looked home and dry only for two injury time Brendan Murtagh goals to bring Westmeath back into it and send the game to extra-time. We eventually got over the line but only after a mammoth battle. Waterford man Jim Greene was over us that year, with John McGrath as S & C coach, and I really enjoyed working with Jim and John. For me, 2008 was probably the most enjoyable year of hurling I had and I felt I was playing really well. In fairness to Jim, he was a great manager and playing under him I felt 10 feet tall, such was the way he dealt with me, and all the players. Jim left after only one year which was a real shame, but I still look back on that period very fondly.

Right now, the body is broken up. I have had every injury going, and the legs are starting to give out now too. I bought a house in Ballinkillen with my wife Ria in 2017 and I now play my hurling there. I will try to prolong the club career for as long as I can, but it's just year by year or even game by game at this stage.

I am so proud to have played hurling for Carlow and to just say that I represented my county. I was part of some great teams and played on some unforgettable days, while also playing with some of the best players to have ever hurled for Carlow. Even talking about the 'Game of my Life', hopefully in years to come, my daughter Scarlett will pick it up and read it and see that I was able to contribute something from my career to the team and the county.

# ROBBIE FOLEY

**CARLOW 1-15 ★ DOWN 0-14**
**Christy Ring Cup Final**
**Croke Park**
**JULY 11, 2009**

*Robbie Foley (sixth from right, back row) and the Carlow team that defeated Down in the 2009 Christy Ring Cup final in Croke Park.*

★ **CARLOW:** F Foley; W Hickey, S Kavanagh (0-1), D Shaw; E Coady (0-1), J Rogers, D Byrne; J Hickey, D Roberts; R Dunbar, M Brennan, C Doyle (0-2); A Gaule (0-1), **R Foley (1-3)**, P Kehoe (0-5). Subs: E Byrne (0-1) for Dunbar, J Coady (0-1) for Kehoe.

★ **DOWN:** G Clarke; F Conway, S Murray, S Ennis; R McGrattan, K Courtney, M Ennis; A Savage, C Woods; C O'Prey (0-1), P Braniff (0-4), S Wilson (0-7); J Coyle (0-1), G Johnson, O Clarke. Subs: A Higgins (0-1) for O Clarke, M Coulter for Coyle.

# THE ACTION

WITH CARLOW AND Down locked in a titanic battle – they were level 11 times – a goal was surely always going to decide the outcome of this final. And it duly arrived in the 69th minute, courtesy of Carlow full-forward Robert Foley. Foley collected a high ball sent in from Andrew Gaule and despite heavy marking managed to swivel and send the ball low and hard to the back of the net.

In front of almost 4,000 fans at Headquarters, Down were left ruing a final wides tally of 11, including seven in the first-half, when the Ulster men could have been well in front. The added bonus of this win for Carlow was a place in the following year's Leinster Championship. Both sides were nervous in the first-half and were level four times. Carlow full-back Shane Kavanagh opened the scoring with a '65' in the third minute, only for Paul Braniff to quickly restore parity and the rest of the half was to follow a similar pattern. Down could have had a goal from Gareth Johnson only for a good save from Frank Foley. Paudie Kehoe and Andrew Gaule were among the first-half scorers for Carlow, while for Down Paul Braniff and Simon Wilson were keeping the umpires busy. At half-time the sides were level 0-7 each.

Down did stretch two points clear early in the second-half before two Paudie Kehoe frees had Carlow back on level terms. Carlow might have thought they missed their chance when Kehoe had a penalty stopped on the line. Likewise, at the other end for Down, when Conor O'Prey kicked a goal chance wide while an unmarked Johnson was screaming for possession. That was to prove costly for Down as with extra-time looming Carlow struck the decisive blow with the winning goal from Foley. Craig Doyle added a point from a free almost straightaway to make sure of the win for Carlow and there was no way back for the Mourne men from there. This was a second Christy Ring Cup title in-a-row for Carlow.

★★★★★

66

MY DREAM WHEN I was a young boy growing up in Myshall was always to play in Croke Park. Playing hurling for Carlow, that never seemed like a realistic ambition. That all changed though when the GAA brought in the Christy Ring, Nicky Rackard, and the Lory Meagher Championships. Straightaway then, Carlow, and plenty of other counties of similar levels, now all had a realistic chance of getting to play a final in Croke Park, which they never had before.

The Christy Ring was introduced ahead of the 2005 season and we were beaten in the semi-final by Down that year, in Parnell Park. A year later, we went one better and reached the final. The tables were turned when we beat Down in the semi-final in Mullingar, which meant that we qualified to play Antrim in the final. I was finally going to get the chance to play in Croke Park. Unfortunately, things didn't go our way that day and we were given a proper hurling lesson by Antrim. To make it worse, the game was live on RTE for everyone to see!

In 2008 we were back in the final again, this time against Westmeath. We all thought we'd be back in Croke Park again, and to try and right the wrongs from the Antrim game. However, that didn't go to plan as when the GAA announced the fixtures, the Christy Ring final was due to be played in Croke Park alright, but on a Friday evening. I had played in Croke Park against Antrim but the dream of getting back there, and to win in Croke Park now seemed to be gone.

Carlow and Westmeath both kicked up a fuss, and rightly so, and both counties said they wouldn't play on a Friday night as it would be impossible for both players and fans to get to the stadium in time. This was supposed to be an All-Ireland final after all. Lads would be coming from work from all different parts of the country and to be expected to get to Croke Park, through rush hour Dublin traffic, and be expected to be there in time, was just too much.

The game was changed in the end although it was moved out of Croke Park altogether and we ended up playing an extra-time thriller in Tullamore, which thankfully we came out the right side of. We were six points up going into injury time before Westmeath got two goals right at the death, so we should have been able to close it out but we pulled it out of the bag after a monumental effort from everyone. There were big celebrations but after a couple of days we were back in training again. We won the Ring final on the Sunday and the following Saturday, six days later, we had to face off against Laois in a promotion/relegation play off.

Looking back, we were just fulfilling a fixture really and we were on a hiding to nothing. We enjoyed that win but at the same time the Laois game was in the back of players' minds and it was a bit of an anti-climax having gone from such a high to be back in training a few days later, and knowing that we could still be back in the same competition again next year. We enjoyed our Christy Ring success that week but we were never really going to beat Laois after that. The Christy Ring Cup the following year was still strong with the likes of Westmeath, Kerry, and Down still there and whatever about Carlow's chances of getting back there again, I knew my chances of getting back were narrowing down as the years were going by. At that stage of my career I was sick of playing Kehoe Cup games in freezing cold January in Wicklow and places like that.

We wanted to go onto the next step and that was winning a championship in Croke Park. We managed to give ourselves a chance of making that dream come through in 2009, when we qualified for another Christy Ring final. We beat Wicklow and Kildare before getting the better of Kerry after a replay in the semi-final, and waiting there for us was Down. When it was confirmed for Croke Park for a Saturday afternoon, it was a little bit of a weight off our shoulders. Unlike 12 months previously, there would be no messing or controversy over the venue so we just had to concentrate on the game itself this time and nothing else. We now had our chance to not only do back-to-back titles, but to do it in Croke Park this time and to right the wrongs after our Antrim performance there three years before.

There might have been about 4,000 at it on the day between the three games – Ring, Rackard, and Meagher finals were all played – but we were playing in Croke Park and there might as well have been a full house at it; it didn't matter to us how many were there.

My own preparation that week in the lead up to the final wasn't great. I was coming towards the end of my career and at that stage I was finding the training hard going. The week of the final I was feeling very run down. I wasn't well that week at all. I was taking vitamins and going to see Dr Tom Foley and trying to get the energy levels up for that game. I did a lot of praying that week as well that I'd improve and thankfully I did.

Over the years I would have gone to a lot of All-Ireland hurling finals and afterwards I'd always go out on the pitch. Everyone else would be celebrating or whatever, but I always used to imagine in my head that I would be doing this or doing that. I'd imagine scoring a goal or a point and getting to win with Carlow there. Standing on the pitch after those games, you'd wonder would you ever get the chance. In that Christy Ring final against Down when I scored the only goal of the game right at the death, all those feelings came out of me right there and then. I couldn't believe it, it was just pure fairytale stuff.

Games between Carlow and Down had always been close enough over the years. They beat us in a Christy Ring semi-final and we beat them in one as well. That final in Croke Park was no different and they had plenty of chances to win the game, but they didn't convert. We stayed in the game and it was pretty much point for point throughout. I think it might have been the 69th minute when we got the goal. We were only a point up at that stage and I remember shouting out to Mark Brennan to just let in the ball first time when he got it, as it wasn't coming in at all. Mark was captain, and was playing centre-forward. We had to try something at that late stage of the game. A couple of minutes later, Andrew 'Duke' Gaule got a ball and he went for a point, but he ended up mishitting his effort and it dropped short. His mishit shot was my good fortune however, as the ball came in perfectly for me at full-forward. I caught it, turned and shot straight for goal. Thankfully, it ended up in the net and it was a great feeling.

To this day, people will still come up to me and tell me where they were when I scored that goal in Croke Park. I might have only met people once or twice over the years since that day but people will still mention it. It's nice that people still remember it and it's nice to be associated with such a day. The dream growing up was to play in Croke Park. Then to win in Croke Park! And, thankfully, I got to do both. Unlike the previous year when we won the Christy Ring, there was to be no play-off this time. This meant that we went up automatically and we would be included in the Leinster and All-Ireland Championship the following year. After back-to-back wins in the Ring Cup, we wanted to show that we were able for the step up. We were able to enjoy the celebrations that bit more knowing that we had no extra game coming down the tracks.

We beat Wexford in the National League then in 2010 and we ran Clare to a point the following week. We had a great team and we were on a roll. We played some great teams but they were the teams we wanted to be playing against. We wanted to be playing against the top teams and I think we showed that we deserved to be up there.

Later that summer, we lost to Laois in Leinster but we ended up drawing them again in the qualifiers in Dr Cullen Park on a lovely warm summer evening and we beat them. That was massive to beat our neighbours. To win a championship game in our first year back up at that level was huge. We were building huge momentum and that Laois win was proof that we weren't just up there to make up the numbers. I was coming to the end of my county career at that stage, but it had been a great few years. When the Christy Ring competition came in, in 2005, Eoin Garvey was in charge. Eoin was a great man to make you believe, but when the Christy Ring came in, our belief stepped up a notch as we now had something big to aim for. We all had that in our heads. We now had a proper championship goal to look forward to.

Eoin came in at a bad time for Carlow. There was one game where Eoin actually had to tog out for us before a 'B' championship game! Once he got settled though, he had all the best hurlers playing for Carlow and we were a different team once he put his stamp on it. Each year came with even more of a professional set up from then on. When we won the first Christy Ring cup in 2008, Waterford's Jim Greene had come in as manager and he had John McGrath as his number two. John McGrath had never played hurling in his life. He was into Kung Fu but he brought that kind of tough mindset to the set up. They made us believe we could do stuff. They kind of brainwashed us in a way to make us think we could do these things, which we eventually did. It was the first time most of us had been involved with dieticians and that kind of thing and it was a very enjoyable time. Jim was a great man manager; he was great to talk to fellas and, of course, he knew his hurling. John McGrath was the opposite. If you threw a sliotar at John he'd throw it straight back and he'd nearly tell you he knew nothing about hurling. His job was fitness and getting our mindset right and he definitely did that. They both worked very well together. Surprisingly, Jim actually didn't stay on for the second year and he ended up stepping down for whatever reason. Kevin Ryan, another Waterford man stepped into the breach and he stepped it up another gear then with his approach. The set up with Jim Greene was very professional but when Kevin came in, it just went up a notch altogether. Kevin brought our hurling skills on so much and that was a massive help when we won the second Christy Ring in 2009.

Looking back on my career as a whole, there is not one thing I would change and I'd do the whole thing all over again if I was able. We had great days playing with both club and county. People might often say to me that I was mad, playing for so long, that I got nothing out of it only broken bones, but that couldn't be further from the truth.

# BRENDAN MURPHY

CARLOW 0-14 ★ LOUTH 0-13
Leinster SFC Quarter-Final
O'Moore Park, Portlaoise
JUNE 12, 2011

*Brendan Murphy (centre) celebrates with Paul Cashin, Sean Gannon and Thomas Walsh after Carlow's epic comeback victory over Louth in the 2011 Leinster Championship.*

★ **CARLOW:** T O'Reilly; A Murphy, C Lawlor, B Kavanagh; P Cashin, S Redmond, K Nolan; **Brendan Murphy (0-3)**, D Foley (0-2); P Hickey (0-1), T Walsh, E Finnegan (0-1); Brian Murphy (0-2), S Gannon (0-1), D St Ledger (0-4). Subs: P Murphy for Kavanagh, C Mullins for Finnegan, J Murphy for Foley, E Ruth for Hickey.

★ **LOUTH:** S Connor; D Byrne, A Hoey, D Finnegan; R Finnegan, M Fanning, L Shevlin; P Keenan (0-2), B Donnolly (0-1); D Crilly (0-1), D Reid (0-1), A Reid; D Maguire (0-1), S Lennon (0-6), JP Rooney. Subs: A McDonnell for Rooney, R Carroll (0-1) for D Reid, P Smith for McDonnell, S Fitzpatrick for Crilly.

## THE ACTION

CARLOW WON THEIR first championship football game in five years with this shock win over Louth, who many people considered the real Leinster champions from 12 months previous. Louth were dealt a big blow in the first-half when corner-back Dessie Finnegan was shown a second yellow card. Carlow, who were massive outsiders with bookies coming into the game, built up a well deserved 0-8 to 0-5 half-time lead.

Louth came out a different team in the second-half and hit three points in the opening six minutes. Both sides swapped points before Shane Lennon put Louth ahead by 0-10 to 0-9 and with just 10 minutes of time remaining, Louth had stretched their lead out to go ahead by 0-13 to 0-10. Instead of pushing on in the final stages, it was Carlow who owned the remainder of the game as they outscored Louth by four points to nil from there until the end.

With eight minutes remaining, Brendan Murphy shot over an outrageous score from a sideline kick to reduce Louth's lead to two and, all of a sudden, Carlow followers were finding their voice. It was the turn of another Murphy then when Brian, Brendan's brother, clipped over a point and now there was just one in it. Full-forward Sean Gannon missed a chance to equalise but a monster free from Daniel St Ledger out near the sideline did level the scores a minute later and the momentum was all with Carlow now. With time almost up, Carlow came forward again and wing back Paul Cashin made a great burst up field before getting his pass off to John Murphy, who in turn found his namesake Brendan, and the big midfielder was in the right place at the right time to get a huge kick away which sailed straight between the posts for the winner. Those last 10 minutes will long be remembered by all Carlow folk in attendance and all players put in a massive shift to get them over the line. However special praise must go to Brendan Murphy and his scores down that final stretch will live long in the memory.

★★★★★

**"**

FOR ME, AND probably a lot of other people too, Louth were the real Leinster football champions of 2010. They were leading all the way in that game against Meath and were robbed right at the end. So, when we were paired to play against them the following year in Leinster, they were big favourites to beat us. Our league campaign was the usual up and down, but we just missed out on promotion from Division Four while Louth had got promoted from Division Three, so they were going into the Championship full of confidence.

It wasn't just beating Louth in the championship that made it so special. It was the manner of it. Coming from three points down late on, to then go and get the winner in the last minute? It was serious stuff. Me personally, I wasn't happy with my own game up to that. I had good passages of play but I was coming in and out of the game and not contributing as much as I'd like. It only takes one moment to switch momentum though and I had a sideline kick over on the stand side and I kicked it over the bar and that seemed to raise the Carlow crowd. That brought us back to within two points.

Daniel St Ledger with a monster of a free and my brother Brian both kicked points and then, all of a sudden, we were level. With time almost up then, Paul Cashin made a run up the field, he off-loaded it to John Murphy and I was running off him. He slipped it to me and I let fly and it went straight over the bar. That was a serious way to top it off because the year before, in Portlaoise as well, we were well beaten by Wicklow.

I remember the Louth goalkeeper taking the kick out after that last point and the full-time whistle going almost straightaway. I just dropped to my knees and everyone just piled in. Going back to that Wicklow game in the championship a year previous where they beat us well; that was my Championship debut for Carlow seniors, as I had come back from Australia at the end of the previous year. To make matters worse, I ended up getting sent off that day. I remember coming home from Portlaoise on the bus that day and a couple of lads were chatting and laughing, and I couldn't get over it after just being hammered by Wicklow.

I was new to the senior set up, but I remember saying it to one of the more senior players on the way home and he just said that, unfortunately, some of us become accustomed to the losses and that was just the way it was. So, to go from that low, to then beating Louth and having the pitch full with supporters, and friends and family after, was brilliant. I suppose, in a way, you could say Louth were ambushed by us. I remember driving out of Portlaoise that day on the bus and it was just class. It was a different bus journey home than the year before, definitely.

Coming in to that championship, the buzz was good in the camp. We had a couple of good results in the league but we had a couple of awful performances too. The way results went, we could have gone up on the last day but it didn't work out. Once a couple of weeks had passed and it was forgotten about, it was all focus on the championship. The league is what Carlow target but there's something special about championship that just gets you going. The long evenings, the fresh cut grass, brand new O'Neill's footballs… the good weather! Championship is different. They are special days.

I remember walking the pitch in Portlaoise before the Louth game with all the lads. There was a song blasting out over the tannoy system and everybody just seemed to be in good form. We never talked about the farcical nature of the previous year's Leinster final and how Louth were treated. We just saw it as Louth, nothing else, and we all said that we'd just go out there and have a real cut off these lads. There is no doubt that Louth weren't expecting it.

They were sick walking off the pitch. They could barely look at us. The Louth midfielder Brian Donnelly, whom I knew as he was over in Australia at the same time as me, just walked straight past me. He didn't even acknowledge me. I have no ill feeling towards Brian and I spent a summer in Boston when he was there after, but he was just shell-shocked.

We played Wexford two weeks later in the Leinster semi-final in Croke Park. I was confident going into that game and it was a great opportunity to make a Leinster final. Carlow and Wexford were always kind of a similar level but we knew at that stage that Wexford were a very good side. We started the game well in the early stages, but what felt like out of nowhere, they hit us with a barrage of quickfire goals. I think Shane Roche ended up with a hat-trick that day. We were a few points down at half-time and really the game was gone. It was hard coming out for the second-half and trying to claw that back. It was disappointing the way that ended. It was hard to stomach in the end because that was as close as any of us had ever been to making a Leinster senior final. I had played in Croke

Park before with the minors, but that Wexford game was my first time playing there with the senior side. Wexford were on a different path at that stage and were used to playing there and winning there, so they had more experience than us in that regard and that definitely helped them on the day. Croke Park is a daunting place to play for lads who don't get to play there often, so you need to be right on the day. It was only three years before that when Wexford were in an All-Ireland semi-final, so they were well used to Croke Park by that stage and the big days.

I often felt in my early years playing with Carlow that teams always felt they could beat us. I suppose that comes back to our history of not winning many things, but even if we were chipping away at a lead, teams always felt they could still beat us. That's why that Louth win was so special because when we were behind, we didn't give up and we actually turned it around and won. Unfortunately, the old failings came back to haunt us the next day out in Croke Park. That same evening as the Wexford game, the qualifier draw was on and we ended up drawing Antrim. Despite the game being in Casement Park, we still felt it was a good draw for us and we went up there expecting to win. At half-time we were a few points down and lads were still buzzing in the dressing-room, but in the end it wasn't to be and we lost by a point.

We might have had trouble putting a couple of good performances together but we could always pull off a championship shock every now and then. In 2012, Luke Dempsey was in his fourth year as Carlow manager and we played Meath in the Leinster Championship in Tullamore. We scored a goal in the last minute to salvage a draw and, only for finishing the game with 13 men, we possibly could have even won it. I felt at the time that we had Meath bet near the end of that game. The following week in training the buzz was great and we genuinely felt we could finish the job the second day out. Once again though, and it's hard to put your finger on it to say why, but we were well beaten a week later in the replay and after that Laois beat us in the qualifiers. Once again, one great performance was followed by a couple of poor ones. A lot of what held us back in Carlow over the years was belief. Just belief in yourself and your county, and actually genuinely believing that you can go out and beat whoever you're up against.

Certainly, when Turlough O'Brien came in as manager a few years later, our mentality did change. Turlough was a proud Carlow man above anything. Even off the field, the way he looked after his players! I have never enjoyed football as much as when Turlough was in charge of Carlow. Even when he brought in Steven Poacher as his number two, it didn't change the dynamic. In fairness to Turlough, he wasn't afraid to ask for help or look for a hand before he called Steven in to work with us. With some managers there might be an ego with them and they might want to be the main man but anything Turlough did was for the betterment of Carlow and he knew what Steven Poacher could bring to the table. As time went on, Steven became very well known in GAA circles but, in a way, I think Turlough might have been happy to let him take the limelight. Like I've said, there was no ego with Turlough and it was all about the players. I was the same as any player. I'd have my good days and bad days. I could be hot and cold but he'd always have your back and he'd always defend you. He'd always have a word with you too if he felt you needed it.

Division Four football, let's call a spade a spade, is not the most attractive football in the world and the team with any bit of organisation and a plan has a great chance of getting promoted – and the two lads working together definitely brought that to the table. In those years, we went into all our games knowing our game-plan and we were confident in every game that we could all do our jobs and do enough to win those games. If teams were getting close to us, we knew how to reset and go again. Turlough and Steven brought a massive organisation and structure to our team and it definitely worked for us during that period. Steven Poacher was the best coach I've worked with, as regards drills etc, but that all came from Turlough. He made that happen.

We ended up getting promoted out of Division Four in 2018 but our performances were not just saved for the league. We had great championship days too. Beating Wexford in Dr Cullen Park in 2017, and going on to play Dublin then. Getting to play Monaghan at home too in front of a huge crowd in the middle of summer, they were all great days to be involved with Carlow. I remember when Garry Kelly got our goal against Monaghan to bring us right back into that qualifier game… and it was like Dr Cullen Park was vibrating. The roars that were heard, I'll never forget. I remember looking around and thinking that this was just unreal. Unfortunately, we didn't get to grips with Monaghan towards the end and we lost out by five points, but those days were special. I've re-watched that Monaghan game back since and for long periods we definitely controlled that game. The people of Carlow at that stage were craving for success. People might look at Carlow and think that just because we've not been that successful that we're not that into football or that there's no passion or love for it. Carlow is a fanatical football county! Obviously, the hurlers have been very successful over the last few years too but from a football point of view, there is as much passion for it in Carlow as anywhere else. Even in Rathvilly, I can't even go up to the shop without someone stopping to talk about football. There was massive pride in the jersey during Turlough's spell in charge. Even when lads were singing the National Anthem there'd be hairs standing up on the back of your neck. Definitely looking back, they were great days and special times for the county.

# JAMES CLARKE

**OLD LEIGHLIN 1-9 ★ ÉIRE ÓG 1-9**
**Carlow SFC Semi-Final**
**Dr Cullen Park, Carlow**
**SEPTEMBER 25, 2011**

*James Clarke was the safest pair of hands for Carlow and Old Leighlin, and he was still in the Carlow jersey in 2019 bringing his son Jack to O'Moore Park.*

★ **OLD LEIGHLIN: J Clarke**; R Burke, M Meaney (BB), G Hickey; D Dowling, J Hayden (0-1), E Fitzgerald (0-1); P Hickey, M Brennan; D Kelly, C Coughlan (0-2), D Bambrick; W Minchin, H Gahan (0-2), S Kinsella (1-3).

★ **ÉIRE ÓG:** M Hennessy; B Kavanagh, C Bolger, V Kavanagh; P McElligott, C McCarthy, J Ryan; E Ruth, M Ware; A O'Brien (0-1), S Gannon (0-1), B Hennessy (0-2); C Mullins, D Hayden, B Carbery(1-5) Subs: T Dowling for Mullins.

# THE ACTION

THIS MIGHT NOT have been the best county football semi-final in living memory but you can be sure that everyone in Dr Cullen Park stayed in their seats right until the end, such was the drama. Both sides will look back and say they should have done things differently and both will look back and say that they could have won the game, but a draw was probably just about the fair result. The football might not have been the best on offer, but in terms of excitement it had plenty.

Old Leighlin hit the front early on when they scored a fortuitous goal, when a Seamus Kinsella free was not dealt with by the Éire Óg defence and the ball was allowed to hop on the ground and crept over the line, at least according to the umpire anyway! Éire Óg were adamant the ball never crossed the line but they were never going to say otherwise. Either way, the goal stood. Typical Éire Óg though, they came back straightaway and with corner-forward Bryan Carbery on fire up front there was always going to be a response. After Ber Hennessy was pulled down, Carbery dispatched his penalty past James Clarke. Eamonn Fitzgerald kicked a point for Old Leighlin to put them into a 1-4 to 1-3 lead at half-time.

The second-half wasn't long started when Carbery once again pointed for Éire Óg before Sean Gannon and Carbery put their side ahead by two. Old Leighlin weren't done yet, however, and points from John Hayden, Cathal Coughlan and Seamus Kinsella put the men from the little village back in front. Just then what looked like a golden opportunity for Éire Óg arrived when they were awarded a second penalty by referee Paud O'Dwyer. Up stepped Carbery again but this time James Clarke guessed right and he dived to keep out the penalty in what was a huge moment in the game. Carbery had a chance shortly after where he possibly could have goaled but he blazed his shot over the bar. With time almost up, Alan O'Brien found himself in space and he made no mistake to send the ball over the bar.

★★★★★

66

IN 2011, OLD LEIGHLIN were going for back-to-back senior football championships. Considering how long it had taken the club to get there – 1997 when they won their only previous one – the big question everyone was asking was would we have the motivation to go back and do it again? That group of players had played a lot of football and had actually reached the final in 2009, but lost to Rathvilly. To reverse that result then a year later and to finally get over the line was brilliant, but when it takes so long to get to the top it can either do two things. You can get the taste for it and be mad to go again, or the one championship might be enough for some lads… so going into 2011, we just didn't know what position we were in as regards lads' appetites to go again.

To win the championship in 2010 was something else. We had soldiered for so long and to finally be county champions, it was great to be able to have that medal no matter what. We all went away on a holiday together and we really made the most of it. We were on such a high and while it took us a while to come down from that, we eventually did and we had another great championship. To be fair to Joe Murphy, he was a great manager and he just took us to a new level and he had it instilled in us that we were the best team in the county.

We came out of the group that year and we qualified for a semi-final meeting with Éire Óg. We had played them in the group stage a few weeks earlier and the game ended up a draw. When we qualified to meet them in the semi-final, both sets of players knew it would be a totally different type of game. It was a lot more intense than our group meeting, but it ended in a draw again. Brian Carbery had two penalties for Éire Óg; he scored one in the first-half and late in the second-half he got another penalty, but I saved it. It was going straight in the bottom corner but I dived to keep it out. It was probably one of the best saves I ever made and definitely the most important. Considering it wasn't the highest scoring game ever and it was so tight, it was a really important save and kept us in the game. I suppose a lot of it comes down to mentality and Joe Murphy just had it in our heads that we were as good, if not better than anybody we came up against. Joe is an avid Éire Óg man but whenever we played them there were no such thing as divided loyalties; he was an Old Leighlin man when he was with us and that was that, it didn't matter who we were playing. I've played under a lot of managers between club and county, but Joe Murphy was the best I ever worked under. During that time, I'd say we were nearly a little bit arrogant as well; not in a bad way, but we just felt that we wouldn't be beaten and if we were beaten, whoever did beat us would know they were in a game.

We won the replay by 2-7 to 1-6 a week later, so we made the most of our second chance. We beat Tinryland in the final by a point which ensured back-to-back titles. I was lucky enough to win an O'Byrne Cup medal playing for Carlow and while that was great, it is hard to beat winning with your club. It's the bread and butter of the GAA. I only joined Old Leighlin in 2004 from St Patrick's, Tullow, and from day one they've always made me feel at home. I ended up getting Player of the Year in the club that season and despite playing really well all through the year, I suppose the penalty save is probably what most people will remember.

After we beat Tinryland in the final, unfortunately we ran into a very strong and very young Athy side up in Newbridge in the Leinster Championship and we were well beaten. That was especially disappointing as the previous year we had put it up to Rhode in Dr Cullen Park and only lost by four points, so to get back to that stage and to just not perform, that was very disappointing.

That was the end of the Joe Murphy era then. I think it is safe to say it was a resounding success, reaching three finals in-a-row and winning two of them. I suppose no matter who came in after Joe, they were going to be under pressure and as it happens that's exactly how it turned out. In fairness to Des Brennan, he was a good trainer and he did things his way but the same hunger was never going to be there when a new manager comes in like that and you're starting from scratch all over again with players and managers getting to know each other. I think most of the lads will tell you that the same hunger just wasn't there for a variety of reasons.

It's funny the way things work out because in 2012 we just didn't have the fire in the bellies, but the year of not being involved in the business end of the championship was probably the thing that did get the fire back, because going into 2013 there was definitely a bit of hunger with lads. Karl O'Dwyer was in charge that year and he just went back to basics really, nothing spectacular. As you can imagine, as a son of Mick O'Dwyer, he wasn't going to be coming up with any major new innovative drills or anything, but what he did he did well. Karl was just pure genuine and lads could relate to him easy. Straightaway, lads were mad eager to impress him and we went on to win the championship again that year.

As I mentioned earlier, playing with Carlow we had a good success in 2002 when we won the O'Byrne Cup. I was actually very lucky to be picked for the final because the way Pat Roe had worked it that year was, he would alternate goalkeepers for the early games; between me and the other goalkeeper Paudge McGrath. We had both played in the group stage, Paudge played in the semi-final and I played in the final. It was just the way it worked out but I was delighted to play of course and to be winning it when I was so young and only really starting out on my county career made it a little bit more special. Pat Roe was a fantastic trainer and there was no second best with Pat, everything you did in training was done fast. Pat wasn't a fella you'd be talking back to and if he saw you not putting in the effort, he'd have no problem calling you out.

I played with Carlow all the way through to 2011, when I called it a day. Luke Dempsey was in charge then; his second spell over us as he had been temporarily in charge for a while in 2004, but he eventually came back for his second coming. Both times when Luke came in, he was a breath of fresh air. He was just so positive and he had a bit of success behind him with Westmeath too so lads listened to him. He was very different to a lot of other managers that had been before him in Carlow. He was very softly spoken but he was a good trainer and like I said, he was just so positive and it was easy to feed off that energy.

When Liam Hayes came after Luke, after 2004, he brought a fiercely professional approach. I remember before the launch of the Leinster Championship, all the managers had a photo shoot and a little press conference and Liam decided to come out with a statement that we were going to win the Leinster Championship! That's just the way Liam was though, he didn't beat around the bush and was straight to the point.

Paul Bealin was another man who came in with a very professional approach. Paul had been there and done that with Dublin so he wasn't coming down to Carlow just for a laugh. When he came in, one of the things he did was get us all new black training gear as he wanted us to train like the All Blacks. Even the hotels we stayed in under Paul were all top class. Maybe, in a way, Paul was a little ahead of his time when he came to Carlow but it was very enjoyable to be part of a set up where nothing is left to chance. Paul only stayed in Carlow for a year before he stepped aside. After Paul left, we were all a little surprised when Luke Dempsey arrived back for his second spell in 2009 but he would end up staying four years with us then.

I had decided in 2010 that it would be my last year playing with Carlow and had my mind made up. However, over the winter going into the next season, the text went out about starting up training again and straightaway, I had itchy feet. I said I'd give it one more go. I didn't want to retire knowing that I should have gone on for another year, so I went back in and I gave it absolutely everything I had. I was watching the diet and really going the extra mile so that when I did finish up, I could have no complaints. The goalkeeping position was between myself and Trevor O'Reilly and even though we were both going for the one position, there was never any rivalry. Trevor helped me out with my game and I'm sure I did the same for him too. I got a few games that year but for the majority of games in the league, Trevor was starting and he started the championship games as well. We beat Louth before being defeated by Wexford in the Leinster semi-final in Croke Park. The qualifier draw brought us up to Casement Park to play Antrim. We lost by a point up in Belfast and I knew that was the end for me then. I went back in the dressing-room and I had my head in my hands… and I think I could have even been crying! I gave it everything and I was still delighted to go back for that last year and to put the shoulder to the wheel for one last push… and I went out on my own terms.

In fairness to Luke, he stood up on the bus on the way home from Belfast and made an announcement to everyone that I was retiring and I got a round of applause. We stopped for a meal on the way back as well and again, he said a few words about me which was really nice. I suppose Luke knew how much it meant to me, so he wanted to make a bit of a fuss.

I suppose at that stage all county set ups were nearly professional and it was totally different to when I first came in. If a manager came in and it wasn't up to standard then very quickly the players would notice the drop off in standards. So, in fairness to the likes of Liam and Paul, they both wanted to do things the right way. Paul was the first man who got in the kit van which would go to all the Carlow games with all the gear in the back and with the name on the side of it. It might sound simple now, but these were all new things at the time. It was actually my father Johnny who was our kit man, so it was his responsibility to be driving the new van and making sure all our stuff was where it was supposed to be on any given day. I got so much enjoyment out of playing county football. Obviously that O'Byrne Cup was the highlight but getting to travel all over the country to play for your county and the amount of people you meet through it, it was a great time… I loved it.

As much as I love Old Leighlin and the huge part the club has played in my life, I started my career playing in Tullow where I grew up and it was a very tough decision to transfer to Old Leighlin. At the time my wife and I had built our home in Old Leighlin and we moved in there in 2002. Going back and forth to Tullow for training a couple of nights a week wasn't easy. My home was in Old Leighlin now. So, in 2004 I decided to bite the bullet and transfer. Thankfully, it all worked out, but I will always have a place in my heart for Tullow.

I played in goal all my life for club and county but people have often reminded me over the years that one of my most famous moments in a jersey actually came when playing outfield. In 2006 Carlow played Wicklow in Dr Cullen Park in the Tommy Murphy Cup. Carlow were long gone out of the championship at this stage so when the Tommy Murphy came around a few lads didn't come back in to play and there were a lot of injuries too, so the panel was very short on numbers. I actually wasn't even on the panel for the championship that year as John Brennan and Gerry McGuill were the two goalkeepers there, but I got asked to go in for this game and of course I accepted. Paul Cashin and I were the only two subs on the night. One of the lads got injured midway through and so Paul went in. A short time later someone else got injured and I remember Liam Hayes looking over at me… 'James you're going on!' I was a little bit worried I have to say but in I went at full-forward anyway. I wasn't long in when Brian Murphy sent in a crossfield ball and I could sense the 'keeper coming behind me so I just got a little touch and it ended up in the net. I couldn't believe it. I didn't even know how to celebrate or anything. About a minute later I received another ball and I stuck it over the bar… 1-1 straightaway and I remember thinking, *Jesus this is easy!* The confidence was sky high then and I thought I could do anything. I got on the end of another ball and I remember thinking, *I'm going to take this on the left foot now, it'll look great.* I'd say I nearly kicked the ball behind me it was so bad! That wasn't long knocking the confidence out of me! We won anyway and I was delighted to have played such a vital part in the win, albeit in different circumstances than what I'd normally have been used to.

After the game I went back to a local pub as a friend of mine was having a birthday party there. A few of them were talking about the match and someone said that an Old Leighlin player had scored 1-1... and could they guess who? They were all naming everybody who they thought it could have been and even lads who weren't even on the panel, but of course my name wasn't mentioned. They couldn't believe it when they were told it was their goalkeeper. It will be a good quiz question in Old Leighlin in the years to come!

# JAMES HICKEY

**MOUNT LEINSTER RANGERS 1-13**
**MIDDLETOWN NA FIANNA 1-11**
**ALL-Ireland IHC CLUB FINAL**
**Croke Park**
**FEBRUARY 11, 2012**

*James Hickey celebrates at the final whistle after Mount Leinster Rangers had defeated Loughgiel Shamrocks in the All-Ireland Club senior semi-final in 2014.*

★ **MLR:** F Foley; G Kelly, B Nolan, K Lawlor; **J Hickey**, R Coady, E Coady; P Nolan, D Byrne; J Coady, D Phelan (0-1), E Byrne (0-1); HP O'Byrne, D Murphy (0-10), E Doyle (1-1). Subs: W Hickey for O'Byrne, P Coady for Murphy.

★ **MIDDLETOWN NA FIANNA:** P Moan; B Mallon, P Gaffney, F Woods; P Hughes, N Curry, B McCann; P McBride (0-1), K McKernan; M Maguire (1-3), C McCann, D Carvill (0-5); C Carvill, R Gaffney, M Moan (0-2) Subs: P McArdle for Hughes, N McCann for D Carvill, S Gaffney for C McCann.

# THE ACTION

CARLOW'S MOUNT LEINSTER Rangers are the All-Ireland intermediate club hurling champions and in doing so are the first team from the county to win an All-Ireland club title. They did so against the odds too, overcoming the loss of red-carded full-back Brian Nolan after 28 minutes to edge out a brilliant Middletown Na Fianna in a high quality final.

Middletown made the early running and were 1-3 to 0-1 ahead after 13 minutes courtesy of a superb Martin Maguire goal. Rangers corner-forward Eoin Doyle managed to nullify that goal, however, with one of his own in the 14th minute, getting in behind a defence that for once was caught napping.

Middletown recovered from that body blow and stormed five points clear again by the 30th minute (1-8 to 1-3) and with Rangers now down to 14 men, it was looking grim for the Carlow men. Five points in-a-row from Denis Murphy – two before the break and three after – and it was definitely game on. From there to the end it was tit for tat, with Rangers using the giant presence of Eddie Byrne to great effect on the edge of the square.

Time and again he drew fouls, each of which were punished by the unerring Murphy. Triumph in the end, by two points, and just about deserved, but kudos to Middletown for their contribution to a fine game. This win was the first time a Carlow club, either football or hurling has won an All-Ireland club title and as a result of this, the Carlow hurling champions from now on will represent their county in the provincial Senior Championship so definitely another massive blow struck for Carlow hurling.

★★★★★

66

FOR ME, THE game of my life was that All-Ireland intermediate club final in 2012. That season had obviously started in 2011, winning the county championship and then going on to the Leinster, and finally culminating in that showdown in Croke Park in 2012. Carlow clubs had been competing at intermediate club level in Leinster since 2008, when things were reshuffled, and in order to start competing at senior level again, a club had to win the All-Ireland intermediate first.

Without that win, there would have been no St Patrick's Day two years later against Portumna in the senior final, and there'd be no Leinster senior club medals in the parish. I think in fairness, it pushed on the other clubs in Carlow too and St Mullins making the Leinster senior final in 2019 was proof of that, and I think all of that came from winning that intermediate All-Ireland.

The Senior Championship in Carlow that decade was shared out between Mount Leinster Rangers and St Mullins. So who's to say if we didn't win the All-Ireland that year that we, or any other club in Carlow, would have been back there again – there's no guarantee and once you get there, you get one chance so you have to make it count. That final though, for us was part of a journey. We had lost the county final in 2010, but we came back and did the three in-a-row after. We won that intermediate All-Ireland in 2012 and then, only two years later, we were back in Croke Park again, this time in the senior final which would have been unthinkable a few years previous. Nobody could have predicted that in their wildest dreams.

That intermediate win, looking back now, was huge. The All-Ireland junior final was on before us, Charleville from Cork were taking on Kilkenny's Ballyraggett and here we were, as part of that double bill. I remember doing an interview before the game and saying that we were going to the Colosseum, because that's what it was, Croke Park was where the gladiators went to play. We had a tough road to even get to Croke Park though. We played Kilkenny champions Danesfort in the Leinster semi-final. They had the likes of Richie Hogan, Paddy Hogan and Paul Murphy, so they were strong, but we went into Nowlan Park and we beat them. We beat Celbridge in the final then and, before we knew it, we were in an All-Ireland semi-final against Robert Emmets from

England. That game was played up in Parnell Park and we were lucky to come out with a win. In the other semi-final, Limerick champions Effin were not only favourites to win their game but to win the competition outright, but there was a major shock when they were overturned by Middletown Na Fianna and, all of a sudden, it was going to a Carlow and Armagh All-Ireland hurling final.

Our manager at the time was Tom Mullally. He was over us for nine seasons overall, and when he came in, he took us to a place, both mentally and physically, but probably more mentally. When Tommy came in, he changed that mindset. I think if anybody else other than Tommy had of been over us that night I don't think we would have won. To be fair to him, he was very casual towards it, not the final as such but in general. For example, I was never a bus man. I'd prefer to go in the car. Of course, I often went on the bus, but on a short journey to Dublin sometimes I just preferred my own space. Garry Doyle was the same and we went to Tommy and explained the situation and in fairness to him, he said to work away and that we would all meet up together when in Dublin in the Green Isle hotel.

Once we met at the hotel, we got on the bus for the short journey into Croke Park and I will never forget that feeling. Coming in on the bus and seeing Croke Park that night. It was February, a real winter's evening, and it was getting dark. It was a great feeling just knowing where we were going and what we were attempting to do. There was a light moment when we were coming around the corner and there was a hearse outside Croke Park. It had a black and white stripe on it. Even better, there was a coffin inside in it and it had a black and red jersey on it… our own colours. The Armagh boys had obviously done it but it lightened the mood a little.

Once the early nerves had settled, we got the game back to maybe three points at half-time and even though we lost our full-back Brian Nolan just before half-time to a red card, we still felt we hadn't really hurled yet. That second-half display was probably one of the best halves of hurling we ever put together. With 14 men against 15 for the second-half, we were going to be up against it but we definitely stood up. Every man did. I remember Eddie Byrne having a stormer that night. Karol Lawlor… Eoin Doyle, who got that massive goal for us just before half time. David Phelan, Padraig Nolan too, all these lads stood up.

Over the years, I've often been asked about my half-time speech in Croke Park that night. I suppose that was kind of blown out of proportion really. I do remember sitting in the dressing-room at half time. There was a television up on the wall and the score was up on the screen. I looked around the dressing-room and there were lads with towels over their heads and it just felt a little flat. I wouldn't say there were harsh words really but we had great leaders in that dressing-room. Lads like Frank Foley, who I hurled with all my life. Eddie Coady, John Coady, my brother Willie. Garry Doyle, who was injured that night but he was still there, Padraig Nolan, David Phelan… they were all leaders. We had so many big men who on any given day would take control of the dressing-room but, for whatever reason that night, it was a little flat.

Look I suppose, I might have hit the table. It might have broken in half!

If we lost, then nobody would remember it. Tommy always painted a great picture for us, though. I remember him saying that night at half-time to us, 'There are people out there now, and they're gone to get their cup of tea and sandwich and they probably think this game is gone but they don't know what's in this dressing-room. They've come up here to see us, and no matter what, we need to put on a big performance for the second 30 minutes'. Basically he told us to leave it all out there. I know that can be a bit of a cliché, but when Tommy Mullally said something, he meant it. Tommy spent nine seasons with us and he always had us tuned in. He always gave us an Everest.

In 2006, we won our first ever Senior Championship title. In the dressing-room after, obviously we are all jumping around but Tommy comes in, serious as you like. He tells us all to sit down and so we do. He pulls a jersey out of the bag and he holds it up. 'The next time you pull on that jersey, you are not representing your club anymore, you are representing Carlow, don't forget that. Don't let yourselves down tonight or between now and the next game.' In the midst of all our celebrating, it just made us all think for a minute but at the same time he was dead right. We never knew if we were going to win the championship again so we had to appreciate it and represent our club and county as best we could. A few years later, when we beat Celbridge to win the Leinster intermediate, he held up a jersey again. 'A few years ago, I told you all you were not representing your club anymore, you were representing Carlow. Well, the next time you put on this jersey again, you are not just representing Carlow… you are representing

Leinster.' Simple stuff yes, but again he was right and it just should showed the progress we were making. After we won the All-Ireland, and I'll never forget it. He held up the jersey again and asked us all, 'Was this it? Was this going to be the end of the road? Do we give ourselves something new to chase?' But like I said, he was always giving us an Everest. It was little things like that.

That night in Croke Park was supposed to be my last night on a field of play. A few months earlier, back in late 2011, after we had won the county final against Naomh Eoin, I said that was it. That was my last time to play in the county championship. I would keep playing until we were beaten but as soon as Rangers got knocked out of the club championship, I was giving it up. At that stage the injuries were just getting too much.

Going back to 2010, I dislocated my shoulder against St Mullins in the championship. The most pain I have ever been in, it was unbelievable. Christy Kealy brought me up to St Luke's in Kilkenny and the doctors told me to do nothing for three weeks and straightaway in my head I was thinking, *Right, the semi-final is in four weeks so yeah, I can be back for that.* The shoulder was put in anyway a few days later and the pain was cruel. At that stage I went to see renowned physio Anthony 'Star' Geoghegan. He told me that if I wanted to play in the semi-final that he'd get me right. I went to the Éire Óg gym in Carlow town every morning before work and worked on getting the shoulder right. I was using the gym for a month and they never once charged me, so I was grateful for that. Anyway, get it right he did and I played in the semi-final against Naomh Eoin. About two minutes left in the game, myself and Damien Roberts collided out near the sideline. It was pure accidental. Whatever way we collided, I snapped my medial ligament. The final was the following week and after coming back from the shoulder and then for the ligaments to go after that, it was another body blow. The week of the final anyway I got an injection. The morning of the final itself, I got four injections but when I was sitting into the car to go to Carlow the leg started shaking and I knew something didn't feel right. I got to Carlow eventually and I played the match and they might as well have played with 14 for all the help I was that day. We lost our county title that day too, so it was a bad day all round.

By the time the following year came around, I said to myself that if the body was good, I'd give it one final rattle in 2011 and if we win it that year, then I'll finish up.

Luckily we won back the county championship and I said once we're beaten after this… I'm gone. A few weeks later, we won the Leinster Intermediate and then in the New Year we won the All-Ireland and I called it quits there and then.

The club won the county championship again in 2012 and were beaten in Leinster by the Offaly champions Kilcormac Killoughey, and I sat out the whole year in football and hurling. I started to get the itch again though and coming into 2013 the body felt good so I said I'd give it another go. We won the county championship again that year and completed the three in-a-row.

We played the Westmeath champions Castletown Geoghegan in the first round of the Leinster Senior Championship in what was a tough game up there in Mullingar. I've heard people since talking about that run and saying that we beat Ballyboden, Oulart the Ballagh, Loughgiel Shamrocks but people never mention that we played Castletown Geoghegan first and it's probably a little bit disrespectful to the Westmeath champions as games between Carlow and Westmeath were always tough. It's dog eat dog stuff and that game was probably our toughest game that year.

We made the All-Ireland senior final anyway and I felt good, the body felt as good as ever. We played Offaly in a challenge game one night out in Fenagh and I did my cruciate ligament that night. Two weeks before the All-Ireland senior final and another massive body blow. I togged out that day in Croke Park though but was in no fit state to come on. That was the last time I togged out in a game. Two retirements, and both in Croke Park!

Looking back, we won the intermediate championship with the club in 1996 and we went senior the following year. The team was mostly full of young lads with the few older fellas still there too. My two brothers Andrew and Willie and I all played Senior Championship hurling with my father Pat in the early days of the club. There were days in the Carlow hurling championship where we were getting bet by 30 points on a regular basis. We couldn't even get challenge games. Despite some tough days at the beginning, there were great people in the club who kept it going during those lean times. People like Eddie Byrne, Mags Byrne, Kieran Lucas, Pat Gallahue, Patsy Nolan and my own father Pat. People like that who still gave of their time despite the results.

Fast forward a few years and by the time I retired we had played the Waterford senior hurling team in two challenge games. We played them in Waterford one night and it was 5-17 to 0-23. We played Offaly another night, Kilkenny under-21s and Kilkenny intermediates. So these were the type of challenge games we were getting by the end. We were playing county teams regularly for our challenge games. The thought of that happening 20 years previously would have been unheard of. I suppose a lot of it comes down to mindset too. Tommy was a great man for instilling that belief into us. When we beat Ballyboden in the Leinster semi-final in 2013, they had seven of the Dublin team which had won Leinster earlier that summer and had pushed Cork all the way in the All-Ireland semi-final. We respected them, of course, but we never feared them, but that's just the belief we had.

Going into the Leinster senior final then a few weeks later, we were given a great boost when we found out that it was to be played in Nowlan Park. Mount Leinster Rangers were never beaten in Nowlan Park. We won five Kilkenny league titles there. We beat Danesfort there in the intermediate semi-final and it was definitely worth a couple of points to us when we found out the venue, there's no doubt about that.

After we beat Oulart The Ballagh in the Leinster final, it was hard to believe that all of a sudden we were Leinster senior champions. It was just crazy. Next thing we're in an All-Ireland senior semi final and playing Loughgiel Shamrocks, the champions of two years previous. We went up to Newry to play them and that was a serious Loughgiel team. In fairness to them they didn't underestimate us. They came with full force and we came with full force, and we came out the right side of a tight and very tough game. We were unlucky in the final in that we ran into Portumna, who were probably one of the best club teams of all time but we gave as good as we got and were still only beaten by a few points in the end.

# ALAN CORCORAN

**CARLOW 1-14 ★ WESTMEATH 0-12**
**National Hurling League Division 2 Final**
**Nowlan Park, Kilkenny**
**APRIL 15, 2012**

*Playing against the biggest and the best on the hurling stage, Alan Corcoran always believed that Carlow could compete and fight for victory.*

★ **CARLOW:** F Foley; **A Corcoran**, E Nolan, D Shaw; J Corcoran, S Kavanagh (0-3), E Coady; J Kavanagh (0-1), R Coady; E Byrne, J Kane, A Gaule (0-2); P. Kehoe (0-3), C Doyle (0-2), M Kavanagh (0-2). Subs: D Roberts (0-1) for Kane, J Rogers for R Coady, M Brennan for M Kavanagh, R Smithers for Gaule, M Clowry (1-0) for Rogers.

★ **WESTMEATH:** S McGovern; C Jordan, A Price, P Fennell; P Gilsenan, J Gilligan, P Dowdall; A Clarke, J Clarke; P Greville, B Murtagh (0-5), D McCormack (0-2); N O'Brien (0-5), J Shaw, D Carty. Subs: R Greville for Shaw, A Mitchell for Gilsenan, D Fennell for Carty, A McGrath for Dowdall.

# THE ACTION

IT WAS FAR from a vintage performance from the Carlow hurlers but they did what they had to do against a lacklustre Westmeath side. This was far from a classic game but in finals it's all about getting the win and Carlow and Westmeath were both desperate to win this title and get up to Division One. However, only one side can go up and it must be said that Carlow were probably the better side on the day overall.

Westmeath were well in it for most of the game though, but the double sending off of Paul Greville (56 minutes) and John Gilligan (64 minutes) certainly hampered their chances. The turning point and the winning of the game was Martin Clowry's late goal. Darren McCormack opened the scoring for Westmeath but the early shooting was very poor. By the 15th minute, eight wides had been shared between both sides. It took Carlow 18 minutes to open their account and that was a fine score from long distance from Jack Kavanagh. Murtagh and McCormack pointed for Westmeath, while Marty and Shane Kavanagh both kept the Carlow scoreboard ticking over. Niall O'Brien and Craig Doyle traded points before Carlow retired at the half-time whistle with a 0-6 to 0-4 lead. Niall O' Brien was switched onto the frees for Westmeath for the second-half and he was accurate as he knocked over a couple of early scores. Still though, it looked like if any team was going to make the breakthrough, it was going to be Carlow.

Andrew Gaule had a goal chance but was denied by a last-minute block, and Daryl Roberts had a chance of a shot but mishit his effort. Carlow started to pull ahead and points from Paudie Kehoe and Roberts gave them a 0-12 to 0-7 lead. With just two minutes remaining the vital score of the game arrived and it went Carlow's way. The Westmeath goalkeeper caught a ball under pressure but he lost possession to Carlow's Ross Smithers, and Smithers passed to his clubmate Clowry, who drove the ball to the back of the net.

★★★★★

66

THERE ARE A number of reasons why that game stands out in my head. Obviously, winning a National League title with your county and getting promoted up to Division One was a big standout moment. It had other significance for me, though.

A few weeks earlier we had beaten Kerry in the league, a game played down in Killarney. I didn't play great that day at all and I was taken off at half-time. Kevin Ryan was our manager at the time and in the dressing room after the game he turns around to me and says, 'It was the worst game I've seen you play in three years'. I doubt he meant it in a negative way as he was half laughing when he said it, but he was just being honest. At the same time, I knew myself he was right as it wasn't the best game I ever played in. I thought that was it then, that I'd be dropped from the team and would struggle to get back in again.

We still had another couple of league games to go after that Kerry game but by the time our last game came around, which was a trip to Aughrim to play Wicklow, we had already qualified for the final. I remember Kevin Ryan saying he was resting a few lads. I was on the bench but I didn't know if that was because I was being rested or if my performance from Killarney was still on Kevin's mind. We met Westmeath two weeks later in the final in Nowlan Park and the whole week leading up to it my stomach was in knots. I ended up starting the game which was a massive relief and a big vote of confidence in me.

The full-back line was myself, Eoin Nolan and Des Shaw. Des Shaw loved a good battle and he loved the full-back line. I can remember running out onto the field before the game and Des pipes up trying to get us psyched up, 'You'll go nowhere without the full-back line lads!' I actually ended up playing well enough on the day, so it was good to get the bad performance out of the system and out of my head as well.

I can remember we were under pressure at one stage and I managed to clear a ball from out under the stand, while at the same time trying not to fall on my arse. Another reason, and probably the biggest one, was that my younger brother John was also playing that day. I was playing right corner-back and he was right half-back, so we were even on the same side of the pitch throughout. John played really well so it was nice to share such an important day for Carlow hurling with your brother on the field. That game was also probably one of the last big games of hurling that John played. A while after that he started to have a little trouble with his breathing and was advised to take a break from sport. He was only young at the time and I've no doubt he would have gone on to become a serious hurler. He tried to go back with the club a few years ago but I don't think he was that much in to it at that time. Thankfully, he's fine now and he has his own family and he's healthy but it was a worry at the time.

The youngest brother David also played for Carlow, but his introduction to senior county hurling was a little different than the usual path you might take. I'm not entirely sure who we played, but it was a challenge match and it was up in Dublin. We were really short this night anyway as we had an awful amount of injuries. David went up to watch the game as he'd go to most of the Carlow games anyway. John Meyler was training us at the time and as the match was going on, John enquired who the fella was watching the game? The lads explained that he was my brother and that he hurled for the club. They got him a bit of gear anyway and he went in and played the challenge match and John kept him on the panel for the rest of the season!

Going up to Division One for 2013 was a massive deal for such a small county. We played some top teams and were unfortunate that a few things went against us. We ran Wexford close. Against Offaly we were leading for long spells, but were caught with a last-minute goal. We played Limerick down in the Gaelic grounds and we ran them to three points. I can remember John Meyler skipping up the line at one stage, he thought we had them. We were so close. A few months later that Limerick team won the Munster Championship for the first time since 1996, so that would have been a massive scalp for us had we gotten over the line.

We had a good few injuries that year and between that and losing a couple of close games it was a tough year. A small break here or there could have been the difference between staying up. We ended up in a relegation play-off against Antrim in the end for the right to stay in Division One but we were beaten by a point. Getting relegated was a huge disappointment after such a big push to get up there but once it was over we still had a championship to prepare for. We beat London well before we were knocked out of the Leinster Championship by Laois. We were drawn to play Wexford in Wexford Park for the second year in-a-row in the qualifiers and it was probably one of the best performances we ever put together. Wexford were huge favourites to not only beat us, but beat us well. We played a fantastic game and were leading Wexford for large periods, including going in at half-time with a four-point lead. We were still going well in the second-half when James Doyle had a great goal chance but it went narrowly wide. From the next attack Wexford got a goal and we ended up losing by two points in the end, 2-16 to 0-20. It was a massive swing in just a couple of minutes.

We had some great days out playing for Carlow around that time though. Going back to 2010 we played Wexford in Dr Cullen Park in the National League and we beat them. The following week we played Clare, again in Dr Cullen Park and we lost to them by a single point. We were so close to winning that game but those two performances definitely made people sit up and take notice. A lot of that Clare team only three years later would be celebrating an All-Ireland win. After our spell in Division One and subsequent relegation, we had a few barren years, I suppose you could say. We got back to the Division Two final again in 2014, '16 and '17 but lost them all. Colm Bonnar came in ahead of the 2017 season and little did we know what lay ahead of us. We lost the league final to Antrim, but made it to the Christy Ring final in Croke Park later that summer, also against Antrim. We beat them comprehensively with James Doyle scoring four goals. James is a serious hurler and his pace is just frightening, and he definitely showed everyone that day what he could do.

In 2018 we won the league final against Westmeath to go back up to Division One and a few weeks later we were back in Croke Park for the second year running for the Joe McDonagh Cup final where once again we beat Westmeath. We played four finals under Colm, winning three and getting to win two championships in Croke Park… it was unreal. The team moral was excellent. After we won the Joe McDonagh in 2018, we got to play an All-Ireland preliminary qualifier. It was against Limerick in Dr Cullen Park and it was only six days after we beat Westmeath in the final. I missed that game as the day after the McDonagh final I headed to America for a holiday. I had been planning it for ages and so I had told management well in advance. I landed in San Francisco for my trip and worked my way down the coast. By the following week, when the Limerick game was on, I was in Universal Studios. I was in a queue to go on one of the rides while listening to the game at the same time. The heat that day was just unbelievable and two women beside me actually collapsed at one stage. I was disappointed to miss that Limerick game and listening to it, there was a part of me that wanted to be back home and playing. At the same time though, the trip had been planned for ages and if I didn't go at that stage then I don't know if it would have ever happened. Limerick went on to win the All-Ireland that year so Carlow got to see first-hand that day just how good they were.

I can remember my first training session with Carlow. Before training all the lads were just pucking the ball across the field to one another and it was James Hickey who pulled me aside and gave me a few words. Other older lads then like Frank Foley, Edward Coady, Robbie Foley, Damien Roberts, Andrew Gaule… they were all very helpful in getting me settled in and it made it that bit easier to feel part of the group. I suppose I was in awe a little going in. I had been in Tullamore when they won the Christy Ring Cup in 2008 and I remember listening to Eddie Coady's great speech. I was there in Croke Park again the following year when they won it again, so to be in training with them same lads was a big thing but, like I said, all the lads were a great help in getting me settled.

I'll always be grateful to Kevin Ryan for giving me my chance and bringing me into the panel. It was great to play under John Meyler then after, such a passionate hurling man. Pat English, such a great Carlow man… he has done great work for both his club and county. It was during Pat's tenure that he made me joint captain alongside Seamus Murphy. That was a big honour and one I was grateful to Pat for. Playing under Colm Bonnar and his management team then was probably the most enjoyable years I had playing for Carlow.

It is hard to forget the day Galway came to Dr Cullen Park in 2019 for a league game and we drew with them, 0-20 each, Martin Kavanagh showing serious nerves with a free in the last minute to draw the game. Martin is still only young now but to step up against a team who were only All-Ireland champions two years before, and nail that free was something else. He was under serious pressure. I remember being on Davy Glennon at the start of the game and obviously you'd expect the pace to be a bit higher, but it was like nothing I'd ever played against. They left a bit of space in front of our full-back line and their forwards were just so fast. I just remember thinking to myself, *This is going to be a long day*. The longer the game went on though we got up to the pace of it and we just kept matching them point for point, and eventually to come away with a draw was just unbelievable.

The same year we played Offaly in the last league game in Carlow. It was absolutely freezing and there was even snow at one stage. It was a hard day to play hurling. They beat us but the following week we played them again, this time in Tullamore in the relegation play-off. At half-time we were eleven points down and a man down as well. It was strange in that there was no panic in the dressing-room. I don't think anybody expected what happened in the second-half, but we came out and turned around that massive deficit to actually come back and win the game and subsequently relegate Offaly.

It was a massive turnaround and a massive victory. That day, as well as the Galway game, showed what we could do up in Division One and how we weren't out of place at all. Those days will always stand out in my memory. It's nice to be able to say that you played against some of the best players and teams around and competed with them… and even beat them on certain days.

# DENIS MURPHY

**MOUNT LEINSTER RANGERS 0-11**
**OULART THE BALLAGH 0-8**
Leinster Club SHC Final
Nowlan Park, Kilkenny
DECEMBER 1, 2013

*Denis Murphy (left) and Richard Coady celebrate after their historic victory over Ballyboden St Enda's, which sent Mount Leinster Rangers into the Leinster senior club final.*

★ **MLR:** F Foley; M Doyle, G Doyle, G Kelly; Diarmuid Byrne (0-1), R Coady, E Coady; Derek Byrne (0-1), P Nolan; D Phelan, P Coady (0-1), E Byrne; E Doyle, J Coady, **D Murphy (0-8)**. Subs: HP O'Byrne for J Coady, J Hickey for E Doyle, W Hickey for P Coady.

★ **OULART:** B O'Connor; E Moore (0-1), K Rossiter, B Kehoe; C Goff, P Roche, L Prendergast; M Jacob, S Murphy; D Nolan (0-1), D Redmond (0-1), D Mythen (0-2); C O'Leary (0-1), G Sinnott, R Jacob (0-2). Subs: N Kirwan for O'Leary, D Stamp for Murphy.

## THE ACTION

MOUNT LEINSTER RANGERS, champions of Carlow, are now the champions of Leinster. Oulart The Ballagh, on the other hand, incredibly, lost their fourth Leinster final in-a-row which only added to the drama in Nowlan Park. The Wexford side had 11 wides on the day with another six balls dropping into the hands of the grateful Frank Foley in the Rangers goal.

It was far from a vintage display from the Carlow champions in the first-half either. They didn't score from play in the opening half and had only 0-3 on the board. Despite this, they still only trailed by two points at the interval. Rangers only scored four points from play in the entire game, but from the thirtieth minute, Oulart didn't score for another 20 minutes and were now really starting to feel the heat. Oulart got the opening point of the second-half to open up a three point lead. Instead of driving them on, it actually seemed to do the opposite as Rangers took over and outscored their fancied opponents by 0-8 to 0-2 from there until the end.

Corner-forward Denis Murphy hit four unanswered points in 10 minutes which edged his side in front. Paul Coady and Rory Jacob traded points, before Diarmuid Byrne scored a fantastic lineball with just over five minutes remaining which was greeted by rapturous applause from the Carlow followers. Denis Murphy completed the scoring on 55 minutes to give Rangers a three point lead. From there on in, Rangers fought for every ball all over the field like their lives depended on it.

★★★★★

66

THE REASON I picked this game over anything else for club or county is probably due to the stature of the competition. It's probably the biggest win I've been involved in anyway. People have always kind of looked down on us in Carlow hurling. It could be someone with zero interest in the sport or GAA in general, but because they're from Kilkenny or Wexford, or wherever, they might look down or talk down about Carlow, despite knowing nothing about us. So to actually win the Leinster Senior Club Championship was huge for the club, and Carlow. This was not a 'B' championship or an Intermediate Championship.

This was the Leinster senior hurling title, the top championship in Leinster... and now a team from Carlow had won it. Coming into the final itself, we had just come off the back of a three in-a-row in Carlow. In the Leinster Championship we travelled up to Mullingar in the first game and we beat the Westmeath champions Castletown Geoghegan. We played very poorly that day and were very lucky to get out of Westmeath with a win. Next up were the Dublin champions Ballyboden St Enda's. Their side was stacked with players who had just won Leinster with Dublin earlier that summer and had rattled Cork in the All Ireland semi-final. They were hugely fancied to beat us easily but that day in Dr Cullen Park, we played arguably one of our best ever games. We only won by two points in the end, 1-17 to 3-9, but we did most of the hurling that day. Despite playing so well though, it still took a save near the end from our keeper Frank Foley to deny Ballyboden a match winning goal. It was a one-on-one but Frank pulled off a great save, and only for that we were out.

The biggest thing coming into that Leinster final against Oulart The Ballagh was, and it could have totally thrown us, was that the night before the game there was a car crash involving a few of the players. Richard Kelly and Conor Hayes were both involved in the accident along with a friend of Richard's who had come up from Clare. Word started to come through that night then that the lads had been in a car crash. It was very worrying but as soon as I found out that they were okay then I kind of tried to switch off from it. That might sound a bit selfish but at those moments you always assume the worst, and of course it was serious, but once I found out they were still alive and the lads would recover, then I was just focusing on the game. It was only later on that I found out more details about the accident. I'm fairly sure that a lot of the players knew a lot more details than me but at the time I kind of blanked it out until after the game. I was ignorant to the situation I suppose in a way, but no matter how much some players did or didn't know, it was definitely on lads minds coming into it. Richard Kelly was part of the panel and was almost certain to play some part on the day of the Leinster final and I know it still breaks his heart to this day that he missed out on that win.

Going into the final against the Wexford champions Oulart The Ballagh, they were massive favourites to beat us but we gave ourselves a big chance going in that day. Looking back on it now, I think that pressure got to them. They had so many missed opportunities in the first-half. They had a good few wides, while they dropped plenty of balls short into Frank Foley's hands too. It was just pure nerves on their part. Not that we were great in that first-half either mind. We were very cagey.

We didn't score from play in the opening period and the half-time score was 0-5 to 0-3 to Oulart. I scored three frees for us which was just keeping us in it. We were working hard though and a lot of the wides from Oulart was down to the pressure we were putting them under. The game was in Nowlan Park and we had played there a few times up to that point. We were in the dressing-rooms at the bottom goal, down at the O'Loughlin Gaels end of the ground; it was our first time using those rooms. It was probably the quietest I've ever seen our dressing-room. Massive game and only two points down, but it was eerily quiet. I don't know if lads were nervous, or if they were concentrating or what. It was hard to know where lads' heads were at.

Tommy Mullally, our manager, came in then and just tore into us which, of course, kind of woke us up. I remember when the second-half started Oulart got the first point to give them a 0-6 to 0-3 lead and everyone expected them to push on from there to win, but it was the opposite. That point from them actually kickstarted us instead and Oulart didn't score for the next 20 minutes. We went from 0-6 to 0-3 down to 0-8 to 0-6 up. During that time, as we were getting closer and eventually going ahead, I think everybody could feel Oulart were getting nervous and that definitely helped us. That Rangers team at that time was very hardened. We had come through so many tough games where we won by a point or two, so we knew how to win tight games. We knew how to grind it out.

The older fellas on the team, the likes of James Hickey, Garry Doyle, Frank

Foley, Willie Hickey, Edward Coady... they had all been around the block a few times, but even the younger lads on the team had come into the side during successful periods, so we all had some kind of experience of big games under our belts. A lot of lads say this now still, but that team probably wasn't our best hurling team ever... but the workrate was savage. It was probably the best team we ever had in the club for workrate. An example of this was Derek Byrne's point. James Hickey, who wasn't long on the field, was going for a 50/50 ball and he slid in on his knees to get the ball. He managed to gain possession, pick it up and offload it to Derek who in turn stuck it over the bar. It was pure determination to get to the ball and win it.

I remember before that also, Edward Coady catching a high ball he had no right to catch and being fouled in the process, but it was instances like that, that showed the workrate in the team. I struck over the resulting free from Edward's foul and scored another about a minute later to put us ahead, and psychologically that was huge. Straightaway then, the tables are turned and then they're chasing you instead of the other way around. I think the longer that game went on the stronger we were getting. I think Oulart were afraid of losing more than wanting to win it.

The scenes at the final whistle were brilliant. Just the emotion and seeing everyone on the field after, it was great. You'd often see games like that, where one team might win a lot, and afterwards you might just see people walking around the pitch and not too excited. After we won, people were crying while doing interviews. When we got back to Borris, it was just jammed, wall to wall people everywhere. The celebrations definitely went on for the week. To be honest though, the celebrations almost kind of merge into one for me, in that they never stick out in my mind. What sticks out for me is the 20 minutes after the final whistle on the field meeting everyone. And when you get back to the dressing-room and it's just you and your teammates. It's talking to your family about what you have just achieved.

The following February we paired off in the All-Ireland semi-final against Loughgiel Shamrocks up in Newry. The Antrim side were All-Ireland champions only two years previous so to go up to Newry and beat them then backed up our Leinster final win. The Leinster semi-final against Ballyboden and the All-Ireland semi-final against Loughgiel were probably two of the best hurling performances we ever gave. The Leinster final in between, we were not great, but finals are different. Both sides were cagey, so it was never going to be a classic.

In hurling terms, the likes of Carlow, Laois and Westmeath would always be around a similar level. After we won the All-Ireland intermediate in 2012, we were probably thinking that if we got back to Leinster again, just to win a game against one of those champions would be a great achievement. There was never any talk of reaching Leinster finals or anything. The first mention of a Leinster final was after we beat Ballyboden, when we actually qualified for it. It was just game by game, but we ended up on a great journey. I actually had a bit of a hamstring injury going into the Leinster final but I wasn't going to miss it. Injuries weren't something new to me however. I've suffered three ACL tears in my career. Two had been before that Oulart game and I tore it again a few months after the All-Ireland senior final playing for Carlow against Laois.

After I tore the knee the third time, I had said then, that was that. I was going to finish it up there and then. Once I got the operation and started the recovery though, the competitiveness takes over and you want to go back again. The pain is just too bad now to carry on though. I feel that I can't play the way I want to, or need to anymore. I can't accelerate or decelerate the way I want too. I can't twist and turn the way I want too, or the way I used too. Recovering from an ACL tear, the amount of time you need to put in for the recovery is massive. After three times, it becomes too much. However, I have been lucky in a way with the time I was born and the teams that I came into. I've had a lot of success with both Mount Leinster Rangers and Carlow but each year is a struggle and right now, it feels the time is right to give it one last go and then quietly slip away.

# BRIAN KELLY

**PALATINE 3-9 ★ ÉIRE ÓG 2-9**
**Carlow SFC Semi-Final**
**Dr Cullen Park, Carlow**
**SEPTEMBER 27, 2015**

*In his long career with Carlow Brian Kelly only had an O'Byrne Cup title to his name, but giving over 20 years of service to Palatine he earned three precious senior championships.*

★ **PALATINE:** C Kearney; B Farrell, C Lawlor, D Kinsella; C Crowley, A Murphy, S Reilly; D Reid, J Kane; P Reid, C Moran (1-1), J Reid (1-1); J Kenny (1-1), L Gordon (0-2), T Kenny (0-1). Subs: S O'Neill (0-1) for Kane, **B Kelly (0-2)** for T Kenny, M Rennick for Gordon, N Reid for Farrell, J Byrne for O' Neill.

★ **ÉIRE ÓG:** R Keating; R Mahon, A Callinan, N Kenny; J Lowry (0-1), M Furey (0-1), B Kavanagh (1-0); S Gannon, M Ware (0-1); C Kelly, D Hayden, E Ruth (0-1); E McCormack (0-1), C Mullins (0-1), N Quinlan (0-2). Subs: M Fitzgerald for Mahon, D O'Brien for Kelly, C Blake (0-1) for Ware, K Chatten for Furey, S Rea (1-0) for McCormack, K Hession for Quinlan.

## THE ACTION

PALATINE QUALIFIED FOR their first county senior football final since 2012 with this victory over Éire Óg and in doing so, they have reversed the earlier championship defeat to the same side in the group stages of the competition. An early burst of 2-2 at the start of the second-half was the platform from where this game was really won.

Palatine goaled first in the game, when Ciarán Moran finished to the net. But Benny Kavanagh responded when he made great ground and finished past Craig Kearney in the Palatine goal. Éire Óg led 1-8 to 1-5 at half time. Palatine made wholesale changes with Brian Kelly, Mark Rennick and Niall Reid all entering the fray. The second-half had barely started when Jamie Kenny had the ball in the Éire Óg net, while Brian Kelly immediately got in the scoring act after his introduction and raised a white flag. Kelly's point put Palatine in the lead and they would hold on to that for the rest of the game.

John Reid sent a bullet past Ricky Keating in the Éire Óg goal, and Brian Kelly kicked another point and, in an astonishing seven-minute spell, Palatine had scored 2-2 without reply. Éire Óg had a lot of wides in the second-half and ultimately were left to rue those missed chances in the end. Palatine then went 10 minutes without scoring, before Ciarán Moran and then Jamie Kenny pointed. Éire Óg had to wait until the fiftieth minute to get their first score of the half through Chris Blake. Éire Óg were then thrown a lifeline when Cormac Mullins was fouled and the referee David Hickey blew for a penalty, which Simon Rea finished to the back of the net after his initial shot was saved. Éire Óg did try hard in those last few minutes but Palatine defended heroically to close out the game.

★★★★★

66

WHEN I THINK back to the 2015 season, it was very shaky at the start and only for small margins we mightn't have had a joyful ending. By that stage there were a few young lads coming onto the senior team while, at the same time, a lot of the older lads such as myself, Bryan Farrell, Joe Byrne, and John and Paul Reid were probably all coming towards the end. We had all been there when we lost the 1997 final so we had played a lot of football, but we still had enough in the legs to be competitive at least.

We had beaten Old Leighlin in the first group game and we were up against Éire Óg in our second game in Dr Cullen Park. They beat us by seven points, and I was livid after I received a straight red card for *nothing*. I was given a one game suspension, so I would miss our next game. With one win and one loss, we were due to play our last group game against Ballinabranna. The group winner went straight to the semi-final and the runner up went to the quarter-final, and obviously our preferred route was to go direct to the semi-final. In order for that to happen we had to beat Ballinabranna by at least 29 points, and to hope that Old Leighlin would beat Éire Óg.

Ballinabranna were out of contention by that stage after two losses so they were in the relegation play-off regardless of what happened against us. With time almost up, Darragh Moran got a goal for us which meant we won by exactly 30 points, 6-20 to 1-5. We waited for confirmation of the other group game between Old Leighlin and Éire Óg and when word came through that Old Leighlin had won, it was confirmation of our place in the semi-final. Éire Óg went to the quarter-final where they beat Kildavin/Clonegal – and when the semi-final draw was made we were pitted against Éire Óg once again.

We had a couple of weeks break before the semi-final and training went well. The day of the semi-final I kind of got the feeling something wasn't right. I felt management were kind of avoiding me. We would normally do our warm-ups in Carlow Rugby Club, which is just up from Dr Cullen Park. Once we got back to the dressing-rooms the starting team was named and I wasn't on it. I was massively disappointed. It wasn't easy to hide that. At that stage I was thinking that I was finished, and that the selectors had lost confidence in me. The team went into the dressing-room at half-time, and the subs stayed out. We were three points down and we weren't going well at all. I was just practising frees while not expecting anything else to happen. Next thing myself and Niall 'Angie' Reid get a call from one of the selectors. so we headed for the tunnel and headed straight to the dressing room. Even though I was playing senior for Palatine for nearly 20 years by that stage, I still remember getting the same butterflies in the stomach going down the tunnel that day knowing that I was coming into the game.

We might have been three points down against a very strong Éire Óg team, but I still felt we could claw it back. I said a few words and, for whatever reason, I ended up going out the door first and leading the team out. Angie Reid was behind me and I remember turning around to him and saying, 'Listen you long b****x, you get up in the skies and you win every ball here now… and kick it anywhere in my direction'. I might have been 37 by that stage but I still felt I had something to offer and could play a part in winning us this game. 'Catch it… Kick it…. Yeah, got it!" he replied

In fairness to Angie he was true to his word. He caught an amount of ball in that second-half and sent them all in my direction. Some of them mightn't have been great balls, but that didn't matter. The pressure was off our defence so that gave them a bit of a break and the more time the ball was up in our forward line then the better. It was a totally different game compared to the first-half. At one stage an Éire Óg defender was coming out with the ball and he was put under pressure from a couple of our forwards. Next thing he hand-passed the ball straight to me. I couldn't believe it… straight to my chest. It was just a sign of the intensity we brought to the second-half which had been missing from the opening 30 minutes.

The one thing that kept going through my head was the previous game against Éire Óg. I felt I had been hard done by that day and didn't deserve to be given a straight red card and subsequently serve a one game ban. It all kept coming back to that. I was going to do everything I could to help us get over the line and in my own head that was driving me on. We won the game by three points in the end to qualify for the county final. When I wasn't starting against Éire Óg that day I felt that was it for me… I was finished playing senior. If Éire Óg had beaten us that day I was going to be finishing up. I would have retired with one county medal. Was that a good enough return for the amount of finals we had been in? Probably not.

After beating Éire Óg we went and bet Old Leighlin in the final, and we ended up winning the championship again in 2016, so to end up with three senior medals felt like a much better return. The funny thing is, I didn't start the final against Old Leighlin either but I wasn't disappointed this time. I knew I had made a contribution to getting us there and I also knew that if the game was in the melting pot that I'd be getting the call at some stage to go in.

Unfortunately, injuries have played a big part in my career down through the years. I can remember breaking a bone in my leg on club duty with Palatine. We were playing Éire Óg and there was about 10 minutes to go and I think we might have been a point down. I'll never forget it. I tried to stand up but I knew something wasn't right straightaway. I remember our manager Mick Lillis running in to me and wondering what the hell was wrong with me? I explained I couldn't walk, never mind run. He grabbed my jersey and said, 'Look Sceach, we need you now more than ever… run it off ta f**k!' I tried to carry on, but once Gerry McGuill came out of goal and hit me a shoulder I just couldn't get up the second time. There was definitely something wrong.

Mick had spent eight seasons with us in Palatine and over that period he was a serious influence on my career, whether that was on or off the field, and we remain very good friends to this day. I had done all my rehab over the winter and had recovered well. My father's birthday was coming up in the New Year but it was clashing with a National League game against Leitrim. A few of us had planned on taking him to St Andrews for a weekend of golf. I had flagged it with management at the very start of the year just, so they knew nice and early. I would rarely ever miss a game or training over the years, so I wanted to flag this clash at the very start. They said that was fine.

This was a couple of months before the game, so there was every chance they might forget but still I wanted to tell them. Once the Leitrim game came upon us I went back to the management again and reminded them of my unavailability. In fairness to Liam Hayes, he was honest and said straight out that they wanted me to stay and really made a case for me to play. We chatted about it and I agreed to come home early from the trip and to play the game on the Sunday. I flew home the Saturday night anyway and fair play to the county board, they covered all expenses. I had played a couple of practice games since the leg break against Éire

Óg and was training away but the Leitrim game was to be my first competitive game since the break. Not long into the game, I got a slap into the side of my leg… the same leg of course. I can remember the pain of it and everything about it. The doctor, Tom Foley came onto the field to see how I was and I just remember saying, 'Tom, my leg is broken!' He was kind of looking at me strange, and asked, 'How do you know it's broken?' I just knew. It was the exact same spot as before and I just knew. I was stretchered off and brought off in the ambulance down to Kilkenny. Came home then with the leg in a cast again. It was a disaster.

Over the years, I've badly done my two ankles. I broke my leg twice. I had a groin operation performed by Gerry McEntee organised through Liam Hayes. I've had a hernia operation. My two collarbones were broken. I fractured my skull, and had an aneurism on my brain. I also finished up my career with a broken hand.

In 2008, Palatine played Kildavin/Clonegal in the county championship in Dr Cullen Park, and that was the day I fractured my skull, but didn't actually realise it at the time. At one stage the ball was kicked out and it went over my head. I could see our half-back Gavin Farrell coming up the field so I turned around and just kind of dived to slap the ball out to him, but my head ended up banging into the knee of one of the Kildavin players. It was pure accidental. Despite getting the bang I could still remember the roar as we had gotten the equalising point. I remember saying to my brother John that night on the way home, 'At least we got the draw!' He explained that Kildavin had actually gone up field and kicked a point soon after to win the game by one. I was in a bad way that night.

I was talking s***e and was vomiting. The strange thing was, I actually felt okay the next morning after I woke up. The only thing that was off was when I was reading a text message, my eye was a little blurry. I went down training on the Thursday or Friday that week. I remember saying to Mick Lillis that I wasn't allowed train under the concussion protocols but I was just going to practice a few frees. Straightaway Mick said, 'You're not going out there at all. If you've a blur in your eye after getting a bang, you better get that checked out'. I went home anyway and by then Mick had organised for me to see a doctor up in Santry. I drove up to Santry the next morning. After I had my MRI the doctor told me I was to go to St Luke's in Kilkenny as I was to get a CAT scan. They could see something but they weren't sure what, so the CAT scan would show up exactly what the problem was. I was to go and get it done straight away.

All of this was happening and I was driving around on my own between these places, which I probably shouldn't have been doing, and with all this uncertainty too. It was a strange time. Once in Kilkenny I had the scan and I knew when I came out of it that something wasn't right, as there were two doctors there to talk to me. They were straight to the point. 'Brian, there's an ambulance waiting for you at the front door. There is a massive bleed on your brain and you need to go up to the neurosurgeon in Beaumont straight away!' I was getting ready to go then and packing up my things to get ready. I made a few phone calls and I just remember thinking that it must be a mistake, as I felt fine. By the time I got to Dublin, my whole family were there to meet me. My parents were away in Clare for a few days and they had come up straightaway once they had heard.

The doctor came in and explained what was going on. I had an aneurism on my brain and they needed to relieve that. I remember asking the doctor how many of these procedures had he done? 'Around 400,' he said. 'And did anyone ever die?' I asked. I remember him laughing and he said, 'Not one Mr. Kelly, not one'. Before the surgery they decided to put me on blood thinners to see if the clot would dissolve before surgery was needed. I ended up staying a week in Beaumont and it did eventually dissolve, so no surgery was needed. The funny thing is that during the whole week up there I felt so good and healthy despite what was going on.

A few weeks after I was released from hospital I went back to see the doctor and he gave me the all clear to return to work. Before I left I wanted to enquire one thing. 'What are the chances of me being able to play football again?'

'Brian, I can't let you back to play football. If you get a bang on that part of your brain again it could spell serious trouble.' In fairness, he did explain that I could go back if I really wanted but I'd have to wear a scrum cap all the time. Training or playing, it had to be on at all times. This would offer some protection for the head. My first reaction was I was going to look like some fool but then, at the same time, I love the game so much that I was willing to do anything to get back playing. After a while I just got used to it and I think everybody else did too.

Three Senior Championship medals was a nice number to finish up with. It was more than we won playing with Carlow, as the O'Byrne Cup in 2002 was the only trophy we picked up over the years. I think the O'Byrne Cup meant more to teams back then and was probably taken a bit more seriously. There was a massive crowd that day in Dr Cullen Park when we beat Wicklow. Cyril Hughes first called me into the Carlow senior football panel when he was manager. I was only young at the time but was delighted to be in there. It was under Pat Roe then that I established myself as a starter. Unfortunately, there was a high turnover of managers with Carlow so we never really got to get a settled squad together.

Probably the closest we had to having all our best players available was in 2005 and '06 under Liam Hayes. Liam was a big players' man, plus he had the link to Carlow through his father and grandfather. Liam's grandfather, also Liam, was actually school principal many years ago in Bennekerry NS, where I went to school; while Liam's father Jim, played for Palatine and Carlow. A few years after he finished up with us, Liam paid me a great compliment in the paper saying I was the best free-taker he had seen, and to have that coming from Liam who had seen and done it all meant a lot. He backed the players every time we went out on the field. After Liam left the whole thing seemed to fall apart and the following season there was a change of manager mid-season, so it was a big come down after a very enjoyable two years.

People have often asked me why did I play on for so long after all my injuries. I just love football. I loved playing it. I loved watching it and it was easy to keep playing until I was nearly 40 when that was the case. Once I did retire, I could look back and say that I did my best for Palatine and Carlow. Was it good enough? At times it was and at times it wasn't, but I enjoyed every minute. Anything I did on the field I couldn't have done without my family. At all times I was lucky to have the support of my parents Gus and Maureen, my brothers John and Mark, and my sister Áine. It is always the lads on the field who get all the plaudits but no player would be able to put in so much effort without the unseen support of those behind the scenes.

# DANIEL ST LEDGER

**MONAGHAN 1-12 ★ CARLOW 1-7**
**All Ireland SFC Qualifiers Round 3**
**Dr Cullen Park, Carlow**
**JULY 15, 2017**

*Shane Redmond and Daniel St Ledger (right) celebrate in Tullamore after Carlow had defeated Kildare by seven points in the 2018 Leinster Championship.*

★ **MONAGHAN:** R Beggan (0-1); F Kelly (1-0), D Wylie, R Wylie; S Carey (0-1), C Walshe, K O'Connell; K Hughes (0-3), D Hughes; N McAdam, D Malone (0-1), G Doogan; O Duffy, J McCarron, C McManus (0-3) Subs: D Mone for D Hughes, C McCarthy (0-2) for McCarron, R McAnespie (0-1) for Duffy, V Corey for McAdam, D Ward for Carey, K Duffy for Doogan.

★ **CARLOW:** R Molloy; C Lawlor, S Redmond, M Rennick; G Kelly (1-0), **D St Ledger**, D Moran; S Murphy, B Murphy (0-2); S Gannon, J Murphy, D Foley; P Broderick (0-5), C Moran, E Ruth. Subs: S Clarke for Kelly, K Nolan for D Moran.

## THE ACTION

MONAGHAN WERE FORCED to dig deep before seeing off the challenge of Carlow in this cracking All-Ireland qualifier played in beautiful conditions in Dr Cullen Park. Fintan Kelly was the hero for Monaghan when the corner-back found the back of the net four minutes from the end, and with it put an end to what has been a glorious summer for Carlow. For long periods it looked like Carlow might actually be in with a shout of winning this game and, indeed, when wing back Garry Kelly scored it actually put the home side in front.

This was as tough a championship encounter as you will see with Carlow every bit as conditioned as their Division One counterparts. It was a proper championship battle and the game was not long on before there was an early dust-up which set the tone for what would be a tough physical encounter. Carlow were buoyed on by a huge home attendance and a huge cheer went up when Paul Broderick put the home side ahead with a free after three minutes. Monaghan responded with points through Conor McManus and Kieran Hughes. Broderick pointed again to level matters, before McManus again and Brendan Murphy exchanged points to tie the sides once again. Two further scores from McManus and Kieran Hughes meant Monaghan went in at the interval with a slender 0-5 to 0-3 lead.

Carlow started the second-half well with Broderick kicking a huge free from about 55 metres out and the Carlow supporters were really starting to believe when Brendan Murphy equalised shortly after. Shane Carey put Monaghan ahead, but not for long as Carlow were about to strike a huge blow. Darragh Foley had a free which just dropped short, but the rebound fell kindly for Garry Kelly and the half-back made no mistake when firing home from close range – Carlow were now ahead by two points. Conor McCarthy and Broderick traded scores but from then on Monaghan really took over, and finally put a bit of daylight between the sides when Fintan Kelly fisted to the net.

★★★★★

66

PLAYING OVER A long period for Carlow, especially during the Turlough O'Brien era, we had some great days. Getting promotion in 2018 and beating Kildare in the championship a few weeks later are hard to beat, but for different reasons it was a game we lost that stands out for me the most. Beating Kildare was absolutely massive and nobody was giving us any chance going into that game. We won by seven points and didn't kick a single wide, so we were convincing winners, but in a way, it felt a little like a freak result. It was a little bit surreal that day. When we played Monaghan in the qualifiers the previous year in Dr Cullen Park, it felt real. For me, it was probably the day I felt that we actually belonged at that level.

Up to that point we had been on a great journey that season; we only just missed out on promotion, but we won our last couple of games so we had a bit of momentum going into the championship. There, we beat Wexford before probably the game where people really started to take notice of us and that, of course, was Dublin in O'Moore Park. We might have lost by 12 points but how often do you see a man on a team losing by 12 points getting the Man of the Match... as happened with Sean Murphy?

We beat London and then Leitrim in the qualifiers, which meant come Round 3 of the qualifiers we were sure to draw a big team and there weren't many better teams around at the time than Monaghan. Similar to the Dublin game, we were back on Sky Sports which again added to the occasion. Dr Cullen Park was packed that evening and the sun was shining and the ground was rock hard. Getting to play live on TV might not be such a big thing for a lot of top inter-county players, but for a lot of us we had never been live on TV before and now here we got to do it twice in the space of a few weeks.

Normally if you were to watch a Division One team up against a Division Four team, you'd be hoping it wouldn't be an embarrassment, but we were going into that match firmly believing we could win. The intensity through that first-half was something else. Early on in the game, I remember Sean Murphy going on one of his solo runs and being met with a big hit from their centre-forward Dermot Malone. Straightaway a few players jumped in and a little bit of a scuffle ensued. The crowd were heightened then and it certainly gets you going as a player too. I think it showed that we weren't going to be bullied about the place, while I think it showed Monaghan they weren't going to have it as easy as they thought they might have. I think it was from that free won by Sean that Paul Broderick put over the resulting kick and that just further lifted everybody and gave great belief. I think it set the tone for the rest of the game.

Midway through the second-half, Garry Kelly came up from half-back to score a goal and the roar from the crowd was unbelievable. The place was rocking. That goal actually put us ahead but, looking back, we might have got the goal too early as I think once we scored it, then it really forced Monaghan to come out and actually play a little more, while instead of it actually pushing us on it kind of had the opposite effect. I remember having the ball at one stage and seeing Brendan Murphy in space and thought I'd give a nice 40 yard outside of the boot pass, but just at the last minute I changed my mind; I went safe and hit a pass on the inside and ballooned it over the line. I think Monaghan got a score from that then. Those little things always stick with you long after the game has gone. I think it was level with around nine minutes to go and we coughed up four turnovers which led to four scores, They got 1-3 out of it and that was roughly the difference between us in the end.

We had just missed out on promotion in 2017; ironically the two games we lost in the league were to London and Leitrim, two teams we beat in that year's qualifiers, but after the highs of that summer we really had no excuse not to get promotion the following year. It would have been a sin not to build on the great summer we had and I think going into 2018, it was all or nothing regarding league promotion. Thankfully, we did get over the line and finally achieved promotion up to Division Three. We had talked about that for so long; every winter we went back it was all about getting out of Division Four. When we finally did get over the line, it kind of felt like the mountain was climbed and the following year was always going to be a hard act to follow. I do think that Monaghan game and that whole campaign was of huge benefit going in that following year and without 2017, then I don't think league promotion in 2018 would have happened. It was a great springboard. Despite having reached our target so early in the season, we didn't rest on our laurels and followed through and had another memorable championship campaign. We beat Louth and then had that famous win over

Kildare, which set us up for a Leinster semi-final against Laois.

That was our third time to play Laois that summer after our regular league tie, followed by the league final in Croke Park and now the championship game, again in Croke Park. Whatever it is about Laois, no matter how well Carlow are playing, we always just seem to struggle against them. Laois beat us on all three occasions that year, which was hard to take. The first time we played, in Dr Cullen Park, we had already achieved promotion while Laois had to win, but they beat us by a point I think, although we had chances. And I think, had we won that game then it might have changed the course of how the other two went. Once Laois won the first day, and then the second day, then they just had a hoodoo on us and no matter what you say, it does get into lads' heads.

Whatever about the first two days, I do think the third day was one that a lot of lads will look back on and regret. How many more times will Carlow footballers get to a Leinster semi-final and be competitive there and only lose by a few points. To be able to say that you played in a Leinster football final would have been the icing on the cake for everybody involved with that team.

After the high of the Kildare game, we were never going to get up to that level again, especially in Croke Park. Laois probably had us well figured out by then. They were very good at keeping the ball as they knew we fed off turnovers and if they kept the ball then there was nothing we could do about it. Laois were patient and they never brought the ball into the tackle. They just kept chipping away and they won by four points in the end. A lot of that is down to good coaching, and while Turlough and Steven Poacher were getting most of the plaudits up to that point, Laois boss John Sugrue probably wasn't getting enough credit as that Laois team were as good as any Laois team we had played. They were very well set up and well organised.

Despite getting relegated in our first year up, we weren't that far off and only got relegated on the last day on scoring difference, so that's how close we were to staying up. I think when we were beaten by Down at home towards the end of the league was when the wheels started to come off and that poor form followed into the championship. We played really well in our final league game against Laois, but still came out the wrong side of the result and despite that we still could have stayed up only for Offaly to kick two injury time scores against Sligo at the same time, which effectively sent us back down after one year up. If we had finished the season on zero points then you'd just say that you're not up to the level and move on but we picked up four points and ended up going down on scoring difference, so that's how close it was.

Definitely, our poor 2019 campaign is one that still sticks in the craw for a lot of lads I would think, and it felt like the end of an era in some ways. While we had a great team around that era, we really only got it together for about two years as lads stepped away, retired or went hurling or whatever. In a small county like Carlow, you just need every single player who is good enough playing and that is not always the case due to different reasons. During Turlough O'Brien's reign with Carlow, and especially when he brought in Steven Poacher as coach, people started to take notice of us a little bit more. We became noted for playing very defensive football. While that may have been the case in certain games, we based our game on who the opposition were and if we might have looked defensive at times, we were well able to score too and we put up some big scores when we got promoted in the league – and even after that we put up 2-17 against Louth, and followed that up with 2-14 against Kildare when we were convincing seven-point winners.

People were talking a good bit about us and we were coming up quite regularly on podcasts, TV, radio and the papers. A lot of it was negative and it was all about the way we were playing the game but in previous years we were getting hammered and no one was talking about us, so the fact people were talking was a good sign; it meant we were relevant, I suppose. In the past when we had a rare championship win, you'd get your couple of minutes on *The Sunday Game* and that was it, but now people were talking about Carlow in the lead up to games. We were happy that people were finally starting to take us seriously, and even seriously enough for people to be criticising us was incredible. People who might point the finger might talk about the Dublin game, or even the Monaghan game and those Laois games as a stick to beat us with, but if you followed the team closely over the years, you'd see we were putting up big scores in Division Four.

We had a proper plan in place and even that was progress in itself and whether we were having good or bad days I would often think back to 2014 when Meath came to Dr Cullen Park and beat us on a scoreline of 7-13 to 0-6. People will often say something is rock bottom after a poor result but that was absolutely rock bottom. We could not have sunk any lower after that. Turlough O'Brien had actually come in as a selector before the championship that year under Anthony Rainbow, but even after that embarrassment he was still mad to get the job for the following year as he had his own ideas and he knew we weren't as bad as what we were showing.

Turlough is such a proud Carlow man and he knew, and we all knew, that he had something to offer. We were shipping very heavy defeats so obviously he saw where we were weak and where needed fixing. He managed to lay a foundation and get some pride back over the following years and nearly all the best players in the county were playing under him during that period. Having said that, there was no quick fix and it was very slow starting; 2015 and '16 were both very slow and bar the odd victory, we weren't doing anything spectacular. Things had kind of stagnated and Turlough knew that and, in fairness, it was then he brought in a new coach in Steven Poacher. Steven came in a couple of weeks before we played Cavan in the qualifiers in 2016 so he didn't have much time to work with us, but it brought a freshness to it again. I'm managing a club now, so I see it from Turlough's point of view but for a manager to decide to bring in someone else takes a lot of courage. Some managers think it's all about them but Turlough wasn't like that, and he didn't care who was front and centre or who was coaching.

In 2020 I decided to hang up the county boots but, really, I played very little club football even after that either. I had suffered a few concussions and had also been diagnosed with epilepsy so I had to step away from everything. It was a massive change to go from playing and training almost every night of the week to, all of a sudden, not playing at all. I was involved with managing my own club Kildavin/Clonegal last year and I'm currently managing Dublin side St Sylvester's, so that takes up a lot of my time at the moment. Actually, truth be told, it probably takes up even more of my time than when I was playing because when you're playing, you're just worried about yourself, but when you're a manager there's so many things you are in charge of and you're always thinking about it.

# PAUL BRODERICK

*Paul Broderick's terrific scoring for Carlow helped the county to historic championship wins and promotion from Division Four of the NFL, and also brought him individual recognition (here he is receiving the GAA/GPA Player of the Month for May 2017).*

★ **CARLOW:** R Molloy; C Crowley, S Redmond, Conor Lawlor; J Morrissey (0-1), D St Ledger, C Moran; B Murphy, S Murphy; S Gannon, D Foley (1-2), E Ruth (0-2); **P Broderick (0-7)**, D O'Brien, J Murphy. Subs: Cian Lawlor for O'Brien, M Rennick for Gannon, B Kavanagh for Morrissey, L Walker for Foley.

★ **ANTRIM:** C Kerr; P Healy, P Gallagher, N Delargy; K O'Boyle, M Sweeney, J Laverty; R Johnston, P McAleer; M Fitzpatrick (0-1), C Murray (0-1), R McCann; CJ McGourty (0-7), C Duffin, R Murray. Subs: K Healy (0-1) for R Murray, S Beatty for O'Boyle, O Eastwood (0-1) for Sweeney, P McBride (0-1) for Laverty.

# THE ACTION

CARLOW FOLLOWERS WILL long remember the name of Corrigan Park, for it was at this West Belfast venue that Carlow senior footballers finally found the last missing piece of the jigsaw, as they clinched promotion out of the basement division. Four away wins showed that they did it the hard way too when they did manage to get over the line. Carlow marksman Paul Broderick was on target with three frees in the opening 10 minutes, but Antrim were soon level with points from Conor Murray and a brace from CJ McGourty. That was as close as Antrim got all day as Carlow were never behind. Broderick landed two more frees, before Darragh Foley hit Carlow's first point from play just before the half hour mark which gave the visitors a 0-6 to 0-4 lead going in at the break.

Within a minute of the restart, Eoghan Ruth extended Carlow's lead and the Carlow supporters who had travelled up were now daring to believe that this could actually be their day. McGourty and Kristan Healy kicked scores for the home side, before Broderick and Foley replied for Carlow. The turning point arrived with just 10 minutes remaining. Paul Broderick stood over a difficult free for Carlow. His well struck effort looked like it was going over, but dropped short and came back off the crossbar. The in-rushing Darragh Foley crashed the ball to the back of the net. Not the best goal you'll ever see, but surely the most important in Foley's career up to that point.

Carlow were now five points up and playing with an extra man; all they had to was hold on. As expected though, Antrim came at Carlow hard in those final minutes. Antrim then kicked three points through McGourty, Eastwood and McBride, while Ruth replied for Carlow to slow things down a little.

★★★★★

66

IN TERMS OF following Carlow football over the years, and then getting to actually play for them, we never really had any games of significance as such. Any big games Carlow had were one-off championship games which we were never really expected to do well in anyway. So you'd build yourself up for that after your league campaign had usually fallen flat. I remember one of my earlier years playing senior football for Carlow. We had just lost our last league game and, while we were having our meal after, we looked at the results and saw the league table. The way results went, we would have actually been in the shake up for promotion had we won

So that Antrim game was my first time playing for Carlow to have something significant in our own hands. To change our position for the following 12 months was big motivation. The players too were all aware of the significance. Later that summer we beat Louth and Kildare in the championship. While it was great to beat our neighbours Kildare, how many cracks have we really had at them? Whereas with the league, we have a crack at it every single year and we'd never got it together like this. Putting six wins together, plus winning our last three league games from the previous season, meant that we were on a great run of consecutive wins in that competition. That year, 2018, was Turlough O'Brien's fourth year in charge. He had come in as a selector in the middle of 2014 when Anthony Rainbow was manager, but this was his fourth year as the main man and that year was probably the first year, for me, that being in with Carlow actually felt like being part of a club team.

The togetherness feeling we had. We were all aware that this opportunity might not come around again for any of us, and having worked so hard to get there we really wanted to take that chance now that we were so close. All the talk was that it had been 33 years since the footballers had been promoted and we did feel that if we made it up to Division 3 that we could go again and have a crack at that too.

The week leading up to the game there had been snowfall and, as the week went on, a lot of games were being called off. We were only hoping that our game wouldn't fall victim to the weather because we had the momentum from playing, and winning, week on week. Plus, we weren't sure what was going to happen if it was called off, so we were all hoping it would go ahead. We travelled up north the night before the game, which was St Patrick's Day and we stayed in a hotel, which was unusual under Turlough's reign for Carlow. It showed that he left no stone unturned to ensure we were ready to go on the day.

In the past when you'd go up to play Antrim, you'd normally be playing in Casement Park but since that has been closed, they've been playing their home games in numerous club grounds around the county. Home advantage, when you get to pick a club ground, is definitely a big thing.

It's funny the things you remember looking back. The week before the game, the county board booked our hotel but without knowing, they booked it in an extremely Loyalist area. We had Steven Poacher with us then as Turlough's number two. Steven, being from Down, knew the area and advised the county board that a change might be best; so we changed our hotel midweek. We ended up in a hotel in Tyrone. It was about a 45-minute journey from there to the ground, so it wasn't too bad.

Of all the games you play over the years, you would never really remember what you talked about before the game on the bus but, like I said, the significance of this game meant that you'd remember the details. On the way to the game, I remember watching a new Ricky Gervais show that had come out on Netflix and that still sticks out in my mind. I was in great form going up to it. I was very relaxed and I didn't really feel the journey at all. Everything went well in the lead up to it. Once we landed at this club pitch, we went inside and while I'd never accuse Antrim of any underhand tactics... this kind of thing had happened us before.

We got into the dressing-room and it must have been about 40 degree Celsius inside. While that heat would have you zonked, it was so cold, and snowing outside that you didn't want to go outside either until you actually had to. In all fairness, it could have all been good natured from Antrim but it was something we could have done without all the same. We had two dressing-rooms together and before the game, lads were doing the usual stuff they'd do before any game. Some lads were stretching, and foam rolling, while others maybe were getting a rub. All the usual carry on. In the meantime, our midfielder Eoghan Ruth in the middle of his pre-match routine had decided to use a water pipe as a lever for some stretch he was doing. It was going across the ceiling of one of the dressing-rooms. After a few pulls he only went and pulled the pipe out of the ceiling and the dressing-room started to flood. It wasn't so bad though as it was the second room we were using, so there weren't as many people in there but still when he came in to tell us, you could see the panic. He was gone pale.

However, that was quickly forgotten about once we got out on the field and pretty quickly the nerves disappeared as we settled in early enough and we got into the game. One of the things during that period that we said we'd always try and do was that we'd stand up for ourselves physically. Not be bullied. We were just so determined to go up that year that we kind of said that we were going to take no messing. If you're shaking someone's hand and he hits you a dunt, then you're going to hit him back. I think at the start of that Antrim game, we set down a marker with that kind of thing. Lads were just throwing their weight around on both sides and really any time it's a game of such significance, you'll see lads grappling on the ground, even before the whistle.

We had a two or three point lead for much of the half and, at times, it just seemed to be point for point. My biggest thing going in to the game was that I was going to be relied on for frees. The pitch was heavy and it had been snowing so it wasn't going to be free-flowing. I knew I wasn't going to get that many shots off from open play on the day so the frees were going to be vital. I was probably going to get maybe six or seven frees during the game and it definitely wasn't going to be a six- or seven-point game, so I knew myself I was going to have to score at least five or six frees when they came my way. I kind of knew going in to the game that I would probably have been earmarked by Antrim. Also, at that stage of my career, I was almost 32 and I'm thinking, *Maybe I can use this to my advantage? Like perhaps if I can lure a second defender, if I delay with the ball and then give a pass to someone who is free, maybe.*

At half-time, I think we were maybe a point or two up. We had played against the breeze and we felt that things were going our way. Despite the game being in West Belfast and the fact some people couldn't make it up that morning due to the heavy snow shower, we still had as many supporters as Antrim up there, so that gave us a great lift too. It felt like things were continuing to go our way as Antrim were reduced to 14 men in the second-half. After the red card, I took the resulting free. It was a really difficult kick but the instructions were to have a go at it, or at least leave it in around the goalmouth. The kick didn't have the distance as it just dropped short, but it was from that, that we got the goal. It was a bit scrappy and while it was still a little bit early to start playing keep ball, the goal meant lads started to believe that this could actually happen.

I'll never forget the final whistle. While beating the likes of Wexford and Kildare in the championship were massive results, and they were *huge*, the Antrim game was just different. It was the end of some larger goal we had been longing to achieve. Your family coming on the field then afterwards and congratulating you, they are memories for a lifetime. The bus journey back to Carlow was great. I wished it would never end. The drive couldn't have been long enough. It was unbelievable.

It was pretty surreal for me playing for Carlow. Playing underage with my club, Tinryland, we won a good few championships all the way up and you kind of expect the same thing to happen when you play senior, but then a number of years pass and you've nothing to show for it, apart from enjoyment. But you still like to win. So to have that bit of success with Carlow then was very welcome. We had some great days out in the championship… beating, Kildare, Wexford, Louth… and putting it up to Dublin were all fond memories. They were all great days but if we lost any of those games by a couple of points we'd get all the usual hard luck pats on the back and we'd forget about it and move on, but the Antrim game was different. We were building for such a long time for that moment. We were fully intent on going up and winning that game, and we all knew we were on the cusp of something great.

We had been on a great run going into that promotion run-in. Going back 12 months to 2017 and we just missed out on promotion as defeats to London and Leitrim came back to haunt us, but I think we won our last three league games. Come championship then, we beat Wexford before putting it up to Dublin for long spells. Two wins in the qualifiers, ironically over London and Leitrim, followed before a narrow defeat to Monaghan at home, so going into 2018 confidence was up.

Going into that penultimate game against Antrim we had five league wins on the bounce and we soon made it six as we confirmed our promotion. It wasn't without the usual few scares though. We were 10 points up against Waterford at one stage before they brought it back to two. Two early goals against Limerick had us well up also, before they came back into it then. These were games we could have lost but when you're coming out the right side of a tight game by a point or two, it's amazing the belief that gives you, as opposed to losing by a point or two. The belief was still there when championship came around and we reached the Leinster semi-final after beating Louth and Kildare… but we ran into Laois again then. That was our third time to face Laois that year and, unfortunately, they all ended up in narrow defeats.

When 2019 finally came around, it was strange to see Carlow operating in Division 3. After two games, we had beaten Sligo and drawn with Westmeath, and I think we might have been on top at that stage. You're looking at the table then and thinking that if we get one more win here, who knows what can happen. As it turned out, one more win was all we managed after that as we beat Louth. The margins between going up and going back down are so minimal. In hindsight, we only needed one more point to stay up that year but, of course, we didn't know that during any of our games at the time. Our second last game was a home clash against Down, the home county of our coach Steven Poacher.

We should have won that day but we were caught right at the end. There was controversy at the end of that game as the referee left the field. Tempers flared up. The feeling after that game was that we were probably looking at relegation even though we still had Laois to play in our last game, but our record against them was really poor. Despite this, we probably put up our best performance that day up in Portlaoise. We started really well, got an early goal and got out ahead of them but Laois, as they always seem to do against us, just did enough. After the final whistle that day, we still had a chance to stay up but we needed Sligo to avoid defeat to Offaly and going into injury time, Sligo were a point up. At that stage we were safe but Offaly struck for two points in injury time to win and that's the way it finished, and ultimately we were back down, but that's how close it was. It was literally seconds.

# JOHN MURPHY

**CARLOW 2-14 ★ KILDARE 1-10**
**Leinster SFC Quarter-Final**
**O' Connor Park, Tullamore**
**MAY 27, 2018**

*John Murphy in action against Laois in the 2018 Leinster semi-final, when Carlow's brilliant summer came to an end.*

★ **CARLOW:** R Molloy; C Crowley, S Redmond, Conor Lawlor (1-0); J Morrissey, D St Ledger (1-0), C Moran (0-1); S Murphy, E Ruth; S Gannon (0-1), D Foley (0-1), D Walsh; P Broderick (0-11), D O'Brien, **J Murphy**. Subs: D Moran for Crowley, Cian Lawlor for Walsh, L Walker for O'Brien, BJ Molloy for Foley.

★ **KILDARE:** M Donnellan; P Kelly, D Hyland, M O'Grady; J Byrne, E Doyle, K Flynn (0-2); K Feely (0-3), P Cribbin (0-3); F Conway, K Cribbin (0-1), P Brophy; E O'Connor, D Flynn (1-1), N Kelly. Subs: C Healy for O'Connor, D Slattery for K Cribbin, T Moolick for Brophy, E Callaghan for Kelly.

# THE ACTION

CARLOW FOOTBALLERS BRIDGED a gap of 65 years, going all the way back to 1953, to the last time they beat Kildare in the Leinster Championship. This was as complete a championship performance as any side could have wished for. Amazingly, Carlow did not kick one wide during the whole game. Kildare will rue the 12 wides they shot over the 70 minutes, but again, a lot of this was due to the fact that they were forced to shoot from long distance. Carlow showed their intent right from the start of this game. From the throw-in, Sean Murphy caught the ball and ran straight at the heart of the Kildare defence, starting the move which was ended by a Paul Broderick score with not even a minute on the clock. Broderick again, this time with a free and Darragh Foley kicked points for Carlow to give them a 0-3 to 0-1 lead before disaster struck. Kildare landed in a high ball and full-forward Daniel Flynn was there to knock the rebound to the net. Where in previous times, Carlow might have wilted but not this time, this was different. Shortly after that sucker-punch Carlow were awarded a free about 50 metres out and Daniel St Ledger's effort went all the way to the Kildare net.

Kildare had a golden opportunity then when they were awarded a penalty after a foul on Niall Kelly. Eanna O'Connor's effort was saved, however, by Robbie Molloy. At half-time, Carlow led 1-8 to 1-3. Paul Broderick started the second half as he had started the first, a fantastic score from play which only showed that Carlow had no intention of slowing down in this game. With the game well into injury time, Carlow made one last sweeping move from their own half with John and Sean Murphy both involved. With most of the Carlow players back in their own half, it was an unexpected man in corner-back Conor Lawlor who collected the ball and with a finish a corner -forward would be proud of, he shot the ball to the back of the net to push Carlow's lead out to 2-14 to 1-10. Game over!

★★★★★

**"**

I CAN REMEMBER Pat Spillane saying before the game, that Division Four teams don't beat Division One teams. Normally they don't I suppose, but we certainly blasted that theory that day anyway.

We had played Dublin and Monaghan the previous season and while we put up big performances in both games, we didn't win. Same with Tyrone a few weeks after the Kildare game, a big performance but we didn't win. That's why beating Kildare was so sweet; to actually beat a Division One team, and not just come away with a moral victory. It showed what could be done.

Lots of things stick out from that day for me. The outstanding moment was probably Conor Lawlor's goal right at the death to seal the win. He came up from corner-back in injury time to score our second goal. It was unique in that he must have run with the ball for nearly 40 yards and only hopped the ball once! When that goal went in, it put us seven points up and I suppose we could kind of celebrate the goal then as we knew we wouldn't be caught at that late stage.

Going into that Kildare game, we were coming off the back of a big win over Division Two opposition in Louth in the previous round. We had beaten them by 2-17 to 0-12 in Portlaoise so were confident of a big performance at the very least, if nothing else against Kildare.

One good thing about having played against Dublin and Monaghan the year before is that it gave us a taste of what is was like to be playing Division One teams and we definitely learned from them. Take Dublin, for example. When they applied a strong press on our kick-out, they turned us over every time and after a while we reverted to type and began to kick it long. Against Kildare, this was identified and we spoke about it in the lead up to the game and we tried a few different things with the kick-outs, took some risks and we started to succeed in winning our own kick again. It was pleasing to see how we had learned from previous failings against the top teams, and how we were able to rectify it. Small details maybe, but these are the things you pick up and learn from while playing Division One teams.

When people talk about that game, one of the other things that always comes up in conversation is that we didn't kick a single wide in the entire game. I remember in the first-half, a pass was over hit into Darragh O'Brien. The ball was going out over the end-line but he slid to keep it in and it went out for a lineball instead. Even though that wouldn't have gone down as a wide as such had it gone out, it still meant that we didn't kick one ball over the end-line and I can't ever remember a team having no wides in a championship match.

We had settled well in the early stages of the game, and were leading by 0-3 to 0-1. Both sides got soft enough goals in the next few minutes. Our goalkeeper Robbie Molloy was unlucky when a ball sent into the square bounced off his chest and Daniel Flynn was on hand, quick as a flash to finish the rebound to the net. We had kind of said to ourselves before the game that Flynn was Kildare's main man and we were going to hit him hard and early. I'd say in the first 10 minutes we got a few good hits in on him. They were hard hits, but fair. We just wanted to let him know that we were there and he wasn't going to get anything easy on the day. Despite this, he still managed to sneak in to get that goal but overall, we did well to nullify his impact on the game.

Our goal was lucky too in that it was a long free from Daniel St Ledger which went all the way to the net, so it evened itself out I suppose. Not long after that then Kildare were awarded a penalty and straight away you're thinking to yourself that, if they get this then we're going to be under serious pressure. If they score, they'll be leading despite playing poorly and we'll be behind having played so well. Eanna O'Connor stepped up, and Robbie Molloy saved brilliantly and almost straightaway we went up field and kicked a score, so that was a massive few minutes in the game.

We progressed from there and tagged on a couple of more scores and then, all of a sudden, we're leading by 1-8 to 1-3 at half-time and then we're all thinking going into the dressing-room that we have a big chance here in this game. We had started the first-half with a score from Paul Broderick after only a few seconds and we repeated the trick again at the start of the second with Broderick again on target, with probably the best score of the day. If you look at the throw-in from the start of the half, there were about five Carlow players all going for the breaking ball. We won it and that's where that early second-half score came from. It just showed the hunger we had on the day and, as well as that, it also showed that we weren't going to die down after our first-half performance and that we were determined to bring the same intensity as we did to the first.

We had a fantastic management team who had drilled that into us at half-time. Turlough O'Brien was a proud Carlow man and a great manager, and Steven Poacher, his right hand man, was a great addition to the set up when he came in. In fairness to Steven, he created a structure and despite being five points up at the break and playing so well, he just kept telling us to stick to the plan, to not let off on the pressure and to just keep doing what we were doing.

People have often commented to me since that we were massively fit that year, but I wouldn't say we were more overly fit than usual. The game plan we had meant that we used the ball wisely and we didn't use up too much energy. Our game plan was defensive no doubt, but we could score as well, and 2-17 against Louth and 2-14 against Kildare was proof of that. We had put up some big scores in the league that year too, so we were well able to score. Scoring 2-14 against a Division One team was no mean feat and we were very proud of that. In fairness, for the second half, not one player dropped their guard and the intensity levels didn't drop one bit. We were ahead all the way through and when Conor Lawlor got that second goal in injury time, we knew we were home and hosed.

The whole 'Carlow Rising' thing, which was everywhere, had kind of started the previous year in 2017. We had just missed out on promotion from the league but we won the last three league games and followed that up with a big championship run. We had played Dublin and Monaghan along the way, both live on TV. We played five championship games altogether that summer. Going into 2018 then, there was still a feel good factor around. We finally got over the line in the league and claimed promotion for the first time in 33 years. We followed that up by beating Louth who were in Division Two at the time, but we beat them comfortably. Normally after a game like that, the underdog fails to shine the next day out and that was probably what was expected of us going into the Kildare game, but we backed up that Louth performance with an even better one the next day out.

The fact that Kildare went on to beat Mayo a few weeks after losing to us, and there was the whole furore with the 'Newbridge or nowhere' saga only proved that Kildare weren't a bad team, but I think it shone our victory over them in an even better light after. Cian O'Neill came in for massive stick after they lost to us. In fairness, he was a very good coach. He had been involved with All-Ireland winning sides with Kerry footballers and Tipperary hurlers, so he didn't become a bad coach overnight by any means and Kildare didn't have a bad team and they showed that with the defeat of Mayo. This was a Mayo side that had only just lost the 2016 and 2017 All-Ireland finals to Dublin so we beat a very good Kildare team.

Our prize for beating Kildare was a Leinster semi-final in Croke Park against Laois. That was to be our third time up against them that year. We had met in the last game of the league, then a week later in the league final in Croke Park and now we were coming together again for a place in the Leinster final. Carlow have always struggled to beat Laois over the years and I think when we played them the first time, in that league clash at home, we lost a great chance that day. We had already been promoted the week before, but Laois needed to beat us or else they would have had a do-or-die clash the following week against Antrim to go up. We lost by a point but we had a great goal chance in the second-half ,and then a chance to level it right at the death, but unfortunately we took neither. If we had beaten Laois that day, then you'd like to think that the rest of the year might have gone differently.

We had a great summer overall but to even win either the Division Four title and lift a trophy in Croke Park or to win the semi-final and qualify for a Leinster final meeting with Dublin would have made it even better. I think by the time that semi-final came around, Laois had probably figured us out a little. They had done their homework on us. They had figured out how to stop our midfielder Sean Murphy and they kind of orchestrated where he went. Sean's runs were a big part of our game. Brendan Murphy was missing from that Leinster semi-final too as he was in America. As well as that, Sean Gannon going off injured at half-time was a massive blow to us. Laois beat us fair and square but, looking back, it was definitely a lost opportunity to make a Leinster final.

# MARTIN KAVANAGH

**ST MULLINS 2-17 ★ MOUNT LEINSTER RANGERS 1-19**
**Carlow SHC Final**
**Dr Cullen Park, Carlow**
**OCTOBER 20, 2019**

*Martin Kavanagh races through the Ballyhale Shamrocks defence in 2019, when St Mullins won through to the Leinster club final in an historic year.*

★ **ST MULLINS:** K Kehoe; C Kavanagh, P Doyle, G Bennett; J Doran, M Walsh, G Coady; J Doyle (0-3), O Boland; P Walsh, S Murphy (1-1), **M Kavanagh (0-10)**; J O'Neill (0-2), P Boland (1-1), P Connors. Subs: P Fortune for P Walsh, O Ryan for P Boland.

★ **MLR:** D Grennan; W Hickey, D Tobin, M Doyle; K McDonald, R Coady, R Kelly; Diarmuid Byrne (0-1), J Murphy; J Nolan (0-2), T Joyce (0-1), D Phelan; D Murphy (1-13), C Nolan (0-2), E Byrne. Subs: P Coady for Phelan, Derek Byrne for Kelly, M Malone for Tobin.

# THE ACTION

WHILE IT'S NEVER fair to single out any one player, by the same token it is hard not to give special praise to Marty Kavanagh after this special performance at Dr Cullen Park. The St Mullins and Carlow sharpshooter ended up with 0-10 to his name, 0-5 of which came from play. To make it even sweeter, Kavanagh also captained his side to victory on the day.

Kavanagh might have been wearing No 12 but he spent more time around his own half-back line and around midfield than the half-forward line. Twelve minutes in and St Mullins had the first goal of the game. Full-forward Patrick Boland was the man to raise the green flag for his side as he kept his eye on a long ball and swung on it the air which put St Mullins into a five-point lead. The high of that goal was quickly followed by a low as only two minutes later Ger Coady was sent off on a straight red card for a high challenge on Rangers' Jon Nolan. It was not long before St Mullins had another goal and this time it was the turn of centre-forward Seamus Murphy who blasted his shot to the net after an excellent run from Marty Kavanagh.

The game was end-to-end now and Rangers were given a real shot in the arm when their top scorer Denis Murphy got in for a goal at the other end. James Doyle, and a brace from Kavanagh saw St Mullins go in leading 2-12 to 1-9 at the break. As expected, Mount Leinster Rangers came out for the second half all guns blazing and they went on a quick scoring blitz as they reeled off five points to bring it back to a one-point game. Rangers never got ahead in that final quarter but they did manage to level it, and as they went in search of a winner they were shut down by a tight marking St Mullins defence. It was clear now that the next score was almost certainly going to be the last and St Mullins desperately went in search of that score. A long high ball was excellently fielded by Seamus Murphy. Instead of trying for his own score, he kept possession and passed to an unmarked Jason O' Neill who still had a bit to do but he made no mistake and put the ball straight over the bar.

★★★★★

66

WHEN THE DUST had settled on the 2019 season, I was lucky enough to have just won my fourth county Senior Championship. Normally you might remember your first a bit more, but for me this season had plenty of talking points, both on and off the field and so it's hard to look past it.

Before we even made the final, there was controversy in the semi-final. We were due to play Ballinkillen but they had a number of players playing football with Kildavin/Clonegal. Kildavin had played an intermediate football game but it had to be replayed, I think the game was called off because of the weather and the football game was refixed for the same weekend as our hurling semi-final. Ballinkillen wouldn't play without their football lads and there weren't many dates left to fit everything in, so when Ballinkillen wouldn't field on the date in question we were given a walkover straight through to the final and Ballinkillen were thrown out.

We didn't want to go into a final that way though and we made it clear we wanted to play the semi-final. If you want to play in a county final, then you have to earn the right to play there so it was only right that we wanted to play the game. Having said that, there was pressure on us to win it having offered the replay and we were very lucky to be in a county final by the end of it.

The game was played a couple of weeks later than originally scheduled. I had a nightmare. I had missed a couple of frees and just felt I didn't play well on the day. Ballinkillen were excellent and they had us beaten. With time almost up, a long ball landed in. I caught it and was pulled down and we were awarded a 21-yard free. I stepped up to take it and had no option but to go for the goal. Thankfully, it went in. Draw game. Straightaway, the momentum was with us and from there on in we were in control for the two periods of extra-time and won well in the end.

Ballinkillen had hurled us off the pitch for 60 minutes and when we got that goal right at the death to bring it to extra-time, I remember thinking that we had it now, we weren't going to lose. Ballinkillen had done all the hurling and now, all of a sudden, they were deflated, while we were elated. After the semi-final there wasn't much of a turnaround as the final against Mount Leinster Rangers was the following week. After our poor performance against Ballinkillen, we were well and truly written off in the week leading up to the final. I'd say nobody was tipping us to win.

Games between both sides were always close though and we just hurled unbelievably on the day. We were dealt a huge blow when we had Ger Coady sent off midway through the first-half which could have de-railed us, but everyman stood up and did his bit... and a little bit extra!

Me personally, I had to listen to a lot of stick that week. Nothing was said to me directly but anyone in sport knows, you hear things and things get back to you. The fact I was captain too that year meant there was an extra bit of pressure on me. I had played poor, by my own standards against Ballinkillen and despite missing a few frees that day, it didn't affect me for the final and I was still eager to right the wrongs of the semi-final. There was no way I was not going to be hitting the frees for the final.

I'd be the type of player that I'd try not to let the pressure get to me and I was happy to take the responsibility on my shoulders again for the final. I did well on the frees and from open play too and I probably ended up playing the best game of hurling I've ever played. To do it in a game of such magnitude and against our biggest rivals made it even better. Things just seemed to go right for me on the day, whereas the previous week they didn't. I was scoring regularly, catching ball, and setting up scores.

As good as winning the final was, there was definitely mixed emotions in the lead up as my brother Jack had been sent-off in the semi-final and so would miss the final. That was hard on Jack and in fairness the club tried everything to get it overturned. He went up to a couple of meetings in Portlaoise and I remember when he came out of the final meeting where he found out that he definitely wouldn't be playing. The hearing was in Portlaoise on the Saturday morning, only 24 hours before the final and he texted me on his way home and just apologised that he wouldn't be playing. I just told him to get behind the lads as best he could on the day and just be a positive influence around the place.

I've never seen a man as happy the next day when we won. That was my fourth county championship but for whatever reason, I'd never seen emotion from our supporters on the field as much until that day. I suppose part of that was the way we won it. We were well on top in the first-half but Rangers came back and it was the very last puck of the game that won it for us, so it was edge of the seat stuff. Jason O'Neill, our corner-forward was the hero for us in the end with his late, *late* point and from the puck out, the ref called full-time.

If you were to write the best way to win a county final then that was definitely it. Playing against your biggest rivals and then to win it with the last score of the game. A county final is special no matter who you're playing against. Finals against your neighbours and biggest rivals though are definitely a little bit more spicy. We've played Mount Leinster Rangers in a number of finals at this stage now and it's definitely special. A lot of us play for Carlow together and there is a good mix of cousins between the two sides also. I went to school in Borris VS too and a lot of my good friends are on the Rangers team.

St Mullins and Mount Leinster Rangers have shared every county title since 2009 so there is a good rivalry there. I don't think it's as raw as it might have been say 20 years ago or more. There was probably a bit of hate there then and lads mightn't have talked to each other sometimes after games. I'd often talk to my father and my uncles about it, and it was definitely a different time when they were playing against each other. The generation now, a lot of the lads would be really good friends and what happens on the pitch tends to stay on the pitch, whereas I don't think that would have tended to happen if you go back a few years.

Obviously, you want to win and you will do anything you can to get over the line but as for falling out with lads over a match, that wouldn't be my cup of tea!

I have to say I enjoy the build up to a county final and 2019 was no different. I enjoy the talk about it, the buzz. Some people can't handle it, but I like it. A county final is not just on the day. It's the week leading up to it and everything right up to the game. The parade around the ground then! It's just an all-round occasion and I love it. I'd always tell lads to just enjoy the build up. Obviously, you can get caught up in the whole thing but I think you should be able to embrace it as you've worked hard to get there and you don't know when you'll be back again. Your career is short, and winning and losing is all part of sport. Any county final I've lost have all been against Rangers and the next day I'd ring the lads and we'd meet up for a drink, and we'd have a chat and a laugh. Having said all that, beating Rangers in that county final was great.

We all thought at the time that that was as good as it got. Little did we know that a couple of months later we'd be playing in a Leinster club hurling final. We had two huge wins over Cuala and then Rathdowney-Errill. All of a sudden then, we're playing Ballyhale Shamrocks in a Leinster final.

It was beyond any of our wildest dreams.

It's amazing when you go on a run like that. You just don't know where a bit of momentum can take you. Those few weeks were unbelievable and something that none of us will ever forget. Beating Cuala in the Leinster quarter-final was something else. They had won back-to-back All-Irelands in previous years, so for us to beat them in Carlow was unreal and it showed what Carlow hurling can do. That game was tinged with sadness though when our own club man Micheal Ryan collapsed up in the stand.

The match was still going on while there was a commotion in the stand but a lot of the players didn't realise what was going on. Micheal's son Oisin had actually come onto the field as a sub with about 10 minutes to go, but once he copped what was happening he went straight back off. Obviously, his emotions were all over the place so he couldn't carry on and so he went over to the sideline to see what was happening. At the time, most of the players knew something was going on but had no idea of exactly what. I thought maybe someone had slipped in the stand and hurt themselves or something, but never did we think that it was something so serious. The game carried on and a few minutes later the final whistle went on one of our greatest ever days, beating the two-time All-Ireland club champions. So, to go from the joy of that to quickly realising then that our selector and one of our dearest friends was actually fighting for his life, that was awful.

The joy of that victory was quickly forgotten about as most St Mullins people there were just in tears over what was happening. The whole team all stayed out on the pitch while the paramedics worked on Michael and then when he was put into the ambulance and taken away. Luckily though, there was a nurse at the game that day up in the stand. She was supporting Cuala and when she saw what happened she went to attend to Michael straightaway.

We went back to the dressing-rooms after and then headed for home with everybody's heads all over the place. Word did come through a couple of hours later that Michael was okay and that he was talking, and that was a massive relief for everyone. Those couple of hours in between were not pleasant though and it's a miracle that Michael is still with us today but, thankfully he is, and that was all down to the paramedics on the day and the people there who helped out in what was a very worrying time for everybody.

That Cuala win put us through to the Leinster semi-final against Rathdowney-

Errill. That was another massive performance for us and James Doyle scored two outrageous points at the death to give us the win. Obviously, we couldn't celebrate after the Cuala win so when we beat Rathdowney, I think we just made up for it then. We definitely celebrated after that. I think everything just came out in people after that. The fact we had just qualified for a Leinster final and the fact that Michael was going to be okay. I'd say we must have been on the pitch for two hours afterwards. It was just unreal. We had won a three in-a-row of county championships from 2014 to '16 and the first two years we were well beaten by the Westmeath champions. In 2016 we beat Westmeath's Raharney and then lost to Cuala in the semi-final, but at least we were improving… we had won a game in the Leinster Championship.

It was a little bit of a monkey off our backs in a way to win a game in Leinster as Mount Leinster Rangers had been doing so well representing Carlow by winning the All-Ireland intermediate and then winning the Leinster senior, and going on to reach the final against Portumna.

I think we showed that then in 2019, just what we could do. It was such an eventful season and full of different emotions. For me personally, the year just kept on getting better. As if captaining your club to county championship success wasn't enough, I received the Man of the Match award in the final. I was voted Carlow Hurler of the Year and went on to win a Leinster Club All Star award as well so it was a great end to the year for the club.

Hurling is in a good place right now in St Mullins, and indeed Carlow. Long may it continue.